Pirates and Buccaneers
of the Atlantic Coast

Pirates and Buccaneers

of the Atlantic Coast

EDWARD ROWE SNOW

Updated by Jeremy D'Entremont

———————— ～ ————————

Issued to commemorate the
centennial of the birth of Edward Rowe Snow

———————— ～ ————————

Commonwealth Editions
Beverly, Massachusetts

Library of Congress Cataloging-in-Publication Data
Snow, Edward Rowe.
  Pirates and buccaneers of the Atlantic Coast / Edward Rowe Snow ; updated by
Jeremy D'Entremont.
    p. cm.
"Issued to commemorate the centennial of the birth of Edward Rowe Snow."
Originally published: Boston : Yankee Pub., 1944.
Includes index.
ISBN 1-889833-71-1
  1. Pirates—Atlantic Coast (U.S.)—History—Anecdotes. 2. Pirates—Atlantic Coast
(U.S.)—Biography—Anecdotes. 3. Buccaneers—History—Anecdotes. 4. Buccaneers—
Biography—Anecdotes. 5. Privateering—Atlantic Coast (U.S.)—History—Anecdotes.
6. Atlantic Coast (U.S.)—History, Naval—Anecdotes. I. D'Entremont, Jeremy. II. Title.
  F106.S673 2004
  910.4'5--dc22

                                                2004000907

Unless noted otherwise, all illustrations are from the 1944 edition
of *Pirates and Buccaneers of the Atlantic Coast.*

Jacket and interior design by Judy Barolak.

Printed in the United States.

Published by Commonwealth Editions,
an imprint of Memoirs Unlimited, Inc.,
266 Cabot Street, Beverly, Massachusetts 01915.

www.commonwealtheditions.com

Contents

Foreword

I grew up with the books of Edward Rowe Snow in a small Midwestern farm town not far from the grasslands of the Great Plains. Today, four decades later, I work on Cape Cod as a historian and director for a museum devoted to a topic very high on Snow's list of interests—the pirate ship *Whydah*.

These two facts are not entirely unconnected.

Writing a foreword for this book has not been easy. On one hand, much of my professional research has gone toward what amounts to a deconstruction of Snow's work, as well as that of many other "popularizers" and "folklorists." On the other hand, I owe him, and them, a profound debt of gratitude for giving me a sense, at a very early age, that there is, indeed, "more beyond."

Some modern maritime historians do not take Snow's work seriously, perhaps because it is easy not to. Edward Rowe Snow wrote—and lived—with neither caution nor a lack of exuberance. It was simply not within his nature, or his grasp, to undertake the sort of erudite books on maritime economics or sociology that are currently all the rage in academia. That was not what he was about.

First and foremost, Snow was a storyteller. Obscuring facts with a good story is not something to be encouraged, but telling a good story can bring history to those who might otherwise scorn it. Good storytelling is hard work, and Snow's stories have played a large part in shaping post-war New England's understanding of its own maritime past. That this maritime folklore may have coincidentally fit his own romantic ideals and adventurous temperament casts its own worthwhile light on the man, the place, and the times in which he wrote.

Pirates and Buccaneers of the Atlantic Coast is one of Snow's best. Filled with drama, these are, as he puts it in the preface, "stories of stark realism." While one might question whether this book is entirely "an accurate account" and "a true and fair picture of the life of a sea-rover," it nonetheless was, and is, better history than many other general-interest volumes on piracy on the Atlantic available in either 1944 or the present. And those readers who fancy themselves aficionados of the "Brethren of the Black Flag" will find scattered here and there nuggets of pure gold well worth the picking.

Not long ago I was "conversing" on the Internet (and one can only imagine how much Snow would have loved *that* invention!) with a teacher about coursework material on black pirates he urgently needed for a freshman class. I could think of nothing better or faster for his purposes than to direct him to a few pages about Charles Gibbs and Thomas Wansley in part three of this volume. "How *do* such characters fall through the cracks?' he asked later.

It is to the eternal credit of Edward Rowe Snow that his work has helped keep so many people, and so many stories, from falling completely through cracks of memory into oblivion. In that sense, he was both a lifesaver and a historian of a very special kind.

Kenneth J. Kinkor
Director of Project Research
Expedition Whydah Sea-Lab and Learning Center
Provincetown, January 2004

Introduction to the 1944 Edition

Pirates were the most picturesque and romantic figures who ever sailed the seven seas. They were also the most terrible. Old as the history of commerce, piracy was one of the first activities connected with early travel and trade, for wherever people go with goods and gold robbery inevitably follows them. The Greeks had a word for piracy—πειρατης.

The Romans called these adventures of the Mediterranean *pirata*. Spellman in his *Glossarium*, Dr. Cowel in his *Interpreter*, and Blount in his law dictionary recount the history of the modern development of piracy. In ancient days the name *pirate* denoted a maritime knight. Gradually the word came to mean an admiral or commander at sea. Lord Edward Coke calls such an individual a man accustomed to the practice of "Roving upon the sea."

Another term for pirate is *buccaneer*, which comes from the French word *boucanier*, "a drier of beef." Men went ashore on West Indian islands where the Spaniards had already murdered most of the population. Here they captured and killed great herds of cattle that were roaming the islands, running wild because of the death of so many of the inhabitants. Drying the beef, they sold it to various traders and merchants. Since the Spanish disapproved of this practice, the buccaneers began to carry arms for defense. Gradually, the buccaneers changed from drying beef to killing the Spanish crews of ships they encountered, pillaging and looting as they went. They eventually organized themselves as "Brethren of the Coast."

One branch of buccaneering was filibustering. The men who practiced this type of piracy were military adventurers operating as freebooters along the American coast without the backing of any country. As a rule the term did not apply to buccaneering north of Cuba.

Pirates, buccaneers, filibusters, and freebooters appeal to the imagination of both young and old. Children have always enjoyed building a raft or manning a leaking rowboat to sail or drift to an uninhabited island not too far from shore, where they pretend to be either Blackbeard or Kidd to their heart's content. Was it not Mark Twain who said that a boy never had a real childhood unless he played as a pirate or buccaneer?

The strange and wild thrill from reading pirate tales is nearly always inherited from childhood. If as Wordsworth says "the child is father of the man," everyone has in his heart a desire for romantic adventure. Age makes little difference in this respect.

My own interest in pirates and buccaneers began when I was about four years old. My older brother Nicholas, then twelve years of age, had been showing a group of his chums Grandfather's collection of foreign curios. They boys were all gathered in our parlor. High on the wall hung a pirate's poison dagger, which my grandfather had captured after a fight with the pirates on the island of Mindanao, near Zamboanga.

"Here is a real pirate's poison dagger," cried Nicholas, pulling the ancient relic from its scabbard. "If I cut you, you'll die a horrible death."

Just then Mother heard the commotion as Nick chased the other boys around the parlor. She ran to the door, almost fainting when she saw what was happening.

"Put that dagger down at once," she screamed. "Let me have it!"

"No, Mother, I'll put it away myself," said the boy. But in the confusion Mother received a gash in her hand.

"Oh, I am cut. What shall I do? The poison will kill me," cried Mother. It was a terrible situation, and I never forgot it. Mother did not die; in fact the cut had not penetrated beyond the outer skin. However, the next day Mother took us all in the parlor and warned us never again to touch the poison dagger. She told us in such a dramatic manner and with such vivid imagery that we never forget her solemn warning.

Later on I passed through an active period of searching for buried treasure on every island near our home. Even today, when I hear of a location where a treasure has been discovered, I find it fascinating to learn what I can about it, visiting the scene and photographing the money or the objects found whenever possible. At the present time there are at least four locations in Massachusetts alone where the prospects of finding coins are good. To be sure, the expenses involved would be more than the net return, but the fun of searching for buried or sunken treasure is much more alluring than any possible financial gain.

It is interesting to conjecture as to how much money the famous pirates of old buried along the Atlantic Coast. A conservative estimate, exclusive of the Oak Island hoard, totals about $35 million, but if five percent of this is recovered within the next century, in spite of the new radio locaters and other devices, it will be a miracle.

Men like Blackbeard are believed to have buried their treasures well. The night before he died, one of his crew asked Blackbeard if anyone knew where his treasure was hidden. His reply was typical. He answered, "Nobody but myself and the Devil knows where it is, and the longest liver shall take all."

Christopher Columbus himself is claimed by some to have been the first pirate in America. Francis Drake was also a pirate—in 1572 he sailed on an expedition into West Indian waters, reaching the Port of Nombre de Dios late one night, where he caused terrible bloodshed.

Some of the great men of piratical history, whose activities centered elsewhere than along the Atlantic Coast, are listed below:

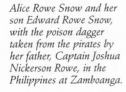

Alice Rowe Snow and her son Edward Rowe Snow, with the poison dagger taken from the pirates by her father, Captain Joshua Nickerson Rowe, in the Philippines at Zamboanga.

Roc the Brazilian; Peter the Great, a French buccaneer; Bartholomy Portuguez, the filibuster (freebooter); John Esquemeling, who writes of his experiences and those of others; Pierre of Tortuga, the pearl pirate; Francis L'Olonnois, the torturer; and Raveneau de Lissan, well known around Cuba. La Fitte, the pirate of the bayous outside of New Orleans, is in a special niche in the Gulf of Mexico's Hall of Fame. Colorful Henry Morgan, in a class by himself for his atrocities and daring around Panama, was one of the greatest buccaneers of all time.

Another great pirate was "Long Ben" Avery. Although his depredations were committed in the Indian Ocean, he visited America to sell his fabulous fortune in diamonds and other precious stones which he had acquired by capturing and plundering ships of the Grat Mogul. When he reached the New World, he changed to a small sloop and scattered his crew along the entire Atlantic Coast, allowing them to go ashore with rich treasure. Avery, however, had concealed the greater part of the fortune in jewels. On his arrival at Boston, he admired the town so much that he planned to settle there. Avery was unable to make the proper contacts in his efforts to dispose of his booty, however, and sailed away to Bristol, England.

There are those who believe he secreted much of his jewelry within a few miles of the Old State House on a lonely island down Boston Bay, but if such is the case it has never been found. The story usually told is that when he returned to Bristol, England, certain "land pirates" persuaded him to turn his immense fortune over to them for quick disposal. They returned a mere pittance to him, and threatened Avery with exposure should he complain. A few weeks later Avery fell ill and died. There was not even enough money found in his possession to buy him a coffin, although the year previous he was worth well over two million dollars!

The shores of New England shall be the location of the first pirate story, an account of the career of the buccaneer Samuel Bellamy, who was wrecked at Cape Cod in 1717.

Dreadful stories they were; about hanging, and walking the plank, and storms at sea, and the Dry Tortugas, and wild deeds, and places on the Spanish Main

Edward Rowe Snow
1944

Introduction to the Snow Centennial Edition

Pirates have plundered and swashbuckled their way through our literature and our imaginations for centuries, and in our age they've achieved new life in movies from Errol Flynn to Johnny Depp. In our minds pirate fact often blurs with pirate fiction. Blackbeard, Long John Silver, Captain Kidd, and Captain Hook all morph into some variation of a rum-swilling, parrot-toting sea dog muttering, "Avast ye mateys!" and forcing cowering captives to walk the plank. What a romantic life they led on the high seas, we think, thumbing their noses at polite society and the powers that be.

Despite our fascination, the last thing any of us would want would be to meet a real pirate in the flesh. Edward Rowe Snow summed up this contradiction in his introduction when he wrote, "Pirates were the most picturesque and romantic figures who ever sailed the seven seas. They were also the most terrible." And Snow didn't hold much back in this volume in deference to the squeamish. Even today's jaded reader will be rightly horrified by some of the descriptions of extreme torture in these pages.

Snow's own interest in pirates reached back to his early childhood. His own grandfather, Joshua Nickerson Rowe, was said to have fought with pirates in the Philippines. This is the first of several books Snow wrote on the subject of piracy, but the later volumes dealt primarily with stories of buried or sunken treasure. This is the most substantial volume he wrote that delves into the bloody details of the lives of the most famous pirates.

Snow's passion for these stories had been rekindled shortly before the writing of this volume. After being wounded in North Africa during World War II, Snow spent a few months in 1943 convalescing in Bristol, England, where he had the opportunity to explore the home port of a number of infamous buccaneers.

Pirate historians may quibble over some of the details presented as fact here. This has often been a problem with pirate history books in general. One of the primary sources for Snow and many other writers has been *A General History of the Robberies and Murders of the Most Notorious Pyrates*, a thick volume first published in 1724. The author was said to be Captain Charles Johnson. We know nothing about the mysterious Captain Johnson, and in 1988 a pair of academics put forth the theory that the true author was Daniel Defoe of *Robinson Crusoe* fame. They made a good argument that convinced many, and the book is now in print with Defoe credited as author.

But others have pointed out that there is no hard evidence linking Defoe with the book. No matter who the author, there is also argument about the book's veracity. Most agree, however, that overall the *General History of the Pyrates* presented a balanced portrait of the lives of the buccaneers. The same can be said of this book, allowing for a healthy dash of romanticism both in the pirates' biographies and the treasure legends associated with them. Snow was first and foremost a raconteur. My advice is to enjoy this book for what it is—a compendium of pirate stories that are largely based on fact.

Snow's fascination with pirates evolved into a lifelong hobby of searching for buried and sunken treasures, and he did unearth two small treasure hoards. It's a pity he wasn't around to see the pirate wreck *Whydah* located in recent years, as well as the discovery of the probable remains of ships once captained by Blackbeard and Captain Kidd. He would have delighted in the new world of high-tech underwater exploration.

Collecting pirate artifacts was another of Snow's passions. Daggers, treasure chests, and even skulls found their way into his Marshfield, Massachusetts, home. His wife, Anna-Myrle, might not always have been totally pleased by these rusty relics, but she certainly looked like she was enjoying herself when she demonstrated a three-pronged pirate dagger for a television show in the 1990s. Their pedigree couldn't be proven, but these curios were seen and handled by thousands at Snow's lectures over the years. There's absolutely no doubt that they sparked the imaginations of countless people. I saw Snow on Boston TV when I was maybe eight years old, telling salty tales with a treasure chest and sack of artifacts by his side. I was hooked for life.

The text presented here is almost entirely as it was written by Snow, with my notes at the ends of the chapters adding pertinent bits of information. There have been some minor corrections to punctuation and spelling, and in some places I've pointed out factual errors. Most of the illustrations from the 1944 edition have been included, along with additional historic illustrations and some modern photos. Another feature of this edition is a new comprehensive index.

Besides the authors cited and the various persons and organizations mentioned in my notes, I want to thank those most responsible for launching this new edition. Webster Bull of Commonwealth Editions truly understands what Edward Rowe Snow means to our region, and his conviction has kept things on course through new editions of five of his most notable volumes. Editor Penny Stratton somehow manages to juggle all the elements while maintaining a invaluably clear overview of each volume. Bob Jannoni has been a catalyst and vital supporter of the effort to return Snow to print. And my friend Dolly Snow Bicknell inherited her father's good humor and athleticism, but—even more important—his positive and caring nature. The legacy of Edward Rowe Snow is alive and well in his daughter and in these pages, as well as in the hearts of those he inspired.

Jeremy D'Entremont
January 2004

PART I

NEW ENGLAND PIRATES

CHAPTER 1

Captain Bellamy,
Wrecked at Cape Cod

Whenever I walk along the great Cape Cod beach from Nauset Coast Guard Station to Highland Light, I always imagine that, when the tide is extremely low, I can make out the remains of the wreck of that great pirate ship, *Whidah*, whose iron caboose was seen showing above the water as late as the Civil War. Of course, I know that the wreck has not been seen above water for over half a century, but it cannot be denied that the old ship, along with Captain Bellamy's treasure of around $100,000 in bullion, is still buried in the shifting sands of Cape Cod.

Captain Samuel Bellamy was notorious up and down the entire length of the great Atlantic Coast as a bloodthirsty buccaneer. The first mention we have of this marauder of the deep is in connection with one Paulsgrave Williams of Nantucket, later a resident of Newport, Rhode Island.* The two men, having heard of the wreck of a Spanish treasure ship in the West Indies, sailed to the location which had been given them. After working many weeks trying to discover treasure, they could not find a single bag of silver which had gone down with the vessel.

---

*Williams was connected more to Block Island than to Nantucket, according to George Andrews Moriarty's "Notes on Block Islanders of the Seventeenth Century" in *The New England Historical and Genealogical Register*, Vol. 105 (1951). —*Ed.*

This discouraged Bellamy and Williams, who had been certain they would become rich. In their disappointment, they decided to turn to an easier but more dangerous profession, piracy on the high seas.

Two other piratically minded sea captains were in the vicinity, Captain Benjamin Thornigold (mentioned elsewhere in this volume) and Captain Louis Lebous.* The four men decided to pool their resources aboard two large sloops, with the 140 men equally divided, 70 on the craft commanded by Thornigold and an equal number sailing with Bellamy. Starting on their buccaneering career, the pirates soon sighted several vessels which were captured and looted. In the fighting twenty-four pirates were killed.

After a few weeks of successful marauding enterprises, during which many unusually rich seizures were made, a dispute arose when Captain Thornigold refused to plunder any more English vessels. This attitude finally led to a break between the pirates, with Samuel Bellamy retaining the majority of the men, ninety in number, leaving Thornigold to sail away in a prize sloop with only twenty-six cutthroats aboard. Captain Lebous joined forces with Bellamy and together they sailed the high seas, spreading to the breeze a large black flag with a skull and crossbones. After several important captures, on December 16 they were sailing off the island of Blanco in the West Indies, when they fell in with a Bristol ship, the *Saint Michael*, bound for Jamaica with provisions. They captured the ship and crew without much trouble, bringing it into the harbor at Blanco. Men from the *Saint Michael* figure prominently with the subsequent career of the pirate.

While at Blanco, they forced into pirate membership four of the crew of the captured vessel, including Thomas Davis, a Welshman. When Davis was informed of the pirates' intention to force him, he cried out in despair that he was undone. One of the pirates overheard his remark and exclaimed, "Damn him, he is a Presbyterian Dog, and should fight for King James." Seeing that Davis was having a hard time with the pirates, Captain Williams of the *Saint Michael* tried to intercede for him. Finally Captain Bellamy agreed that Davis would be put on the next vessel that was taken.

On January 9, 1717, Davis was placed with fourteen other forced men aboard the *Sultana*, which had been made into a galley after its capture

---

*Captain Thornigold was usually referred to in documents of the period as "Hornigold," "Hornygold," or "Hornogold."—*Ed.*

a short time before. The pirate fleet sailed for Testagos, where they put the ships in order, after which they parted company with Captain Lebous. Reaching St. Croix, they blew up a French pirate ship.*

Toward the end of the month of February 1717, a fine galley, the *Whidah*, was sighted making her way through the Windward Passage between Cuba and Porto Rico for London from Jamaica.† Having just completed a successful trading voyage along the Guinea coast, the *Whidah* was loaded with a rich cargo of indigo, Jesuit's bark, elephant's teeth, gold dust, sugar, and other commodities. Captain Lawrence Prince was in command of the *Whidah*, and his action on being challenged by the pirates stamps him as an extremely timid man.

Three long days and nights the pirates pursued the *Whidah*, finally maneuvering close enough at the end of the third day to fire a shot at the galley. To Bellamy's amazement, the *Whidah* promptly hauled down her flag in surrender, offering no resistance of any kind. The pirate leader chose a prize crew to go aboard the galley, and the three vessels then sailed for the Bahama Islands. Here Bellamy transferred several of his guns to the *Whidah* and told Captain Prince he could sail for home on the *Sultana*, loading aboard her any of the goods not desired by the pirates. Bellamy gave the captain twenty pounds in silver and gold as a farewell token of friendship, and then Captain Prince sailed the *Sultana* over the horizon to England.

Thomas Davis, the forced man who had been promised his freedom, requested permission to sail with Prince before he started, but was turned down. When Captain Bellamy agreed to leave it up to the pirate crew, the men voted against Davis leaving them, as they said Davis was a carpenter and badly needed aboard. "Damn him," said the company, "rather than let him go he should be shot or whipped to Death at the Mast."

Incidentally, the spelling of the pirate craft is controversial. George Francis Dow and John Henry Edmonds, in their masterly work on New

---

*According to Whydah Museum director Ken Kinkor, this is based on a misreading of depositions submitted at the trial of the pirates. What actually happened is that Bellamy's men arrived at St. Croix shortly after HMS *Scarborough* had sunk a ship belonging to the pirate crew of John Martel.—*Ed.*

†Snow was mistaken: The Windward Passage is between Cuba and Haiti, not between Cuba and Puerto Rico. Also, that the *Whydah* landed at Jamaica on this voyage is not supported by Jamaican records.—*Ed.*

England pirates, use the spelling *Whidaw*, while Sidney Perley, historian of Salem, chooses *Whidah*. In the booklet issued after the execution of the six pirates, the spelling *Whido* is preferred, but the most fantastic possibility was suggested some years ago that the *Whidah* actually was the *Quedah*, a vessel captured by Captain Kidd himself. Many other spellings are known. We never shall, of course, be certain of the real spelling.*

About twenty thousand pounds in money had been taken in the *Whidah*'s capture, and this rich prize was stored between decks without a guard. As there were 180 men aboard, the money was divided into 180 bags, each weighing fifty pounds.

Five more ships were encountered. Bellamy's buccaneers stopped an English vessel, laden with sugar and indigo, looted it, and allowed the craft to proceed. Then two Scottish ships were taken and, the next day, a vessel from Bristol, England, where many of the pirates hailed from. Finally, they sighted the last of the five ships, a craft from Scotland loaded with rum and sugar, but leaking badly; in fact, it was in such deplorable condition that when a prize crew sent aboard refused to continue the journey, a vote was taken to abandon her. A scow captured previously was now brought alongside so that the crew could be transferred before they scuttled the leaking rum ship.

During the afternoon when the sea marauders were sending the Scottish rum ship to the bottom, the first flashes of lightning could be seen in the distance, and before long a severe thunderstorm had descended upon the pirate fleet. Captain Bellamy ordered his men to take in all small canvas and Captain Paulsgrave Williams, on the other ship, double-reefed his mainsail. The storm was of such violence that in one fearful gust of wind the *Whidah* nearly capsized, and it was only by expert seamanship that she was saved. The wind was northwest, driving the pirate fleet away from the American coast. Great towering waves, with white, dangerous crests, were everywhere encountered, and the fearful wind forced Bellamy to scud along with only the goosewings of the foresail set. As night came on, the tempest increased in fury. To quote from a contemporary account in Johnson's *History of the Pirates* [attributed by many to *Robinson Crusoe* author Daniel Defoe—*Ed.*], the storm in its fearful intensity

---

*Now that the bell from the ship has been recovered, the accepted spelling is *Whydah*. The name comes from a trading post of the same name on the Gold Coast of West Africa. Throughout, however, we are retaining Snow's spelling, which was commonly accepted at the time, in his own text.—*Ed.*

obliged the Whidaw *to bring her yards aportland, and all they could do with Tackles to the Goose Neck of the Tiler, four Men in the Gun Room, and two at the Wheel, was to keep her Head to the Sea, for had she once broach'd to, they must infallibly have founder'd. The Heavens, in the mean while, were covered with Sheets of Lightning, which the Sea by the Agitation of the saline Particles seem'd to imitate; the Darkness of the Night was such, as the Scripture says, as might be felt; the terrible hollow roarings of the Winds, cou'd be only equalled by the repeated, I may say, incessant Claps of Thunder, sufficient to strike a Dread of the supream Being, who commands the Sea and the Winds, one would imagine in every Heart; but among the Wretches, the Effect was different, for they endeavored by their Blasphemies, Oaths, and horrid Imprecations, to drown the Uproar of jarring Elements. Bellamy swore he was sorry he could not run out his Guns to return the Salute, meaning the Thunder, that he fancied the Gods had got drunk over the Tipple, and were gone together by the Ears.*

The vessels sailed the night through under bare poles, the mainmast of the *Whidah* was cut down after being sprung in the step, and the mizzenmast went by the board. "These misfortunes," says Johnson, "made the Ship ring with Blasphemy," which was increased when the *Whidah* was found to be leaking badly. The sloop was also in a weakened condition. The storm continued for four days and three nights before it abated. Then the wind, which had been shifting all around the compass, turned to north-northeast, and diminished in intensity, so the pirates were allowed a breathing spell from the elements.

But the *Whidah* continued to leak severely. The lee pump had to be manned continually, day and night, in order to keep the water at a constant level. The carpenter finally crawled up in the bows to find the leak. After considerable effort and much piratical profanity, the carpenter located the break, repaired it, and clambered back from the bows. The pirates could now rest from their pumping labors. It was agreed that a run to Ocracoke Inlet off the coast of Carolina should be attempted, but the pirates encountered a southerly wind that made them change their plans completely. They decided instead to try to reach the waters of southern New England where they could visit friends in Rhode Island.* One sunny

---

*Paulsgrave Williams' mother and sisters lived on Block Island.—*Ed.*

day, as these wastrels of the deep were relaxing on board, the lookout spotted a sloop in the distance. Quickly overtaking her, they found that the sloop was from Boston and commanded by a Rhode Island man named Beer. After a short skirmish Captain Beer surrendered. The pirates made fast work of the task of plundering his vessel. Although both Captain Bellamy and Paulsgrave Williams were in favor of allowing Beer to keep his sloop, the others outvoted them and the vessel was sent to the bottom. Johnson tells us of Captain Bellamy's conversation with Beer:

> *Damn my Blood* [says he], *I am sorry that they won't let you have your Sloop again, for I scorn to do any one a Mischief, when it is not for my Advantage; damn the Sloop, we must sink her, and she might be of Use to you. Tho', damn ye, you are a sneaking Puppy, and so are all those who will submit to be governed by laws which rich Men have made for their own Security, for the cowardly Whelps have not the Courage otherwise what they get by their Knavery; but damn ye altogether; Damn them for a Pack of crafty Rascals, and you, who serve them, for a Parcel of hen-hearted Numskuls. They villify us, the Scoundrels do, when there is only this Difference, they rob the Poor under the Cover of Law, forsooth, and we plunder the Rich under the Protection of our own Courage; had you not better make One of us, than sneak after these Villians for Employment?*

Captain Bellamy had done his best to make Beer join his pirate band, but Beer declined the doubtful compliment. Bellamy then spoke as follows:

> *You are a develish Conscience Rascal, damn ye. I am a free prince, and I have as much Authority to make War on the whole World, as he who has a hundred Sail of Ships at Sea, and an Army of 100,000 Men in Field; and this my Conscience tells me, but there is no arguing with such sniveling Puppies, who allow Superiors to kick them about Deck at Pleasure; and pin their Faith upon a Pimp of a Parson; a Squab, who neither practices or believes what he puts upon the chuckle-headed Fools he preaches to.* *

---

*Primary source evidence indicates that Beer was captured by Williams rather than Bellamy. In any event, Johnson (or Defoe) was taking liberal creative license with this exchange.—*Ed.*

The buccaneers then put Beer in a small boat and landed him at Block Island. There he obtained passage to Rhode Island, reaching his Newport home on the first day of May, when he told his astonished friends of the misfortunes which he had suffered.

We now approach the time of the dramatic shipwreck of the *Whidah* on the white sands of the great beach at Cape Cod. Early on Friday morning, April 26, the ships were about halfway between Nantucket Shoals and the George's Banks, sailing along at a steady clip, when suddenly the lookout sighted a vessel, which soon was overtaken and captured. It proved to be the wine pink, *Mary Ann*, from Dublin, Ireland, in command of Captain Andrew Crumpstey, and bound for New York.* Her entire cargo was Madeira wine. Captain Crumpstey and five of his crew were ordered aboard the *Whidah*, and seven armed men took over the pink.

When news of the type of cargo aboard the *Mary Ann* became known, a small boat was sent across to bring back some wine, and the craft returned to the *Whidah* with several dozen bottles of the beverage. Orders were given to steer a course northwest by north, but before long another vessel hove into sight. This was a Virginia sloop, which was promptly captured and manned by the pirates. The buccaneer fleet now consisted of four vessels. As evening approached, they all put out lights astern and made sail, keeping together.

Aboard the wine pink *Mary Ann*, the pirates lost no time in getting gloriously drunk, each taking a turn at the wheel while the others went below to indulge. As the night passed, the pink was discovered to be leaking badly, and several of the pirates were forced to man the pumps. To make matters more serious, a storm from the east, which had been threatening for some time, suddenly broke loose in all its fury, and the rain came down so hard that the ships completely lost touch with each other in the gale.

It was shortly after this that the buccaneers aboard the pink heard that most feared of all sounds at sea—breakers on a lee shore. All hands rushed to trim headsail but it was too late. Before any steps could be taken to prevent it, the *Mary Ann* hit heavily on a sandy

---

*Snow's original text refers to the *Mary Ann* as a pinky, but it was a pink. A pink was a small ship for transporting light goods designed for maximum maneuverability, while a pinky, sometimes spelled *pinkie*, was a type of sharp-sterned nineteenth-century New England fishing schooner. We have changed the term to pink throughout.—*Ed.*

shore. It was Cape Cod where the pirate craft struck, at a point just opposite Sluttsbush back of Stage Harbor. The location is now in Orleans, Massachusetts. Pirate Thomas Baker, the commander of the pink, ordered the masts cut away, and the vessel soon drove up on the beach.

Some of the pirates, realizing that either the sea or the people of Massachusetts would soon have them, asked Captain Baker to read out loud from a prayer book. Baker, also believing that the situation was one of extreme gravity, took them down in the hold, where he read from the Book of Common Prayer for a full hour. Daylight came, however, without the pink's breaking up, and at low tide the men all jumped down to a dry beach. They found themselves on Pochet Island, now a part of the Orleans mainland.

In need of sustenance, they ate sweetmeats [fruits preserved in sugar—*Ed.*] which had washed ashore in a chest, and drank some more wine from part of the cargo which had come up on the beach. Looking oceanward, the unhappy buccaneers noticed the masts and spars of the snow and the sloop, which had both ridden out the storm. The great flagship *Whidah* could not be seen anywhere, and the seven men rightfully concluded Bellamy had also met disaster.

At ten o'clock that morning, John Cole and another man who had seen the wreck from the mainland paddled out to the island by canoe and took all seven of the pirates ashore to Cole's home. The pirates later decided to try to escape to Rhode Island, where in those days they had many friends, and asked Cole how to reach that destination.

The forced men then started trouble for the pirates. Mackconachy, the cook aboard the pink, bravely denounced the seven pirates for what they were when they reached Cole's home. As soon as possible, Cole sent a messenger to Justice Joseph Doane of Eastham. This good man told his deputy sheriff to organize a posse at once. Meanwhile, the pirates had reached the tavern at Eastham, where they were indulging in refreshments. A short time later, in the midst of their repast, the posse crashed in on them from all sides and made the buccaneers surrender. Their journey continued in the direction of Rhode Island, it is true, but it came to a sudden stop at the Barnstable jail, where the pirates were imprisoned.*

---

*They were interrogated at the Barnstable jail, but the records were said to be lost in a courthouse fire around 1820.—*Ed.*

The buccaneers aboard the *Whidah* fared no better. Their lot, with the exception of two men, was death in the ocean. The old Wellfleet Life Saving Station, about twelve miles north of Orleans, is the nearest modern-day marker by which we can identify the present location of the pirate wreck. The *Whidah* was pushed toward the breakers near this place, finally coming to grief about two miles south of the Wellfleet Life Saving site. Whether the *Whidah* was caught in the trough of the sea or whether she split in two cannot be ascertained.* Although Captain Bellamy attempted to anchor off the breakers, the sea was so boisterous that the pirates cut the cable and tried to work their way off shore, but the great ship soon struck heavily on the bar, probably capsizing shortly afterwards. Of the 146 men aboard the *Whidah* all except two perished beneath the waves.† Thus death by drowning off the Cape Cod beach was the end of the notorious Captain Samuel Bellamy, a typical pirate of colonial times.

One of the two men who successfully accomplished the swim ashore in the great combers was Thomas Davis, who had been forced from the *Saint Michael* the preceding December. The other survivor was John Julian, a Cape Cod Indian, who was thrown ashore by the sea almost at his own doorstep.

A controversy raged a few months later as to how the prisoners aboard the *Whidah* met their death. Preaching from the pulpit one Sunday morning, Cotton Mather expressed his belief that the pirates had murdered all of the sixteen prisoners, including Captain Crumpstey, just before their own death, but no testimony agrees with him. Anyone who has seen dead bodies after the battering of a few hours in a heavy surf can understand why Mather believed the prisoners had been murdered, but as Davis, the only white survivor, does not mention this possibility, it is safe to think that all aboard were drowned together with the two exceptions.

Local tradition around Cape Cod has another tale about the pirates, supported by the *Boston News-Letter* of April 29–May 6, 1717. In this version, the captive master of the Irish pink ran her ashore while the pirates were all drunk below deck. The only trouble with this theory is

---

*Recent archaeological study of the remains of the *Whydah* indicate that the ship may have broken up into at least three sections.—*Ed.*

†More precisely, only two are known to have survived.—*Ed.*

that Captain Crumpstey of the pink was taken aboard the *Whidah* at the time of capture, and later drowned from the *Whidah* when she hit ten miles up the beach and thus could not possibly have been on the pink when she was wrecked.

The Massachusetts Historical Society's collections of 1793 include an account of the history of Wellfleet, in which it is stated that Bellamy's entire fleet was decoyed to Cape Cod, where it was cast on shore there by the clever plans of the captain of a snow, captured the day before.

Reverend Cotton Mather, pastor of the Second Church in Boston, 1685–1728. Mather had an intense interest in pirates and their executions.

The tale goes on, saying that a lantern was hung in the shrouds of the snow, as the night was dark, and one by one the vessels piled up on the beach. In actuality, however, only two vessels were wrecked, the disasters which we have already described. The town historian then comments on the treasure which sank with the *Whidah*, telling of the money which was picked up prior to the year 1793.

The shifting sands often exposed the iron caboose of the *Whidah* on the outer bar at dead low tide. "Uncle Jack" Newcomb told Henry David Thoreau that he had seen the iron caboose at low tide many times but it is not believed that anyone has seen a portion of the old pirate chieftain's flagship above water since the 1860s. Thoreau and his companion, according to Perley, found some of the treasure on the bar years ago.

The above digression from our narrative left Justice Doane and his sheriff's posse rounding up the seven pirates from the pink. Just about the time Justice Doane believed his work was finished, news came to him of the wreck of the other vessel, the *Whidah*, ten miles farther up the beach, but it was Sunday before he reached the second wreck. We recall that only two men reached shore alive from the *Whidah*. As soon as he could make out where he was, Thomas Davis, the white survivor, discerned a house two miles away, and made his way to it. It was the home of Samuel Harding, who quickly showed the usual Cape Cod reaction to a shipwreck. Harnessing his horse and wagon at once, he drove down to the scene with Davis. With the Indian's help, the men made several trips from the wreck to Harding's home, and it is believed Harding had obtained the best merchandise from the cargo by the time other active Cape Codders arrived at the scene of the disaster. All day long Saturday, the mooncussers and beachcombers worked at their interesting avocation, until, when the first streaks of Sunday's dawn arrived, the beach had been stripped clean of all important material from the cargo. No gold or silver, as far as we can tell, had come ashore by this time, as the bar was some distance off the shore. Dead bodies, however, began to come up on the beach in alarming numbers. Their disposal later caused Cyprian Southack much trouble.

Reaching the beach Sunday morning, Justice Doane found it picked clean, with the exception of a few articles seen drifting ashore in the surf. Davis and Julian surrendered to Justice Doane, and they joined the others at the Barnstable jail. Later in the week the nine men, under heavy guard, were sent to Boston by horseback. This means of conveyance the

British sailors from the wrecked *Somerset* would have appreciated in 1778, when they were forced to hike all the way from Cape Cod to Boston.*

The next day the people of Boston were startled to hear of the wreck of a pirate treasure ship on the sands of Cape Cod, and Governor Samuel Shute went to bed that night dreaming of pirate gold. He should have been warned by the embarrassing experiences of his predecessor, Bellomont, whose relationships with Captain Kidd caused him many anxious moments. Shute's thoughts of great riches from the buccaneer ship spurred him on, however. Issuing a proclamation to His Majesty's officers and subjects to take and hold all pirates, treasure, and other goods from the wreck, Shute quickly looked over his available maritime gentry for a person of daring and courage who could go at once to the scene of the wreck.

Captain Cyprian Southack was the ideal mariner for this task. A very interesting sailor he was. Then in his fifty-sixth year, he was already planning the first real chart of Massachusetts Bay and its surrounding area, part of which is contained in this volume. He was artist, cartographer, fighter, and seaman. Captain of the *Province Galley*, his sketch of Boston Light is well known to antiquarians, while his chart of the coast was a necessity for all mariners for the next hundred years. Such were the accomplishments of this interesting Boston mariner of two centuries ago. We shall see, however, that they were of little avail against the traditions of Cape Cod people, especially when it came to a pirate shipwreck.

Captain Cyprian Southack, now fully informed as to his mission, prepared to reach the scene. Hiring a small sloop, the *Nathaniel*, Southack left Boston on May 1, 1717. Five long and eventful days had passed since the wreckage was scattered by the storm along the great beach. Handicapped by a south wind, the sloop did not reach Cape Cod until the afternoon following its sailing, making six days in all since the wreck had occurred. Commandeering a whale boat at Cape Cod Harbor, he sent two men ahead to obtain horses in Truro. The men, mounted on horses, reached the scene of the wreck at seven in the evening, but it had been six long, profitable days for the men of Cape Cod, and by this time all movable goods from the *Whidah* had been

---

*Snow's original text refers to the *Somerset* as a frigate, but technically it was a larger ship, a warship carrying sixty-four guns.—*Ed.*

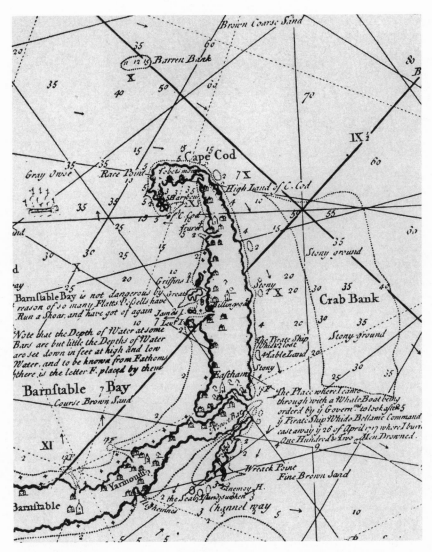

Map showing location of Bellamy's treasure ship Whydah, *drawn by Captain Cyprian Southack around 1735*

stored in cellars, locked in barns, and secreted in attics. Even Captain Williams of the pirate fleet had returned to join in the search for sunken booty, anchoring his ship off the shore and rowing in, but so many Cape Codders were there that he did not tarry long.*

Meanwhile, Captain Southack started out in his whaleboat from Provincetown Harbor, finally reaching Boat Meadow Creek in Orleans. From here he sailed up to a natural canal, which at that time crossed Cape Cod. The canal was located between Orleans and Eastham, and has been called both Jeremy's Dream [or "Drean," apparently meaning "drain"—*Ed*.] and Jeremiah Gutter. It is clearly drawn on Southack's map in this volume.

Captain Southack did not expect a cordial reception from the men of Cape Cod, and in this he was not disappointed. In his own words, he found the "Pepol very Stife and will not [surrender] one thing of what they Gott on the Rack." Caleb Hopkins of Freetown was very indignant, and the two men almost came to blows, while Samuel Harding, to whose house Thomas Davis had journeyed the morning of the wreck, said that Davis had ordered him not to part with any of the spoils from the sea. "I find the said Harding is as Gilty as the Pirates saved," was Captain Southack's conclusion.

The governor allowed Southack extraordinary powers. He could "go into any house, shop, cellar, warehouse, room or other place and in case of resistance to break open any door, chests, trunks," or other objects to get the pirate goods.† With all this authority, however, Cyprian Southack was unable to gather much merchandise and for all the time he was at Cape Cod, comparatively little ever reached Boston. That he did a thorough job no one can question, especially if he reads through the lengthy epistles which Southack dispatched from time to time to Governor Shute and others. The letters are still on file at the Boston State House [now Massachusetts Archives—*Ed*.].

After waiting at the beach to recover the various articles and wreckage which came up on the shore from time to time, and gathering

---

*Later testimony from some of Williams' crew captured in New York indicates that it was not Williams' ship that had anchored offshore of the wreck, according to Ken Kinkor of the Whydah Museum.—Ed.

†This was apparently the first of the infamous "writs of assistance" issued in the Massachusetts colony.—*Ed*.

together the material which one or two timid Cape Codders relinquished, Captain Southack sent for the sloop *Swan*, commanded by Captain Doggett, to sail the meager booty back to Boston. Scarcely had Doggett cleared Boston Harbor when he was pursued by another pirate, who promptly boarded the *Swan*, took goods valued at eighty pounds, and then allowed Doggett to proceed to Provincetown with the vessel.

As the bodies of the dead pirates continued to come up on the Cape Cod beach, some means of taking care of them had to be agreed upon. The coroner and his jury ordered the burial of the victims, and with Cyprian Southack right on the scene, he asked that Southack pay the expenses. The fighting and wrangling over the bodies of the buccaneers is almost beyond belief. As more and more of the dead pirates came upon the beach, new arrangements had to be made. Southack finally refused to have anything further to do with the expenses, whereupon the coroner posted an attachment on some of the goods which Southack had just collected from the wreck, and received his money.

The attempts which Southack made to reach the treasure were exacting and tedious. Day after day he rowed out to the scene, trying to discover the bags of silver and gold down through the muddy waters, but since the heavy rain continued almost every day the water stayed muddy. He finally abandoned his search in the vicinity of the bar off the beach and returned to Boston with the goods he was able to secure. It is to be questioned whether Governor Samuel Shute profited much from this unusual adventure of the drowned pirates of Cape Cod. In his disappointment, he probably obtained little comfort from the fact that Governor Bellomont back in 1700 had concluded his experiences with Captain Kidd with even greater trouble and embarrassment.

The men accused of piracy, with the exception of Mackconachy, who was evidently released at Cape Cod, were all taken to Boston and placed in jail there.

The pirates were allowed to languish in jail all that long summer of 1717. It was not until October 18 that they were brought to trial in the Admiralty Court at Boston. John Julian never came to trial, and was either let off or died in jail.* Thomas Davis convinced the court of his innocence in any wrongdoing, and when pardoned sank to his knees

---

*In later works, Snow indicated that Julian was sold to the John Quincy family of Braintree, Massachusetts.—*Ed.*

on the courtroom floor, "thanked the Court and was dismissed with a suitable admonition." The others were found guilty.

Cotton Mather, who often visited the pirates in their jail cells, became so thoroughly convinced of the innocence of one of them, Thomas South of Boston, England, that he obtained a reprieve for him on November 2, thirteen days before the other six were executed.* The unusual interest Mather showed in the pirates is indicated in the good man's diary for November 15, 1717, the day the last members of the Bellamy crew were hanged.

> *15 G. D. There is good this day to be done, on a very solemn Occa-sion. Six pirates were this day executed. I took a long and sad walk with them, from the Prison, to the Place of Execution. I successively bestowed the best Instructions I could, pray'd with them, and with the vast Assembly of Spectators, as pertinently and as profitably as I could.*

The six pirates were Simon Van Vorst, of New York, John Brown of Jamaica, Thomas Baker of Holland, Hendrick Quintor of Amsterdam, Peter Hoof of Sweden, and John Sheean ["Shuan" in the trial records—*Ed.*] of Nantes. On November 15, 1717, they were taken down to the Charlestown Ferry, and there rowed out to a scaffolding erected out over the water. Baker and Hoof were penitent and humble. Hoof joined with Van Vorst at the last minute in singing a Dutch psalm, while John Brown broke out into furious oaths, but afterwards began to read from the prayer book. Then Brown made a speech to the great assemblage.

"Beware of wicked living," said Brown to his listeners. "Also, if you fall into the hands of pirates, as I did, have a care into which country they come to." Then the scaffolding fell, and the six outlaws of the sea met their fate.

After the execution Mather wrote a pamphlet on the incident, but his regular printer refused to print it, so John Allen printed 1200 copies of *A Brief Relation of* REMARKABLES *in the Shipwreck of Above One Hundred Pirates, Who were Cast away in the Ship Whido, on the Coast of*

---

*South was acquitted at trial. The pirate for whom Mather requested a reprieve may have been Simon Van Vorst of Tappan, New York, according to Ken Kinkor of the Whydah Museum.—*Ed.*

New-England, April 26, 1717. The book had a good sale, but is a very rare volume today.

The various sermons, pamphlets, and discourses with the condemned men gave Mather a peculiar pedestal to occupy in the mind of the average pirate at sea. Cotton Mather later admitted that he learned of several victims of the men who had gone on the account who were forced to curse Cotton Mather as part of their punishment. This strange ritual which befell those captured by pirates on the high seas must have disturbed Cotton Mather, for later in life when called by a pirate to pray for him, Mather said, "The Pyrates now strangely fallen into the Hands of Justice here, make me the first man, whose Visits and Counsils and Prayers they beg for." Nevertheless, his unusual interest in matters pertaining to pirates and their executions must have surprised some of the other good people of America's leading seaport.

———————— ～ ————————

Some might take issue with Snow's characterization of Bellamy as "bloodthirsty," since there's no real evidence to support such a harsh adjective. In fact, others have romanticized the pirate and presented a "softer" image. An oft-repeated gem of Cape Cod folklore is the tale involving Samuel Bellamy's romance with a sixteen-year-old Eastham girl named Maria Hallett. According to the legend, Maria's parents didn't think Bellamy worthy of their daughter, so he became a pirate in order to gain a fortune that would impress the Halletts. After Bellamy's departure, Maria Hallett gave birth to a child who subsequently died, and she was thrown into jail, where she went mad. She eventually lived in a shack on the beach and was considered a witch.

According to the story as it is sometimes told, Bellamy was coming back to see Maria when the *Whydah* met its doom. As the vessel broke apart, Maria Hallett watched from the beach, giving thanks to the Devil for vengeance against the man who had deserted her. She then retrieved a treasure chest from the ship and hid it away, never revealing its whereabouts to anyone. Some say the ghost of Maria Hallett still walks the windy bluffs overlooking the *Whydah* wreck. The story has inspired romance novels and plays, but of course there's no evidence that any of it really happened.

The *Whydah*, launched in England in 1716, was a three-masted ship approximately 100 feet in length, weighing about 300 tons. The pirates added eighteen additional guns to the *Whydah*'s original ten.

Snow estimated the treasure on board the *Whydah* at "around $100,000 in bullion." Whydah Museum director Ken Kinkor says that this estimate was apparently based on a conversion of twenty thousand pounds sterling to U.S. dollars; the working ratio at the time Snow was writing was 1:5.

Snow's assertion that Captain Lawrence Prince, who was in command of the *Whydah* when it was taken by the pirates, was "an extremely timid man" is debatable. Most merchant captains during this period surrendered without incident when challenged by pirates.

In an ironic twist, four days before the six pirates were hanged in Boston, news reached the city that a British warship had arrived in New York. The ship was carrying a royal pardon for which the condemned men qualified.

John Julian was a Muscheta, or "Mosquito," Indian from the coast of Central America. To discourage escape attempts, captured Indians from the north were usually traded south, and southern Indians were often traded north. According to Snow's 1960 book *New England Sea Tragedies,* after his *Whydah* experience Julian was sold into domestic slavery in the home of Major John Quincy of Braintree, Massachusetts. He later escaped from a subsequent owner and, after killing a pursuer, was eventually captured. He was hanged at Boston Neck on March 22, 1733.

Whether Thoreau and his companion found coins from the *Whydah* is questionable, since there were other eighteenth-century wrecks in the area, and one of the coins found by Thoreau was dated thirty years after the sinking of the *Whydah*. It also can't be known with any certainty that the "iron caboose" seen by Newcomb was that of the *Whydah*.

In the 1940s Edward Rowe Snow's research—and love for adventure—led him to mount the earliest concerted effort to recover material from the lost galley. He wrote in his 1951 book *True Tales of Buried Treasure* that he had "spent the equivalent of a small treasure hoard at the scene of the pirate ship's wreck." Snow built a diving platform at what he believed to be the wreck site, but all diver Jack Poole was able to recover was an encrustation containing a few pieces of eight. The operation was halted when a storm smashed the diving platform to pieces.

According to Arthur T. Vanderbilt's *Treasure Wreck: The Fortunes and Fate of the Pirate Ship Whydah,* Oscar Snow of Provincetown was part of this expedition. Oscar Snow said that he could see three cannon in the vicinity of the wreck, but his efforts to bring them ashore failed.

Snow was discouraged and wrote that it would be a "very lucky treasure hunter who ever does more than pay expenses while attempting to find the elusive gold and silver still aboard the *Whidah*." Today, those words can be seen on a sign hanging in the offices of Expedition Whydah, the group that has successfully recovered much from the pirate ship.

Snow could not have foreseen the tremendous technological advances in the underwater salvage field in recent years. A tenacious underwater explorer and Cape Cod native named Barry Clifford, who grew up listening to the romantic tales of Black Sam Bellamy and Maria Hallett, has now spent nearly two decades bringing up an estimated 200,000 individual items from the wreck site, including a bell inscribed "The Whydah Galley 1716." Among the recovered objects are thousands of pieces of eight, cannons and smaller weapons, and articles of clothing. Also recovered were twenty-eight lead gaming pieces, reminding us, as historian David Cordingly wrote in *Under the Black Flag*, that "gambling was almost as popular as drinking among seamen."

According to pirate historian and Whydah Museum director Ken Kinkor, "The site has proved to be much larger and more widespread than originally thought by either Edward Rowe Snow or Barry Clifford. As Snow learned to his chagrin, it is also an extremely difficult site to work, given that it is very close to an exposed coast with treacherous and unpredictable seas." It can't be known, according to Kinkor, whether the coins recovered by Snow and Poole were from the *Whydah*. "The fact that he even attempted such salvage," says Kinkor, "is a tremendous testimonial to the man's optimism and spirit."

Edward Rowe Snow pointing out the location of the pirate ship Whydah *at Cape Cod*

A selection of the artifacts recovered by Clifford and his team are now displayed in a museum on MacMillan Wharf in Provincetown. The wreck and recovery of the *Whydah* treasure has been the subject of several books, including Clifford's own *Expedition Whydah.*

Diver Jack Poole, who brought up material from what may have been the wreck of the Whydah *while working with Edward Rowe Snow in the 1940s (from Snow's* Mysteries and Adventures along the Atlantic Coast, *1948)*

CHAPTER 2

Captain Quelch,
Who Brought Gold into New England

Marblehead, Massachusetts, is known today for its annual exhibitions of yacht racing. All New England sailing enthusiasts, young and old, gather here once a year to test their respective nautical abilities. Two hundred years ago, however, the situation along the Marblehead waterfront was different, with fishermen, merchantmen, and pirates sailing in and out of this prosperous New England port. The mariners were always ready for privateering, and many a pert sloop left Marblehead in search of French and Spanish vessels to capture and destroy.

On July 13, 1703, Governor Joseph Dudley of Massachusetts commissioned the brigantine *Charles* as a privateer to prey upon French shipping. Owned by five of the leading Boston citizens, the eighty-eight-ton vessel was under the command of Captain Daniel Plowman. Toward the end of the month the captain, then aboard the *Charles* in Marblehead Harbor, became seriously ill, finally sending word to his owners that he was too sick to sail. It is possible that Daniel Plowman was already worried about the character of his crew, for in a rather cryptic letter he asked the owners to come at once to Marblehead to save "what we can."

The Bostonians met to discuss the situation. They decided to send the brigantine to sea under another captain, but when Plowman heard this he implored them to forget any future plans, urging the owners to get the vessel up to Boston at once, where the guns and stores could be unloaded. By this time Plowman was in great fear of the crew. Before any action was taken, however, the sailors, headed by Anthony Holding, committed their first act of piracy by locking the sick captain in his cabin. As soon as this was accomplished, John Quelch, the vessel's lieutenant commander, came aboard, and after deliberating with Holding and the others, agreed to take command. The *Charles* sailed out of Marblehead Harbor, slipping by Marblehead Rock and Cat Island until Halfway Rock was dead ahead. We cannot say whether any of the superstitious sailors aboard followed the prevailing custom of the period by scaling good-luck pennies across to land on the barnacle-covered back of Halfway Rock, but it is reasonable to believe they did.

Safely out of the harbor and away from interference, the pirates descended to the cabin, where they pulled the sick captain from his bunk. After carrying him up on deck, the buccaneers unceremoniously threw Captain Daniel Plowman into the waters of Boston Bay. There were those who later claimed that the captain died of natural causes before this drastic event occurred, but there is no reason to believe them. Captain Plowman was deliberately drowned by the pirates.

Sailing southward until he reached the waters off Brazil, Captain John Quelch began a career of piracy and murder which made his name one to be feared in all the South Atlantic. He boarded and captured ship after ship, until by March of 1704, nine Portuguese vessels had fallen to his black flag—two fishing boats, a ship, five brigantines, and a shallop. While all this was going on, however, England and Portugal had signed an alliance. This act was unknown to Quelch, who considered himself a privateer. Thus he actually became a pirate without his knowledge, according to Quelch.

Quelch, his brigantine filled with spoil from his encounters with the unfortunate ships which he captured, now decided to return home to Marblehead Harbor. The fact that his decision was voluntary seems to prove to many that he did not fear capture or punishment for his activity in the Atlantic, and that he probably did not even consider he had been anything but a privateer commissioned by Governor Dudley.

Reaching Boston Bay in May 1704, Quelch anchored off Marblehead. As soon as he paid his crew, he allowed them to go ashore, and in a short time was on dry land himself. After a voyage of nine months, especially if the sailors were not in the habit of carrying substantial sums of money with them, there were bound to be repercussions when a score or more of swaggering bloodthirsty individuals with bulging pockets full of money are turned loose and allowed to roam at will through the streets of a village. This occasion was no exception. The pirates squandered their money at the local taverns, visited women of easy acquaintance, and attracted attention everywhere they went.

Within a few days news reached Boston of the return of the *Charles*. America's first maritime reporter inserted into the pages of America's earliest newspaper (first published the preceding month) the following item:

> *Arrived at Marblehead, Capt. Quelch in the Brigantine that Capt. Plowman went out in, and said to come from New-Spain & have made a good voyage.*

The paper, a weekly, reached the streets May 23, 1704. The two owners of the *Charles*, John Colman and William Clarke, had been frantic with surprise and disappointment when the vessel disappeared from Marblehead Harbor months before, and this was the first report of the return of their stolen ship. The two men filed a complaint at once with the Secretary of the Province and Attorney General Paul Dudley, son of the governor, accusing John Quelch of piracy.

Young Dudley acted with wisdom and alacrity, hurrying over to the North Shore at once. On that same day diary-minded Samuel Sewall was returning from a journey to Newbury, and stopped for refreshments at Lewis's in Lynn, where he found that Dudley had already captured one of the pirates, sending him on up to Boston.

Lieutenant Governor Povey, who commanded the fort at Castle Island, issued a proclamation the next day. It named the forty-one pirates, accusing them of importing "a considerable Quantity of Gold dust which they are violently suspected to have gotten & obtained by Felony and Piracy, from some of Her Majesty's Friends and Allies."

Two days later John Quelch was safe in the Boston prison. John Lambert, whom we shall discuss later, John Miller, John Clifford, John Dorothy, James Parrot, and William Wiles had also been brought to the town jail on what is now Court Street, Boston. James Austin was in prison at Piscataqua, while another pirate was confined in Salem. Another member of the crew was on the way from Newport.

By this time the governor had returned to Boston, and at once issued a new proclamation, which stated the money the outlaws carried had been taken from Portuguese vessels. The paper included the name of

Christopher Scudamore among the pirate suspects. Others mentioned were Richard Lawrence and Matthew Primer.

The unusual interest shown by the officials in their efforts to capture members of the pirate crew may have been due to the fact that each hunted man was carrying valuable gold dust taken from the Portuguese vessels. On June 6, Governor Dudley, afraid that the gold would not reach him intact, commissioned three prominent Bostonians, Samuel Sewall, Nathaniel Byfield, and Paul Dudley, to journey to Marblehead to begin an investigation as to what was happening to the gold dust and the rest of the treasure.

Arriving in Salem the next day, the three men found to their dismay that a Captain Larramore, of the *Larramore Galley*, had been so impressed by the pirate stories that he had turned pirate, going "on the account" himself. Samuel Wakefield, a customhouse officer, was instructed to apprehend Larramore before he left Cape Ann.* In a severe rainstorm, the three commissioners rode to Marblehead, where they held court before a roaring fire in the great living room at Captain Brown's home. They retired that evening, and the next morning were awakened at six o'clock by a messenger from Cape Ann, bringing the information that a group of pirates had been seen in a "Lone-house there."

Colonel Legg of Marblehead was ordered by the governor to call out his Essex South Regiment, and Colonel Wainwright was given instructions to recruit his Essex North Regiment. Judges Sewall and Byfield then journeyed to Salem to make plans for the apprehension of the pirates.

It was agreed that Major Stephen Sewall and twenty of his militia stationed at Salem Fort should proceed to Cape Ann by water, while Samuel Sewall and Byfield, escorted by a troop of horsemen, journeyed overland. Sewall tells us that the muster of the Beverly troops was already beginning, while at Manchester the men were forming at the crest of a huge rock. There was much excitement, but the idea of hunting pirates was suppressed and kept in the background as much as possible.

When Attorney General Dudley and Colonel Legg reached Gloucester, they found that Captain Larramore and the pirates who were living at Snake Island had already sailed away. It was believed that they were trying to reach the Isles of Shoals off the New Hampshire coast.

---

*At least eleven members of Quelch's crew from the *Charles* had joined with Captain Larramore.—*Ed.*

A decision now had to be made. Should or should not these half-trained soldiers and militia men leave their families and put out from land in an attempt to capture bloodthirsty men who were at home on the high seas?

It is interesting to watch the various reactions of the men of New England when they were told of the dangerous situation that confronted them. Captain Herrick pleaded earnestly that his men be

Judge Samuel Sewall,. appointed by Governor Dudley to investigate piracy aboard the Charles

excused. Other officers also presented what they considered good rea-sons for not going. "Matters went on heavily," says Samuel Sewall in his diary. "'Twas difficult to get men."

Sewall's own brother Stephen finally offered to go, and after that sev-eral other resolute men agreed to act company him. With this beginning many of the more timid individuals decided to join the group, until there were forty-three in all. Without question, it was a hazardous undertaking which confronted these brave men of Massachusetts. The wind dropped completely as they were about to sail, and the men were forced to row out of Gloucester Harbor. They skirted Ten Pound Island and rounded Eastern Point, heading for the open sea. A great cheer went up from the assemblage gathered on the beach as the shallop passed.

The throngs on the shores of Gloucester who had shouted cheers of encouragement to their loved ones went home to worry and pray. The women were upset, Sewall mentioning in his diary that he

> dined with Sister, who was very thoughtful what would become of her Husband. The Wickedness and despair of the company they pur-sued, their Great Guns and other war like Preparations, were a ter-ror to her and to most of the Town; concluded they would not be taken without Blood. Comforted ourselves and them as well as we could.

Special prayers were offered by Mr. White and Mr. Cheever in the Gloucester meeting house. In the meantime, the shallop had passed Thacher's Island, rounded the Dry Salvages, and, with the aid of a sub-stantial breeze, began the twenty-five mile sail across the sea to the Isles of Shoals. At seven o'clock the masts of the galley were sighted.

Stephen Sewall now was confronted with the problem of planning the strategy for capturing the pirates. All hands aboard the Sewall shal-lop were sent below with the exception of four, who pretended they were fishermen, and stayed in view. Just as the soldiers approached the other vessel, the pirates were observed to send a small boat ashore, which was a lucky break for the men of Massachusetts. As the shallop reached a position within a few rods of the outlaw vessel, the pirates left on the deck of the *Larramore Galley* detected the true state of events, and made a rush for their guns, pulling off the aprons and withdrawing the tampions. Promptly Major Sewall ordered his company of forty-two to rise in a group with their firearms ready. It was such a terrific surprise to the buccaneers that all resistance stopped aboard the pirate ship. The buccaneers saw that the game was up, and quickly surrendered. The sea rovers who had gone ashore for the purpose of burying treasure were also apprehended. When they reached the shallop, the entire group was placed in irons. Forty-five ounces of gold dust was taken from the pirates at this time. After all was made ready for the trip to the mainland, Sewall's shallop began the sail back to Massachusetts with the *Larramore Galley* in tow, reaching Salem the next day. Major Sewall, discovering that many of the *Larramore* crew were not in the plot, permitted the innocent ones to go free.

In all, twenty-five pirates of the original forty-three aboard the *Charles* were eventually confined in the Boston jail, while eighteen escaped the Yankee dragnet completely, never appearing in New England again.

A Court of Admiralty was now set up. On Tuesday, June 13, 1704, the arraignment began where the Old State House stands today, with Governor Dudley as President of the Court. John Usher, Lieutenant Governor of New Hampshire; Nathaniel Byfield, Judge of the Vice Admiralty; Jahlael Brenton, Customs Collector for New England; Isaac Addington, Province Secretary; and Lieutenant Governor Povey all sat with him on that unusual occasion.

It was a solemn moment with everyone awaiting the beginning of the pirate trial in complete silence. Then the Court of Admiralty for the Trial of Pirates was opened. A warrant was sent to the keeper of the prison, after which the dignitaries adjourned until three o'clock to enjoy their dinners in comfort. During the afternoon session three of the pirates agreed to turn against their associates and help the court, or as the language of the period indicated, to "stand within the Bar, and to be Sworn as Witnesses on Her Majesty's behalf." They were Matthew Primer, John Clifford, and James Parrot, who were eventually pardoned.

All eyes were now on the next prisoner as Captain John Quelch, heavily ironed, was escorted into the room and walked up to the bar. In a firm voice he asked for counsel. Although the court did not admit that he was entitled to counsel, they assigned James Menzies to help him. Twenty other prisoners were arraigned before the court adjourned that day.

The following Monday John Quelch, his irons temporarily removed, was brought to trial for his life. Charged with piracy, robbery, and murder, Quelch was also accused of neglecting the orders of the owners. In addition he had refused to set ashore Matthew Primer and John Clifford when they asked to be let go, and had sailed for Fernando Island off

Brazil, capturing several vessels belonging to the king of Portugal, a good ally of Her Majesty. One of the queen's witnesses testified that Christopher Scudamore, the pirate cooper, had killed the Portuguese captain with a petard. It was also claimed that the ringleader had not been Quelch, but pirate Anthony Holding, who was never captured. Of course Holding started the mutiny, but actually retired to the background after Quelch had accepted the captaincy, so the claim was only partially correct.

Quelch, Lambert (a Salem man), Scudamore, Miller, Peterson, Roach, and Francis King were condemned to death. Fifteen others in the crew withdrew their plea of innocence and asked for the mercy of the court. They were all later released to enter the queen's service.

Every minister in Boston tried to get the pirates to repent prior to their death. The Reverend Cotton Mather preached a sermon in which he warned the pirates to seek forgiveness before their final judgment was decided. In other pulpits as well, ministers held the pirates up as examples of sin.

On Friday, June 30, 1704, the condemned men were marched from the jail down to Scarlett's Wharf, then at the foot of Fleet Street. It was an awesome procession. Preceded by a man carrying the silver oar emblematic of the British Admiralty, the pirates were accompanied by Cotton Mather himself, who never willingly missed an occasion of this type. The condemned men, guarded by the provost marshal with forty soldiers, walked slowly along the last bitter mile, which was to end in eternity.

The crowds had gathered early that morning at the top of Broughton's Hill, where the Copp's Hill Cemetery stands today. The gallows had been set up between the rise and fall of the tide off the shore. This was before the days of the Charles River Dam, and the area was known as part of the river. Samuel Sewall was an eyewitness. His account is as follows:

> *When I came to see how the River was cover'd with People, I was amazed: Some say there were 100 Boats. 150 Boats and Canoes, saith Cousin Moodey of York [who probably had made the journey for the event] Mr. Cotton Mather came with Capt. Quelch and six others for Execution from the Prison to Scarlett's Wharf, and from thence in the Boat to the place of Execution about midway between Hanson's point and Broughton's Warehouse. Mr. Mather pray'd for*

> *them standing upon the Boat. Ropes were all fasten'd to the Gallows*
> *(save King, who was Repriev'd). When the Scaffold was let to sink,*
> *there was such a Screech of the Women that my wife heard it sitting*
> *in our Entry next the Orchard, and was much surprised at it; yet the*
> *wind was sou-west. Our house is a full mile from the place.*

We cannot say whether Bird Island or Nix's Mate Island was the scene where the dead pirates were eventually strung up in chains to warn prospective buccaneers, as there is no record indicating either place. The body of one man, however, never left the mainland. He was John Lambert, of prominent Salem antecedents. Lambert's body was cut down late that night, and his remains were taken up to the King's Chapel Burial Grounds, where at midnight they were interred in the ground by the side of other members of his family. Tens of thousands pass the graveyard daily, but few realize that a real pirate is buried on the other side of the high iron fence that runs along the Tremont Street side of this historic cemetery. There was much gold involved in the proceedings and everyone who had anything at all to do with the capture and trial of the pirates received adequate pay in addition to his regular salary or wages. After seven hundred twenty-six pounds had been paid to various people for their part in the pirates' capture, the gold dust and silver were allowed to remain in Massachusetts until October 1705, when 788 ounces of the precious mineral were placed in five leather bags and shipped to England. How much more escaped the ocean journey cannot be estimated. Some years later, however, Cotton Mather and Governor Dudley quarreled, whereupon Mather published a volume in which he accused the "treacherous Governor" of allowing odd collusions with the pirates. We read that the pirates paid the equivalent of $140 for the privilege of exercising within the prison yard for a period of two or three days.

Captain John Quelch, of course, has his side of the story. His trial has actually been called "one of the clearest cases of judicial murder done in our American annals," according to Dow and Edmonds. There is no evidence that he was ever given the benefit of a doubt. His final words, uttered a moment or two before he was to meet his Maker, were as follows:

> *Gentlemen, Tis but little I have to speak; what I have to say is this,*
> *I desire to be informed for what I have done. I am Condemned only*
> *upon Circumstances. I forgive all the World, so the Lord be merciful to*

*my Soul. . . . They should also take care how they bring money into
New England, to be Hanged for it.*

Thus we receive the impression that Quelch believed himself innocent and a wronged man. It seems to me, however, that any sailor who
agrees to countenance the horrible activity which took place in Marblehead Harbor and out in the Bay is guilty of piracy and was justly
hanged.

Governor Joseph Dudley, who officiated at the trial of Captain John Quelch

The competition for the souls of the condemned pirates among local clergy was undoubtedly fierce, but none were a match for Cotton Mather. "We have told you often," Mather sermonized, "we have told you weeping, that you have by sin outdone yourselves; That you were born Sinners, That you have lived Sinners, That your Sins have been many and mighty, and that the Sins for which you are now to Dy are of no common aggravation." Mather's attack on Governor Dudley, *The Deplorable State of New England, By Reason of a Covetous and Treacherous Governor*, was published in 1708 in London.

In his book *Raiders and Rebels: The Golden Age of Piracy*, Frank Sherry points out that pirates were more loyal to each other than to their country of origin, religion, or race. Of Quelch's crewmembers that were tried in 1704, thirteen were English, four Irish, one Swiss, one Dutch, and three American.

In *Piracy, Mutiny and Murder*, Snow wrote that in the spring of 1958, Arthur Tonneatti of Gloucester, Mr. and Mrs. Napoleon Couette of Fitchburg, and Alton Hall Blackington, a radio personality and writer who was a friend of Snow's, set out for Snake Island, where they believed Larramore and his crew had buried 320 ounces of gold dust in 1704. They uncovered nothing but an ancient stove on the island before they decided they were on the wrong Snake Island—there are several with that name along the coast. Snow wrote that Mr. Tonneatti was planning an expedition to another Snake Island "when he met his death in a tragic accident."

In the book *Buried Treasures of the Atlantic Coast*, W. C. Jameson has written that Star Island in the Isles of Shoals off New Hampshire was the hiding place of Quelch's plunder, but there appears to be little evidence to back this claim. For years many Marbleheaders, wrote Robert Ellis Cahill in *Pirates and Lost Treasures*, clung to the belief that Quelch buried substantial loot just offshore from their town landing. In fact, according to Cahill, this spawned a yearly "Treasure Hunter's Day" celebrated each May in the town for many years.

CHAPTER 3

William Fly, Hanged in Boston

Everyone sailing down Boston Harbor passes by an ominous black and white pyramidal marker atop a granite sea wall at Nix's Mate Island. There are many legends and stories told about this unusual island. But as the last resting place of innumerable pirates, Nix's Mate does not need fiction or legend to glamorize it. History itself has done that well. Of all the pirates whose bodies have been hanged in chains at Nix's Mate, William Fly was undoubtedly the most blasphemous.

Captain Fly was from England, hailing from suburban Bristol. He went to sea early in life, working his way up to the position of petty officer. Nothing is known either of his parents or of his education, but it is probable that his schooling was extremely meager and his background poor.

While at Jamaica, Fly was offered the position of boatswain by a short-handed master of a Bristol slaver, Captain John Green, who was planning a voyage on his snow *Elizabeth* to the Guinea coast. After a few weeks aboard the slaver, Fly developed a hatred of Captain Green, and discussed with certain others in the crew the possible advantage of seizing the snow for themselves. All accounts agree that Captain Green was admittedly a villain in his own right. Fly and the rest of the crew particularly hated the captain and the mate. They resolved to murder both of them, and sail away on a piratical cruise.

The mutineers planned to seize the snow in the early morning hours of May 27, 1726. When one o'clock came, William Fly, followed by his fellow conspirators, walked aft to Moris Cundon [also spelled Maurice Condon—*Ed*.], the man at the wheel. The helmsman was surrounded. Fly told him in no uncertain terms that they were seizing the *Elizabeth*, and that if he shouted or spoke a word they would blow out his brains. The man agreed to remain quiet. William Fly's next problem was Captain Green. Rolling up his sleeves, Fly seized a great cutlass and, accompanied by Alexander Mitchell, rushed into the cabin of the master.

"What in the devil is the matter?" exclaimed Captain Green, as the two mutineers rudely shook him awake.

"We have no time to answer impertinent questions," answered Mitchell. "You are to go on deck at once, and if you refuse we will be at the trouble of scraping the cabin to clean up your blood. Captain Fly has been chosen commander so we cannot have another captain on board or waste provisions to feed useless men." Captain Green, fearing that he was lost, made a final plea, asking that he be put ashore somewhere; meanwhile he would agree to be placed in irons.

"Ay, God damn ye," said Fly, "to live and hang us, if we are ever taken. No! No! Walk up and be damn'd, that bite won't take. It has hanged many an honest fellow already." So the two men pulled the captain out of his warm bed, dragged him into the steerage, and finally threw him on the deck, William Fly taking particular delight in prodding constantly the man he hated with the point of his cutlass.

The pirates told the captain that he could have a choice of either jumping overboard like a brave fellow or being tossed into eternity as a sneaking rascal. Evidently the captain's sins were many, for he implored the mutineers, "For the Lord's sake, don't throw me overboard, boatswain, for if you do, you throw me into Hell immediately."

"Damn you," Fly replied, "since he's so devilish godly, we'll give him time to say his prayers and I'll be parson. Say after me, Lord, have mercy on my soul, short prayers are best, and then over with him, my lads."

When the pirates attempted to throw him overboard, Captain Green grabbed at the mainsheet. Promptly, pirate Thomas Winthrop severed Green's wrist with one blow of his broadax, and the captain fell into the sea and was gone.

Meanwhile the mutineers seized and brought Mate Thomas Jenkins up on deck. He was told that since the captain had already been thrown overboard the mate should join him for company, for as they were both of the captain's mess, they should drink together. All gave a toss and threw him into the water. Coming to the surface, the mate cried out to the ship's doctor to throw him a line. Since the doctor was already in irons, however, along with the gunner and carpenter, Jenkins soon drowned.

Helmsman Cundon and Seaman Thomas Streator were told to report to Captain Fly. Fly informed them that they were rascals, and should have been thrown overboard after the captain and mate, but instead they were to be placed in irons for security. The mutineers, their success apparent, celebrated the victory in copious draughts of punch, and Captain Fly announced that henceforth the *Elizabeth* would be called the *Fame's Revenge*.

While the pirates were still formulating their plans, they sighted a sail in the gathering daylight, later identified as the *Pompey*, which had left Bristol at the same time as the *Elizabeth*. A hail of inquiry came from the *Pompey*, asking about the health of Captain Green.

"He is very well," answered Fly. "At your service." Fearing to attack such a large vessel, the pirates sailed away. It was agreed that the ship should be headed for the North Carolina coast. Reaching their destination on June 3, they came upon a sloop, the *John and Hannah*, captained by pilot John Fulker, lying at anchor inside the bar. When Fly stood for the inner harbor, Captain John Fulker rowed out to Fly with his mate and three others to offer his services as pilot. One of the others was Captain William Atkinson, formerly of the brigantine *Boneta*.

Reaching the snow, Captain Fulker was invited aboard. Captain Fly took the four men into the cabin to share a bowl of punch. As the punch was brought in Fly suddenly announced that he was not one to mince words, for he and his comrades were "Gentlemen of Fortune." Fly was interested in Fulker's sloop on the other side of the bar. If she could beat the snow, then Fly wanted her. Anchoring the *Fame's Revenge* a league away, the pirate captain ordered Fulker to take six men and bring out the sloop. But the wind was in the wrong quarter. After considerable effort, the attempt was abandoned. Captain Fulker returned under guard to the pirate vessel. Furious because of the captain's failure to sail the sloop out to him, Fly punished the American severely. Captain John Fulker tried to explain that a bar ran between the two vessels. Not wishing to wreck the sloop, he had been unable to carry out his orders because of a contrary wind.

"Damn ye," replied Fly, "you lie like a Dog, but damn my Blood, your Hide shall pay for your Roguery and if I can't bring her off I'll burn her where she lies." Fulker was then taken to the gears, where he was stripped to the waist and given a terrible beating with a cat-of-nine tails, until blood ran down his body and filled his shoes.

Another attempt was made to bring off the sloop. The crew, afraid of what might happen should they fail in their orders, sailed the sloop right across the bar, where she hit, ripped open her bottom, and sank. Realizing that the accident was his own fault, Fly concealed his rage over the loss as best he could.

Two days later the buccaneer set sail for further conquests. About this time Captain John Gale was coming up the coast aboard the ship *John and Betty* taking her from Barbados to Virginia. Captain William Fly, cruising in the vicinity, sighted the ship and gave chase at once, but when the *John and Betty* proved the better sailor, Fly hoisted a flag of distress.

The suspicious Captain Gale rightly interpreted this ruse, and stayed on his course. Fly crowded on all sail possible, doggedly following the *John and Betty*. A bit of pirate luck now helped the Bristol buccaneer. The wind slackened, allowing Fly to drift within gunshot. Hoisting his Jolly Roger, Captain William Fly ordered the cannons fired several times at the ship. Captain John Gale, realizing his hopeless position, surrendered, striking his colors. Fly went aboard his longboat, which carried a unique metal throwing device called a *pateraro* in the bow, and rowed over to the ship, where he soon had the captain and crew prisoners. After forcing six of the crew to join him Fly let the ship sail away, but held Captain Fulker and some of the others who refused to sign articles. Captain William Atkinson, who had rowed out with Fulker from the sloop, was detained because of his superior knowledge of navigation. Atkinson, about whom we shall learn more later, asked why he was being kept aboard the *Fame's Revenge*. Fly's reply, probably the result of a limited vocabulary, should not be read by the too fastidious:

> *Look ye, Captain Atkinson, it is not that we care for your Company, God damn ye, God damn my Soul, if you don't act like an honest Man, God damn ye, and offer to play us any Rogue's Tricks, by God, and God sink me, but I'll blow your brains out; God damn me if I don't. Now, Captain Atkinson, you may pilot us wrong, which God damn ye, would be a rascally trick, by God, because you would betray Men who trust in you; but, by the eternal Jesus, you shan't live to see us hang'd. . . . If you will be a Villain and betray your trust,*

may God strike me dead, and may I drink a Bowl of Brimstone and Fire with the Devil, if I don't send you head-long to Hell, God damn me; and so there needs no more Arguments, by God, for I've told you my Mind, and here's all the Ship's Crew for Witnesses, that if I do blow your Brains out, you may blame no Body but your self, God damn ye.

Fearing Atkinson might talk and plan with some of the other pressed seamen, Fly forbade him to engage in any sort of conversation with them. And as a further precaution he ordered a hammock swung in the cabin in which the former master of the *Boneta* could sleep.

The sloop *Rachel* was next encountered. Captain Samuel Harris had fifty Scotch-Irish passengers aboard, bound for Pennsylvania. Captain Fly had the sloop boarded. A day later the pirates, after taking and forcing James Benbrook, allowed it to proceed.

Captain William Fly now desired to sail northward toward the island of Martha's Vineyard, where he intended to procure water and rest, before his voyage to the Guinea coast. Atkinson was the navigator, however, and purposely carried the *Fame's Revenge* off the coast and out into the bay. Fly finally realized that Atkinson was misleading him.

"God damn you," shouted Fly, "you are an obstinate villain." Pulling out a pistol, Fly was about to fire it at Atkinson when pirate Mitchell stepped in and pleaded with Fly, thus saving the life of Atkinson.

The next encounter of the pirate ship was the fishing schooner *James*, then sailing near Brown's Bank, located about two hundred miles off Cape Ann. The pirate hoisted his black flag and fired a shot across her bows, whereupon Captain George Girdler of the *James* went aboard the pirate vessel. As they were on the fishing grounds, several other schooners soon came in sight, and Fly decided to divide his men in an attempt to make more captures. As later events proved, this was Fly's fatal mistake, for when he sent six of his pirates aboard the *James* to follow the fishermen, there were only three of his buccaneers aboard the *Fame's Revenge*, one of whom was in irons for suspected mutiny!

Atkinson's golden opportunity was now at hand. He had already indulged in certain preliminary conversations with Samuel Walker and Thomas Streator, and the former revealed Atkinson's plans to Benbrook. Almost a dozen forced men were aboard the *Fame's Revenge*. When several other sails were seen in the distance, Atkinson knew the hour to strike had come. Captain Fly kept his arsenal of guns and cutlasses aft on the quarter deck with him, but when Atkinson and the others called out in glowing terms about the new sails which they sighted on the horizon, Captain Fly finally overcame his usual caution to walk forward toward the bow, where he might see for himself. This proved his undoing.

"If you were but here, Sir, with your glass, ahead, you would easily see them all," Atkinson called from the bow, whereupon Fly walked to the windlass, sat down on it, and with his telescope scanned the seas. As he sat there Benbrook and Walker came up behind him, suggesting that he focus his attention a point or two to one side. Meanwhile, Atkinson quickly ran aft, reaching the arsenal where he obtained a brace of guns. At a given signal Benbrook and Walker grabbed Fly, broke the captain's sword, and pinioned his arms. Atkinson rushed back to the three men, where at gunpoint he called upon Fly to surrender at once, or else he would be a dead man.

When Pirate Grenville showed his head above the companion hatchway, Atkinson promptly broke his skull with his pistol butt. The other pirates were quickly subdued and put in irons, thus giving the ship to the forced men. When confined by the side of his three confederates, Fly began to curse as only he could. It is said his swearing and blasphemy far exceeded all his previous records. But it was of no avail this time, and four days later the *Fame's Revenge* sailed in by Nix's Mate, where Fly was later to be gibbeted, and anchored in Boston Harbor. The four buccaneers were still in irons below deck.

One of the great events of Boston's pirate history began on the following July 4 when the sailors were all brought to trial in what is now the old State House. The Admiralty Court had as its presiding officer Lieutenant Governor William Dummer, and diarist Samuel Sewall was one of the Admiralty Court judges in the proceedings.

Captain Atkinson was tried first. As there was no question of his innocence, Atkinson was acquitted at once. Joseph Marshall and William Ferguson of the *James* then came before the magistrates. They also were quickly freed. Next to face the Admiralty Court were the six men who had been forced from the *John and Betty*. After their statements had been given, they were permitted the right to walk out of court as free men. Three other sailors were interrogated, Edward Apthorp of the *John and Hannah*, Moris Cundon, helmsman on the *Elizabeth*, and James Benbrook, who had helped seize Fly. All were acquitted. The fate of Walker, Benbrook's fellow conspirator, is not apparent.

As was the custom, the four known pirates were the last to be tried. Fly had been planning his defense in the meantime. As Mitchell and his mates had not been heard from since they sailed away in search of the fishermen off Brown's Bank, Fly decided to blame him for all his troubles.

"I can't charge myself with Murder," he said. "I did not strike or wound the Master or Mate. It was Mitchell did it." Regardless of this statement, the Court's judgment was that he should die. Samuel Cole, pirate quartermaster, was next heard. He was father of seven children. A month before, Cole had been suspected by Fly of mutiny and given a terrible lashing with one hundred strokes. Because of this he was still in great agony, but he was, nevertheless, sentenced to die. George Condick, a young drunkard, who had never been more than the ship's cook, was pardoned. Nothing in favor of Henry Grenville, another married man, could be found, so he was sentenced. Fly, Cole, and Grenville then received their judgment. They were to be hanged at the usual place of execution, near what is now fittingly enough the Boston Harbor Police Station 8.

The Reverend Cotton Mather, without whom no execution seemed complete in those stirring days, interviewed the doomed men on July 6, 1726. The results of his interview, together with a sermon preached at that time, he published in a book called *The Vial poured out upon the Sea.* While much of the material is of no importance in our particular survey, a paragraph or two is of interest. His speech to the pirates follows:

> *Unhappy Men:—Yet not hopeless of Eternal Happiness:—A Marvellous Providence of GOD has put a Quickstop to a Swift Carriere you were taking in the paths of the Destroyer. But had you been at once cut off in your Wickedness, what had become of you? A merciful God has not only given you a space to Repent, but has ordered your being brought into a place where such means of Instruction will be Employ'd upon you, and such pains will be taken for the Salvation of your Souls, as are not commonly Elsewhere to be met withal, May this Goodness of God lead you to Repentance:—Among other and greater proofs of This, you will accept this Visit, which I now intend you.*
>
> *We thank you, Syr, replied the pirates.*

Somehow, it would seem that the above reply of the pirates has been changed, perhaps just a little, by the good minister, when he wrote the account.

Captain William Fly soon behaved in a manner which justified his record. He shocked Reverend Mr. Mather by his downright refusal to listen to the sermon in the Old North Church, a sermon which had been especially prepared for the pirates, and members of the congregation were disappointed when he didn't appear. Captain William Fly stuck by his guns, however, saying that he did not wish the mob to gaze at him. The other pirates attended and sat through what was probably a two-hour sermon on the subject, *They Dy even without Wisdom.* Tuesday, July 12, arrived, the date of the execution. The usual thousands of spectators had thronged to Copp's Hill from the entire countryside around the leading seaport of America to watch the pirates die. At about three o'clock that afternoon the doomed men climbed to the wooden platform, where three black-gowned ministers from the town offered lengthy prayers.

Captain William Fly was determined to go to his death bravely. He wished to be remembered as one who did not fear execution. Cotton Mather is the authority for the fact that Fly carried a nosegay in his hand, and spoke to people in the crowd, whenever he found the occasion opportune. Rowed out to the gallows, "he nimbly mounted the stage," smiling and joking with those about him. The hangman, evidently a new man, fumbled with the knots while preparing the trap, and Fly reproached him for "not understanding his Trade, and with his own hands rectified matters," according to Mather.

The *Boston News-Letter*, number 1172, for the week of July 7–14, 1726, carried an account of the occasion, which we reproduce:

> *On Tuesday, the 12th Instant, about 3 P.M. were Executed here for Piracy, Murder, & c. Three of the Condemned Persons mentioned in our last, viz. William Fly, Capt. Samuel Cole, Quarter-Master, and Henry Greenvill, the other viz. George Condick, was Repriv'd at the Place of Execution, for a Twelve Month and a Day, and is to be recommended to His Majesty's Grace & Favour. Fly behav'd himself very unbecoming even to the last; however, advised Masters of Vessels not to be Severe and Barbarous to their Men, which might be a reason why so many turn'd Pirates: the other Two seem'd Penitent, beg'd that others might be warn'd by 'em. Their Bodies were carried in a Boat to a small Island call'd Nicks's-Mate, about 2 Leagues from the Town, where the above said Fly was hung up in Irons, as a Spectacle for the Warning of others, especially Sea-faring Men; the other Two were buried there.*

Two hundred years later I went ashore on the bar which surrounds the granite wall and pyramid now known as Nix's Mate, and carefully explored the shifting sands, rocks, and silt which comprise part of what is left of the pirate island. After several days of searching and digging I located what probably was the spot where Fly was gibbeted, for a frag-

Edward Rowe Snow (waving) and friends at Nix's Mate in Boston Harbor, where the bodies of pirates like William Fly were strung up in chains as a warning to all (photo by Howard White, from Snow's Piracy, Mutiny and Murder, *1959)*

ment of the iron band and several links of chain were uncovered. This was all that could be found which recalled in any way the nefarious and villainous Captain William Fly, who, according to Dow and Edmonds, "only wanted skill and power to become as infamous as any who had scoured the seas."

William Fly's seamanship skills were questionable, and he didn't amass the riches of other famous pirates—but his prodigious cruelty and profanity secured him an elevated place in pirate lore. Fly had a short career even by pirate standards—only thirty-five days—and according to some sources was a mere twenty-seven years old when executed.

Snow interpreted Fly's performance at the gallows as an effort to exhibit courage, but historian David Cordingly, in his book *Under the Black Flag*, viewed it more as a final act of rebellion. "A surprising number of pirates," wrote Cordingly, "showed defiance at the end and refused to die in the contrite and penitent manner expected of them."

A daybeacon has marked Nix's Mate Island since 1805, when one was first erected by the Boston Marine Society. The black and white pyramidal marker was in disrepair and was slated for removal in 2001 by the U.S. Coast Guard, who planned to replace it with a "steel pipe tower with dayboards." After the Friends of the Boston Harbor Islands (the marker is the model for their logo) and others made a plea for its preservation, the Coast Guard agreed to repair the marker instead.

The island itself, once at least eleven acres, is now worn down to a small S-shaped spit that is submerged at high tide. According to local legend, the first mate of a Captain Nix was hanged on the island after being blamed for the murder of his captain. Just before his execution the mate proclaimed that as proof of his innocence the island would disappear—and it did.

CHAPTER 4

Philip Ashton,
Whose Story Surpasses Robinson Crusoe

We should not trust in ourselves, but in God who delivered us from so great a Death, and doth deliver; in whom we trust, that he will yet deliver us.

The passage above, taken from the Bible, was placed on the title page of a small book written about the strange adventures of Philip Ashton of Marblehead, Massachusetts, who was captured by the pirates, forced to become one himself, eventually escaping from them, and who finally returned to Marblehead after many months of hardships and suffering.

This young Marblehead sailor began his adventures while with the fishing fleet then in waters off Cape Sable. At that time, 1722, it was customary for the entire fleet to stop fishing on Friday afternoon and sail into Port Roseway, near what is now Shelburne, Nova Scotia, to await the Sabbath and properly observe it there. Philip Ashton was aboard a shallop that entered Port Roseway late that Friday afternoon, June 15, 1722. Besides the usual number of fishermen in the harbor, he noticed a brigantine, which he incorrectly assumed to be an inward-bound West Indiaman. After Ashton's shallop had been at anchor for a few hours, a boat from the brigantine came alongside his fishing vessel.

Suddenly the men in the boat jumped aboard, pulling cutlasses and pistols from under their clothing, and soon overcame the astonished fishermen on the shallop's deck. Time after time they repeated this identical maneuver, until over twelve fishing vessels anchored in the harbor had been captured.

A worse shock was in store for the fishermen, however, for when they were brought aboard the brigantine, they found that it was commanded by none other than the infamous villain, Captain Edward Low, whose adventures are given elsewhere in this volume. Philip Ashton was soon sent for, and he went aft to meet the great pirate. Confronted by the man whose name alone was enough to strike terror in the hearts of all honest sailors, Ashton was asked to sign articles and come along on a voyage. In his own words, Philip Ashton tells us what then occurred:

> I told him, No; I could by no means consent to go with them. I should be glad if he would give me my Liberty, and put me on board any Vessel, or set me on shoar there. For indeed my dislike of their Company and Actions, my concern for my Parents, and my fears of being found in such Bad Company, made me dread the thoughts of being carried away by them; so that I had not the least Inclination to continue with them.

Of course, when Ashton refused to join up and sign articles with Captain Low, he was roughly handled and thrown down into the hold. While in the hold he heard the various crews of the fishing fleet brought over to the brigantine, one by one, and realized that there was little hope of assistance from the other vessels. The next day about thirty or forty of the fishermen who had refused to join up were placed on Mr. Orn's fishing schooner, which was turned into a floating prison for the dissenters.

At noon on Sunday Quartermaster John Russel boarded the schooner and took six of the fishermen away. They were Nicholas Merritt and Lawrence Fabens, both of whom later escaped; Joseph Libbie, who finally became a pirate and was hanged at Newport; Philip Ashton; and two other men whose names are not known. The fishermen were rowed over to the pirate chieftain's flagship, where they lined up on the quarterdeck. All of them were under twenty-one years of age.

Captain Ned Low approached them, pistol in hand.

"Are any of you married men?" asked Low. The question, unexpected as it was, struck the listeners dumb at the moment. The silence infuriated the great pirate, and he cocked his pistol, shoving it against the head of poor Philip Ashton.

"You dog," cried Low, "Why don't you answer me? I shall shoot you through the head unless you . . . tell me now if you are married or not." Ashton, greatly frightened, stammered that he was not married, and the rest of the group also answered that they were still single. Low then walked away from them. Ashton later found out that the pirate's concern was due to Low's wife having died, leaving a small child, which even then was living at Boston.

Later in the day Low again interviewed the six men, asking them to sign papers, and all six refused. Still later he had each man sent for, singly, whereupon he asked the same question. Each fisherman again refused. Then Philip Ashton was taken below into the steerage, where the quartermaster tried to tempt him with stories of great riches and wealth. Other pirates gathered about him, and tried to be friendly, to win his confidence, and asked him to

> *drink with them, not doubting but that this wile would sufficiently entangle me, and so they should prevail with me to do that in my Cups, which they perceived they could not bring me to do while I was Sober; but . . . I had no Inclination to drown my Sorrows with my Senses in their Inebriating Bowls, and so refused their Drink, as well as their Proposals.*

After his final refusal, Ashton was taken up on deck again, where Captain Low threatened him with death unless he changed his mind. Ashton said that whatever happened he could not join the pirate band, but finally Low signed him on anyway as a forced man, together with the names of all his companions.

The following Tuesday the buccaneers chose a schooner belonging to Joseph Dolliber of Marblehead as the new flagship, and all the pirates went aboard her. With the exception of the six forced men and four others who had joined from the Isles of Shoals, the prisoners were sent over to the brigantine and allowed to proceed to Boston. This was discouraging to Philip Ashton, who made one final attempt to appeal for freedom. Together with Nicholas Merrit, he went to Low, and the two young men fell on their knees before the pirate captain, asking for release. Low scornfully refused, telling them if they attempted to break away they would be shot. The brigantine soon sailed off, and the forced sailors were alone with the highwaymen of the sea.

Just as Ashton had given up all thought of deliverance, an accident occurred which gave him hope. One of the pirates had come back to the ship, leaving a dog on the beach, and the dog began to howl dismally. Low, hearing the disturbance, ordered that the dog be brought out. Two Marblehead boys volunteered to row in and get him, and nineteen-year-old Philip Ashton decided this was a good chance to escape. He

Pirates boarding a ship

rushed to the side of the ship and was about to jump into the boat when Quartermaster Russel caught hold of his shoulder, saying that two men were sufficient to bring out one dog.

Surely enough, the pirates watched the boat land on the shore and the Marblehead men walk inland away from it. They never returned, and the pirates lost their boat as well, while the dog soon wandered off and was not seen again. Of course, Quartermaster Russel now believed that Ashton had tried to join the two, knowing that they had planned to escape, but the truth was that while Ashton had planned to escape himself, he did not know the other two had the same objective. Nevertheless, the quartermaster was so infuriated that he attempted to kill Ashton then and there.

The buccaneer seized Philip Ashton by the shoulder, clapped his great pistol against the skull of the boy, and pulled the trigger; the gun missed fire. Again and again the quartermaster snapped the pistol, but each time it failed to go off. Disgusted with his firearm, Quartermaster Russel went over to the side of the ship. Standing by the rail, he reset the pistol, pulled the trigger, and fired the gun successfully into the ocean. The exasperated pirate now drew his cutlass and lunged for the boy. Terrified, Ashton ran down into the hold, where he cowered in the midst of a group of the other pirates, and thus escaped Russel's wrath.

It was a hard lot which lay ahead for the Marblehead lad, and he soon learned to hide in the hold most of the time. Once a week, however, he was brought up under examination and asked to sign articles, and every time he refused. Thrashed and beaten with sword and cane after each refusal, Ashton would escape to the hold as soon as he could to nurse his cuts and bruises for another week. Probably some of the kinderhearted rogues took care of this poor lad in their crude way, so that he was able to get something to eat every day.

But week after week passed without hope, and despair made Ashton utterly miserable. In his book he speaks of Low's narrow escape from an encounter with a British man-of-war in the very harbor of Saint John's, Newfoundland, mentioning the seizure of seven or eight vessels the next day. Later a captured sloop manned by impressed pirates ran away from Low and was never seen again. Nicholas Merrit, one of Ashton's Marblehead friends, was aboard this vessel. The schooner and a captured pink were careened at the island of Bonavista, after which seven or eight forced men from the pink went ashore to hunt. They never returned to the ship. Ashton felt that with so many escaping from Low, his chance would eventually come, and in this he was not mistaken.

A terrible storm caught the pirates shortly afterwards, and for five days and nights Ashton feared that they would all go to the bottom. Even the most foul of the buccaneers was afraid during the fearful tempest, as Ashton recorded one of the bloodthirsty ruffian's exclaiming in his particular moment of spiritual anguish, "Oh! I wish I were at Home."

At last the storm went down, and the pirates headed for the three islands called the Triangles, located in the West Indies about forty leagues from Surinam. Captain Low decided that another careening was necessary. In heaving down the pink, so many hands climbed into the shrouds that it threw her open ports under water. Low and the doctor, then below in the cabin, almost drowned, but managed to get out in time. The vessel went over on her beam ends in forty feet of water throwing the men into the sea. As the vessel righted itself, the men climbed back into the shrouds. The entire hull remained far under water. It had been a narrow escape for the notorious Captain Low.

In the excitement two men drowned, and Ashton, who was a poor swimmer, almost perished before he was rescued. The pink had carried most of the provisions and the drinking water, both of which were lost, so every sailor transferred to the schooner, which at once put out to sea.

Reaching the island of Grand Grenada, eighteen leagues westward of Tobago, they went ashore for water. The French on the island suspected them of being in the smuggling trade, so sailed out to capture Low and his men. When Low saw them coming, he ordered all the pirates to their stations, and the French sloop was quickly seized and made one of the pirate fleet. The buccaneers captured seven or eight vessels in short order, after which they took two sloops off Santa Cruz.

Low now desired a doctor's chest, and sent four Frenchmen ashore at St. Thomas, demanding a chest of instruments and medicines of the residents with the alternative of having their town sacked and burned. The doctor's chest arrived within twenty-four hours, and the Frenchmen who had been prisoners were allowed to sail away in one of the captured sloops. From Santa Cruz they sailed to Curaçao, but then fell in with two ships, an English man-of-war and a "Guinea-Man." Low escaped only by sailing over some shallows on which the man-of-war ran aground. On this occasion Ashton was aboard the schooner, under command of Quartermaster Farrington Spriggs. The two pirate vessels separated in the chase, and Spriggs headed for the island of Utilla, near Roatan. Having lost Low completely, Spriggs decided to sail up through the Gulf of Mexico to New England, where he could increase his small company and reprovision his schooner.

There were eight forced men out of Spriggs' entire crew of twenty-two who secretly plotted to capture the schooner. The scheme was to get the pirates drunk under the hatches as soon as the *Happy Delivery* approached the shores of New England. The forced men would then sail into the nearest harbor and throw themselves on the mercy of the government.

It was a good plan, but the men never had a chance to try it out. Sailing away from Utilla, they fell in with a large sloop, which bore down on them, opening fire as it approached. Spriggs did not come about, however, running for a possible escape instead. Then pirate colors were hoisted from the sloop. At this the regular pirates aboard Spriggs' vessel broke out into cheers, for it was none other than Low's famous ensign which fluttered high above the stranger's decks. Soon the two old cronies were together again, and all was well except for the forced men whose scheming came to an end. As it was five weeks since Low and Spriggs had parted, the forced men had been hopeful that they had seen the last of the villain, but such was not the case. To make matters worse, one of the forced men eventually informed on the others. Spriggs was in favor of shooting them down, but Low laughed it off.

On returning to the schooner, Spriggs told Ashton he deserved to be hanged from the yardarm, but Ashton informed the schooner's captain that his only desire was to be free of the pirate vessel, and he intended to harm no one. The incident was soon forgotten.

Low now steered a course for Roatan Harbor, in the Bay of Honduras. The pirate chieftain quickly went ashore, where he indulged in drinking and carousing to his heart's content for a few days while his buccaneers were occupied in careening and scraping the vessels. The schooner was loaded with logwood and sent out in charge of one John Blaze with four men aboard. When Low and Spriggs, together with many of the pirate leaders, went off to another island, Ashton's hopes were raised again. He would try to escape.

Saturday, March 9, 1723, was an eventful and thrilling day for Philip Ashton of Marblehead. Noticing the cooper with six men getting ready to row ashore from Spriggs' vessel, he asked to be taken with them, as he had not been on land since his capture almost nine months before.

Since the island was desolate and uninhabited, the cooper finally gave in to the pitiful pleadings of the lad from Marblehead, and into the long-boat jumped young Philip. As it happened, Ashton had asked the cooper on the impulse of the moment, and was dressed

> *with only an Ozenbrigs Frock and Trousers on, and a Mill'd Cap upon my Head, having neither Shirt, Shoes, not Stockings, nor any thing else about me; whereas, had I been aware of such an Opportunity, but one quarter of an Hour before, I could have provided my self something better. However, thought I, if I can but once get footing on Terra-Firma, tho' in never so bad Circumstances, I shall call it a happy Deliverance; for I was resolved, come what would, never to come on board again.*

When the longboat landed, Ashton was the most active worker of all in moving the heavy casks up on the beach, so when the task was over he naturally went off by himself as if to rest, strolling along the beach, picking up stones and shells as we all do along the seashore, until he was quite a distance from the others. Then he walked toward the edge of the woods, whereupon the cooper called out to him, asking where he was going.

"I'm going to get some coconuts," was Ashton's reply, and soon reached the forest. Once out of sight of the pirates, he broke out in a keen run, reminding us for all the world of Stevenson's hero in *Treasure Island*, for whom he possibly served as a model.

In the meantime the pirates had filled the water casks and were ready to return to the ship. Ashton huddled in the dense forest, burrowing into a thicket, while the cries sounded out around him, calling him back to the longboat. Of course Ashton kept a discreet silence. After a long time, the pirates gave up and rowed out to their ship.

Philip Ashton was thus left alone on a desolate and uninhabited island. When he was sure the pirates had left him, Ashton ventured forth from his hiding place, appearing down on the beach about a mile from the watering place, where he could observe what went on aboard the pirate vessels. Five days later they sailed away, leaving him very much alone on the island. His thoughts follow:

> *I began to reflect upon myself, and my present Condition; I was upon an island from whence I could not get off; I knew of no*

*Humane Creature within many scores of Miles of me; I had but a
Scanty Cloathing, and no possibility of getting more; I was destitute
of all Provision for my Support, and knew not how I should come at
any. . . .*

Ashton walked around the island, estimating it to be some thirty
miles in length.* The reader can easily locate it on any modern map or
chart, situated to the north of Cape Honduras in Central America. Try
as he would, however, Ashton could find no signs of human habitation.
Later he located a great grove of lime trees, and near them some broken
fragments of earthen pots, from which he concluded Indians had formerly lived at the island.

Wild figs, grapes, and coconuts were plentiful, but Ashton found no
way of opening the coconut husks, although I have seen them split off
from their covering by striking them longitudinally on a sharp rock.
Then he discovered an oval-shaped fruit, larger than an orange, which
was red inside, and contained two or three stones slightly smaller than
a walnut. Fearing he might be poisoned, Ashton kept away from them
until one day he chanced upon a group of wild hogs devouring the fruit,
after which he sampled them and found them delicious. He called them
"Mammees Supporters," but when I went through Panama in 1927 they
were known as papayas. Sundry other fruits and herbs were also discovered by Ashton, although he avoided the "Mangeneil Apple," which
he claimed would have killed him.

Deer, wild hogs, lizards, ducks, "Teil," curlews, "geldings," snakes,
pelicans, boobies, pigeons, and parrots, with tortoises along the
beaches, made up the wild life at the island of Roatan. Ashton could not
take advantage of the situation, however, for he had no knife or
weapon of any kind, and was without means of making a fire. But he
did discover hundreds of tortoise eggs in nests which he found on the
beach, and grew very fond of this change in his fruit and vegetable diet.
He became quite a naturalist in observing the habits of the tortoise,
noticing that the creatures lay their eggs in the sand above the high-
water mark, depositing them in a hollow which they dig to a depth of
from twelve to eighteen inches. After laying the eggs, the tortoise fills
the hole and smoothes over the sand. The eggs, Ashton found, usually

---

*Ashton's estimate of the island's length was approximately correct; the island
is less than four miles wide at its widest point.—*Ed.*

hatch in about eighteen to twenty days, after which the young turtles make a rush for the water.

The giant lizards were as big around as "a Man's wast," and about twelve to fourteen feet long. Ashton's first encounter was a terrible experience, for he mistook it for a log, whereupon it opened its mouth wide enough "to have thrown a Hat into it, and blew out its Breath at me." There were smaller serpents on the island, some of them poisonous, especially a snake called the "Barber's Pole, being streaked White and Yellow. But I met with no Rattle-Snakes there, unless the Pirates," concluded Ashton.

The flies bothered Ashton greatly, in particular the small black flies. These insects and the mosquitoes were very bothersome. He found that a certain key located off the island was free from all flies and insects, but being a poor swimmer, he had to construct a bamboo life preserver to insure his arriving safely at the island.

With his frock and trousers bound to his head, he swam across, donning his clothes on reaching the island. Unfortunately, he never was able to bring out enough wood or branches to construct a hut there, or he might have made the low treeless key his permanent abode. His new home the young adventurer called the Day Island and his older residence the Night Island.

One time, however, just as he reached his Day Island, he was severely hit from behind, and to his astonishment found the shock was caused by a huge shovel-nosed shark, which had grounded itself in the shallow water and could not seize him. Later Ashton became more and more experienced in swimming, but he never forgot that narrow escape from death.

The greatest trial Ashton had to bear was the lack of shoes. His bare feet were soon masses of ugly bruises and cuts from the sticks and stones away from the beach, and the sharp fragments of shell on the shore itself. Often he walked along as tenderly as he could, when suddenly he would step on a sharp rock or shell which would

> run into the Old Wounds, & the Anguish of it would strike me down
> as suddenly as if I had been shot thro', & oblige me to set down and
> Weep by the hour together at the extremity of my Pain.

At one time he fell ill, and when in this condition was attacked by one of the wild boars. Managing to climb part of the way up a tree,

Ashton felt the tusks of the boar as they ripped through his clothing and tore a substantial section of the cloth away. The boar then left the scene. Incidentally, this was the only time a wild beast bothered him in any way, but it almost proved fatal. Growing worse instead of better, he despaired of life itself and in his sickness and unhappiness longed for the sight of his parents.

The rains began during October and continued for five months. Throughout this time the air was raw and cold, similar to that of a New England northeasterly storm. During these months he wished for fire more than ever, but was never able to produce it while alone on the island.

An amazing incident took place in November 1723, when Ashton sighted a craft of some type approaching him in the distance. Drawing closer, it resolved itself into a canoe, with one man paddling it. Ashton, still very feeble at the time, made no effort to conceal himself. The canoeist paddled close to shore and observed Ashton at the edge of the beach. Shouting to the Marblehead sailor, the canoeist queried him about who he was and what he was doing. Ashton soon told his story, after which the stranger, whose name Ashton never found out, came ashore and shook hands with the sick islander.

It was a happy occasion for poor Philip Ashton when he could actually see and talk with another human being. The man, who was English, had been living with the Spaniards for the last twenty-two years, but when, for some undisclosed reason, they wished to burn him alive, he fled to Roatan Island. Building a fire for Ashton, for he had tongs and a flint, the Englishman told the sick Marbleheader that he would paddle out and hunt venison for him, planning to return in a few days. He gave Ashton his knife, the tongs and flint, five pounds of pork, and a bottle of powder before taking his departure three days later.

Ashton never saw him again, for within an hour after the canoe disappeared in the distance, a terrific storm hit the island, and probably drowned the Englishman at sea. A canoe drifted ashore some time later, but after careful examination Ashton decided it was not that of the Britisher.

With the aid of the tools and implements which his friend had given him, Philip Ashton was soon eating a more balanced diet, and the fire kept him comfortable during the bad weather. Slowly regaining his strength, he would walk along the beach, watching the crabs in the shallow water. Ashton finally developed a manner of catching them at night, by lighting a torch and wading waist deep with it in the water. The crabs, attracted by the light, would hasten to it, whereupon Ashton would spear them with a sharpened stick he carried in his other hand.

Growing stronger daily, Ashton made plans which involved the canoe he had found on the beach. He then thought himself "Admiral of the Neighbouring Seas," and decided to make a tour of some of the more distant islands. Storing up a supply of grapes, figs, tortoise, and other eatables, with his precious flint box safely packed away, he set out for the island of Bonaca [usually spelled Bonacca—*Ed.*], some six leagues westward.

Approaching the distant land, Ashton noticed a sloop off the eastern shore, so pulled his craft up on the beach at the western end of Bonaca. Making his way overland, he walked to the other side of the island, but could not make out the sloop. Tired from his journey, he sat down at the foot of a large tree located near the shore and went to sleep.

Suddenly awakened by gunfire, he jumped to his feet to find nine large canoes, filled with Spaniards, coming up on the beach in front of him, with several of the men discharging their guns at him. He ran for the nearest thicket, whereupon they all landed and went after him. But he was adept at concealing himself by this time, so after searching for several hours, the Spanish sailors paddled away from the vicinity, and Ashton went down on the shore. He noticed the tree where he had fallen asleep, and saw that there were several bullet holes uncomfortably near where his head had been. It took him three days to return to his canoe, for his rush into the thicket had opened up his old wounds. But he found the canoe unharmed, and was soon paddling away from the island. His experiences while there made him eager to return to Roatan Island, which he reached without accident.

Seven long months then passed. Finally, in June 1724, when he was out on his Day Island off the shore, two large canoes approached, and the men aboard noticed the smoke from Ashton's fire. Ashton fled to the Night Island in his canoe at once. Glancing back, he saw that the canoes were slowly following ashore, indicating that they were as afraid of Ashton as he was of them.

Observing their extreme caution, Ashton decided they could not be pirates, so went openly down on the shore to find out what he could. The visitors then leaned back on their oars and paddles and asked Ashton who he was.

> *I told them I was an English Man, and had Run away from the Pirates. Upon this they drew something nearer and enquired who was there besides my self; I assured them I was alone. . . . They told me they were Bay-men, come from the Bay [Honduras]. This was comfortable News to me; so I bid them pull ashoar, there was no danger.*

They first sent one man ashore, whom Ashton went down to meet. When the visitor saw such a "Poor, Ragged, Lean, Wan, Forlorn, Wild, Miserable, Object so near him," he started back, frightened from the shock, but on recovering shook hands with Ashton, who embraced him with joy. Then the sailor picked poor Ashton up in his arms and carried him down to the canoes, where the entire company soon surrounded him in wonderment. When Ashton told them he had been living on the island for sixteen months, the group were amazed. After they gave Ashton a small amount of rum, he fell down insensible, overcome by the effects of the drink to which he was unaccustomed, but he revived slowly and later was as well as could be expected.

The Bay men told him that they had fled from the Spaniards, who, they feared, were about to assault them. They soon moved everything ashore, and within a short time had erected a substantial dwelling a little distance away on one of the windswept keys. They named this new home the Castle of Comfort. Ashton recovered his strength and spirits aided by the presence of so many human beings around him, and was soon joining in hunting expeditions. He made a good friend of an old man the Bay men called Father Hope, who told him of his many experiences, finally revealing that he had buried a small treasure chest in the woods.

Six months later, however, the pirates appeared. At the time, Ashton had gone over to Bonaca to hunt with three other men. Returning one night to Roatan Island, they were surprised at the sound of heavy firing, and on coming into the moonlit harbor they noticed that a large vessel was besieging the "Castle of Comfort." Taking down their sail as rapidly as possible, the four islanders rowed out of the harbor, but unfortunately they had been detected. Soon a canoe was chasing them, with eight or ten men in it. Drawing closer to the fleeing men, the invaders discharged a swivel gun mounted in the bow of the canoe. The shot landed in the water ahead.

The attacking party were actually pirates from Spriggs' vessel, the same from which Ashton had escaped. Reaching shore before the buccaneers could catch them, the islanders fled into the woods. The disappointed pirates landed on the beach, taking the canoe which the men had left on the shore, and then departed from the island. Ashton described what happened when his friends surrendered:

> *Accordingly they took all the Men ashoar, and with them an Indian Woman and Child; those of them that were ashoar abused the Woman shamefully. They killed one Man after they were come ashoar, and threw him into one of the Baymens Canoes, where their Tar was, and set Fire to it, and burnt him in it. Then they carried our People on Board their Vessels, where they were barbarously treated.*

Learning of a treasure in the woods which had been hidden by old Father Hope, the pirates beat Hope unmercifully until he revealed the location. They found the treasure and took it away with them. Before leaving, the pirates gave the Bay men a craft of about five tons to sail to the Bay in, but made them promise not to communicate with Ashton or his group. Then the pirates sailed away for good.

Father Hope decided a bad promise was better broken than kept, so came at once to the hiding place of Ashton and his friends, where a conference was held on plans for the future. All except Ashton, John Symonds, and an African slave belonging to Symonds wished to leave at once for the Bay. Ashton at first was tempted to go, but decided that the chances for a ship were better at the island. Farewells were made, and the Bay men left in their small craft.

The season was now approaching for the Jamaica Traders to sail in the vicinity, and as Bonaca was a favorite watering place for the traders, the three men went over to the other island. On the fifth day they were there a great storm came up, which blew hard for three days, and when the worst of the gale had passed, Ashton noticed a large fleet of vessels standing for the island's harbor. The larger vessels anchored off, but a brigantine came in over the shoals, making for the watering place. Three Englishmen, as Ashton could tell by their dress, rowed a longboat into shore, so Ashton ran down on the beach. Seeing the queer apparition, the men stopped rowing and asked Ashton who he was. He joyfully answered, "An English man run away from pirates!" They were satisfied, and came to the beach. Ashton soon found that the ships were the British man-of-war *Diamond*, with a fleet of traders in convoy, bound to Jamaica, and that they were ashore to get fresh water, as many sailors were very sick aboard ship. After a short time Mr. Symonds showed himself. He had been careful to keep out of sight for fear of alarming the sailors.

Ashton found that a chance of a trip home presented itself when the brigantine proved to be from Salem, Massachusetts, less than three miles from his father's home! The master of the brigantine, Captain Dove, was shorthanded, and signed Ashton on at once. It was a sad farewell with Symonds that Ashton experienced on the beach a few days later, but as Ashton said, "I was forced to go thro' for the Joy of getting Home."

One can imagine the thoughts that passed through Ashton's mind on the sail up through the Gulf of Florida, and finally the thrill which ran through his body when the brigantine first came abeam of Halfway Rock and headed for the passageway between Baker's Island and the Miseries. He had been away from home two years, ten months, and fifteen days. As soon as the ship landed, he journeyed at once to his home in Marblehead, where his family, who had long ago given him up for lost, joyously greeted him.

Thus ends the remarkable story of Philip Ashton, who saw adventuresome days over two hundred years ago, when the pirates of the high seas almost ended his career on many occasions. When he had recovered his health and strength, Ashton related his experiences to the Reverend John Barnard, who had preached a timely sermon in honor of the boy's return, choosing as his text "God's Ability to Save His People from All Danger." No reader can claim that Barnard did not have a good subject for his sermon that Sunday morning.

———————————— ～ ————————————

Reverend John Barnard, the influential pastor of Marblehead's Old North Church and a Harvard graduate, published Philip Ashton's story in a sixty-six-page book called *Ashton's Memorial—An History of the Strange Adventures and Signal Deliverances of Mr. Philip Ashton*. Barnard was somewhat of an adventurer himself and had sailed to England and the West Indies, so it's no wonder Ashton's saga appealed to him. All four known surviving copies of the original American edition of *Ashton's Memorial* are housed in Massachusetts, as are the two surviving copies of the London edition.

Roatan, sometimes called Rattan on old maps, was visited by Christopher Columbus in 1512. The Payan (and possibly Mayan) Indians who lived on the island were removed by Spanish slavers, leaving Roatan almost completely depopulated by the time pirates arrived in the seventeenth century. The island, about forty miles off the north coast of Honduras, today is home to about 30,000 people with origins in several cultures including English, Spanish, and Payan Indian. Many of the residents are descended from rebellious slaves left on the island by the British during the height of the slave trade. The island is now served by ferry and air service and is a prime destination for scuba diving and fishing.

CHAPTER 5

Thomas Pound,
Who Escaped the Hangman's Noose

Shortly before midnight on the night of August 8, 1689, the dim out-
lines of seven persons could be seen as they passed along Bull's Wharf
in Boston, today the busy city terminal of the South Station. The leader
of the group was Thomas Pound, Boston Harbor cartographer and pirate
unique, who was soon to take an unusual part in the attempt to help Sir
Edmund Andros escape from New England.

Looking back over the 255 years which have passed since the event,
one finds the history of the Boston rebellion against Sir Edmund Andros
blurred and confused in many places, and Thomas Pound's part is as difficult to understand as any other.

Sir Edmund Andros, governor of the Dominion of New England, was
captured and imprisoned by a group of citizens on April 18, 1689,
shortly after the arrival of news that King James II had been deposed
from his throne. As nearly as can be ascertained, Pound and his friends
gathered at the Bull Tavern that August evening for the express purpose
of working out a scheme to help Andros make a successful escape. Their
plan apparently was to sail out of Boston and capture ships and supplies
while off the coast in an effort to give the government frigate *Rose* an
excuse to sail out and pursue the pirate ship. As the *Rose* would actually
be manned by Andros sympathizers, the two ships were to unite and
sail for Rhode Island, where the governor expected to flee. With Andros

aboard, the two vessels would then sail for France where Andros could come to the aid of his deposed leader. One must go back a few years into Massachusetts history to understand the events of the period. The reader may recall that the Massachusetts Bay Charter of 1629 was voided in 1684. The people on losing their control over the colonial government became greatly dissatisfied with the general situation as time went on. In November 1685, Edward Randolph, the unpopular collector of customs, left England in the frigate *Rose*, which was commanded by Captain John George. Randolph was carrying a commission for Joseph Dudley to become the president of the Council for New England. In the Colonial Society's *Publications* John H. Edmonds tells us of the occasion:

> *Randolph notes that Captain George was a civil person, that the* Rose *was the biggest first rate [ship] yet one of the worst for sailing and had six months provisions aboard. This the* Rose *surely needed, as she did not arrive at Nantasket until May 14,1686. . . . Dudley and his Councillors were duly installed, but Randolph, as godfather to the new government, naturally tried to keep things in his own hands, but with ill success.*

Randolph soon found that he was going to have considerable trouble in his position of "godfather." President Dudley granted his own son, a minor, the post of Clerk of the County Court, giving him three-quarters of the gratuities of Randolph's secretarial office, while Captain George started a scandal about Randolph's wife, and challenged Randolph to a duel. The duel, however, was not fought, as friends of both parties interceded. The arrival of the frigate *Dartmouth* from Bermuda did not help matters because the master became involved in a quarrel with Randolph almost at once. Although the duel had been avoided, a rough-and-tumble fight actually did develop on one of Boston's main streets between Captain George and Captain Saintlow of the *Dartmouth* on one side and Randolph and his constable on the other. Not only were there troubles of a personal nature; the political situation was going from bad to worse.

Matters became so serious that Sir Edmund Andros arrived from England as the new governor in December 1686. The following May he sent Captain George to cruise aboard the *Rose* as far north as Pemaquid, keeping a watchful eye for pirates and the like. Thomas Pound, who was an expert cartographer and mariner in his own right, was appointed pilot for the expedition and continued in this capacity off and on through the years 1687 and 1688.

The first news of the entry of William of Orange into England as the new king reached America in January of 1689, when Sir Edmund Andros was at Pemaquid with 1,000 soldiers. Andros immediately ordered all men under him along the coast to be alerted for possible invasion. He returned to Boston later, and on April 4 the royal proclamation of William of Orange arrived in town, and was reprinted by Richard Pierce.

Sir Edmund Andros tried hard to suppress the publication of this proclamation, putting Pierce in jail as a penalty for printing it. But the news became generally known, and the inhabitants began a rebellion against Andros. Captain George of the *Rose* was ashore at the time, and the citizens quickly seized him. The ensigns fluttered to the breeze on the beacon atop Beacon Hill as a signal for the men of Charlestown to cross over to Boston at once. Both Dudley and Andros were made prisoners. Fearing he might help Andros escape, the rebels would not release Captain George.

Out on the frigate *Rose*, Lieutenant David Condon was preparing to shell Boston, but the townspeople notified him that they were holding Captain George as a hostage, and if one shot was fired from the frigate, George would be executed at once. The next day four strongholds trained their guns on the frigate—the North and South Batteries, Castle Island, and Fort Hill. Lieutenant Condon saw the hopelessness of further resistance and allowed the frigate to have her topmasts struck. Her sails were carried ashore as a precaution, with the crew, one by one, declaring their allegiance to King William and Queen Mary.

Word finally came from England that William and Mary had acceded to the throne, and most Bostonians breathed easier. But there was still bitterness about the frigate *Rose*, for when pirates were reported off the coast and it was suggested the *Rose* be refitted to chase them, objections were made on the grounds that Captain George was not loyal to their new majesties. The townspeople still thought it dangerous to permit him to sail out of the harbor.

Most evidence which can be found points to the probability that Captain Thomas Pound and Captain John George agreed to a scheme whereby Pound would pretend to become a pirate, making so much trouble near Boston Harbor that the town would have to send Captain

George aboard the frigate *Rose* in pursuit of him. Then Pound and George would join forces to sail to Rhode Island, where Sir Edmund Andros would be waiting after his escape from Boston's Castle Island.

Governor Edmund Andros escaped from Castle Island on August 3 according to plan, and Thomas Pound and his crew made their way from Bull's Wharf five days later, as we have already related. Pound, not knowing that Andros had by that time been captured, sailed away believing the scheme would be successful.

Early on the morning of August 10, 1689, a Bermuda-type vessel with the pretended pirates aboard anchored off the shores of Lovell's Island in Boston's Outer Harbor, where a small boat from the island was expected.

Thomas Hawkins, who actually owned the ship, was now told by Pound to await the arrival of the small boat. Originally, Hawkins had merely agreed to sail to Nantasket with Pound and his group, but once under way, Pound took over the vessel and there was nothing Hawkins could do about it. Finally the noise of a boat being pulled over the rocks was heard, and one of the men in Pound's crew shouted out, "There they are!" Soon the small boat came alongside with five heavily armed men, who climbed aboard.

Pound ordered all the fishing casks thrown overboard, and an easterly course set. The Brewster Islands faded away in the distance as the coast was left far behind. By this time Hawkins realized that Pound was bent on a piratical cruise, and he seems to have been forced to serve as sailing master, while Pound commanded the expedition.

The first vessel which the pirates encountered was a small fishing sloop, commanded by Captain Isaac Prince of Hull, who was then about ten leagues off the Brewsters. Hawkins hailed the sloop, asking him for eight penny worth of fish and three or four gallons of water. As the exchange was made, fisherman Prince noticed that Hawkins did not bring his vessel alongside, but held his craft bow-on by the quarter of the fishing craft. Evidently Pound did not wish Prince to see the extra men aboard his vessel.

Some of Prince's crew, however, noticed ten or twelve sailors lurking out of the way on the sloop, so Captain Prince asked Hawkins where he was bound.

"Billingsgate," replied Hawkins.

"How come you are so far to the northward?" asked the astonished Prince.

"It's all one to me," replied Hawkins, and the two vessels soon parted. When Prince reached Boston, he reported the incident at once.

After parting with the sloop, Hawkins reached the vicinity of Halfway Rock off Salem, where he fell in with the ketch *Mary*, commanded by Captain Helen Chard, homeward bound with a cargo of fish. Hawkins boarded the ketch and seized the wheel, announcing that he was taking the vessel. After a few days, Hawkins and the pirate crew transferred to the ketch, and allowed the captain and two men to go free. John Darby willingly joined the pirates, while another lad was forced. Chard noticed one of the pirates limping quite a bit, and recognized him as a former acquaintance. Thomas Johnson, the "limping privateer," was a well-known waterfront scoundrel of Boston.

Chard arrived at Salem the following Monday with the news that the pirates had taken his ketch. Promptly a vessel manned by North Shore militia sailed out in search of the *Mary*, but came back to port without having sighted the pirates at any time.

There was a good reason why the pirate ketch was not sighted, for by that time she was well on her way up the coast, bound for Casco, Maine. Anchoring in Casco Bay some four miles below the fort there, three of the pirates went ashore in a longboat to Fort Loyal. While two of the men filled their water casks, the third, John Darby of the *Mary*, reported to the fort's commander that the ketch had been taken off Cape Sable and robbed by a privateer.

John Darby also gave certain details of an encounter in which Captain Chard had been injured, saying that a doctor was needed aboard. When the physician arrived on the pirate vessel, he did not find Captain Chard, but he received a proposal that he become the pirate doctor, and sail with the Boston buccaneers on the high seas. This exciting life appealed to him, but the fort physician, although agreeing to recruit for the pirates, finally lost his nerve and did not accept. When he went ashore, he told several stories about what was going on aboard the pirate ketch, thus being responsible for numerous versions of the event.

The doctor communicated with the soldiers at Fort Loyal in a manner to arouse the suspicions of the commanding officer, who placed a special guard around the fort. Unfortunately, the very men chosen were those who later escaped, seven soldiers in all. As soon as the fort was quiet for the night, these guards robbed the other sleeping men of everything they could, then took all the ammunition and a brass gun. Arriving aboard the ketch, the soldiers from Fort Loyal joined up with the pirates. Fort Loyal, left without ammunition and poorly manned, was attacked and captured by the Indians [and the French—*Ed.*] the following spring, with the women, children, and wounded soldiers slaughtered in cold blood.

Pound's delay in leaving the bay when the wind failed gave Commander Davis a chance to send out a canoe to demand the return of the deserting soldiers. Ignoring the request, Pound went ashore on an island whence he took a calf and three sheep, after which he sailed for Cape Cod, capturing the Nantucket-bound sloop *Goodspeed* in sight of Race Point, where the lighthouse stands today. The pirates swapped ketch for sloop, and then asked Captain John Smart of the *Goodspeed* to sail for Boston at once with the message to the government there that if the government sloop sailed out after them it would "find hott work for they wd die every man before they would be taken."

Of course, Pound expected the *Rose* frigate to come out in response to his dare, but instead the government sent out the sloop *Resolution*. The sloop never did fall in with the pirates. Meanwhile Pound had sent Hawkins ashore with some men at Cape Cod to obtain fresh meat and they returned with four pigs. After this they sailed for "Martyr's Vineyard Sound" sighting a brigantine at "Homes Hole." Pound ran up his pirate emblem, and Captain John Kent of Newbury surrendered his vessel, the *Merrimack*. The *Merrimack* was allowed to sail away after Pound had robbed it of food and supplies.

Pushed by a northeaster into Virginia waters, Pound sailed up the York River. Here Pound and Hawkins went ashore, where they met two likely fellows who joined up with the pirates, bringing aboard a Negro lad and several articles of value. When Pound sailed away, he noticed another sloop following which the pirates quickly outdistanced. Soon the stranger tacked and returned to the James River.

Once again Pound headed for the Massachusetts coast, although by this time he must have known that any chance of carrying Sir Edmund Andros to France or of enticing the *Rose* frigate to come out was merely wishful thinking. Whatever reason he had to start his piratical cruise, he was now an adjudged pirate, a rover on the high seas who was a menace to all honest sailors.

Reaching Naushon Island in Vineyard Sound, the pirates went ashore at Tarpaulin Cove to fill their water casks. Hawkins went aboard a Salem bark also at anchor, trading the Negro and some sugar for an anchor and money. Later in the week Pound chased a small ketch into

Martha's Vineyard Harbor, where the inhabitants helped defend the ketch against the pirates, who finally gave up and sailed away. In the fight Thomas Hawkins had been recognized by several Boston sailors, who told him that if he ever came to Boston he would be hanged.

Pound reached Race Point again, where Hawkins, who had been brooding over his fate, went ashore and deserted the ship, telling the others that he had been worrying about being recognized at Tarpaulin Cove. This had shaken him so much that he had decided to jump ship at once, hoping that if he kept out of sight for a while he might be forgotten.

Hawkins was due for a rude awakening, for he fell in with some native fishermen from Nauset, Massachusetts, to whom he told his hard luck story of escaping from Pound and the other pirates. The fisherman grabbed him quickly, took all his money and valuables, and then left him to perish. The next person Hawkins encountered was a Portuguese whaler named Captain Jacobus Loper, who was then planning a voyage to Boston.

Explaining to the captain that he had originally intended to go to St. Thomas for a privateering commission when he had sailed away from Boston, Hawkins told Loper how he had been tricked. When Captain Loper asked how they could possibly have reached the West Indies in that small Bermuda boat, Hawkins became embarrassed and was silent. In the Boston Court House Loper's testimony still exists, deep in the records of the Suffolk Court files.

> *[undated]*
>
> *I Jacobus Loper aged forty years testifieth that in the time of my bring Thomas hawkins to boston prison from his pyracy heard him say that noses [Nauset] men ware a pasel of Roughes & that if he got Cleer at boston that he would be Revenged on them for thaire base dealing for said he they be wors pirts then pounds & Johnson. . . . Then sd I did you meen to Goe theather [to the West Indies] with your letter boate: he was upon this Surprised & wholly Silent: I ferther told him that it apeerd by his words that he would first take a biger vessell as he before said & did: & that he was a fool & would hang him self by his much discorce then he answered, by God they kant hang me for what has bin don for no blood has been shed to the above truths I subscribe.*
>
> *Jacobus Loper*

Realizing that Hawkins was not returning to the pirate vessel, Captain Pound sailed away shortly afterwards. Soon the buccaneers fell in with a Pennsylvania sloop, which they chased for a considerable time, finally taking her "under" or south of the Cape. Pound let her go after trying to get salt pork from the cargo, and then captured the sloop *Brothers Adventure*, which supplied the hungry pirates with the food they were after. Three barrels of beef, a good quantity of peas and corn, butter, and cheese, with thirty-seven barrels of salt pork made up the booty.

Now able to make his cruise into southern waters, Pound anchored at Tarpaulin Cove again, making final preparations for a voyage. Unknown to him, the governor in Boston, informed of Pound's whereabouts by Governor Matthew Mayhew of Martha's Vineyard Island, ordered Captain Samuel Pease of the sloop *Mary* to make ready for sea in order to capture him. With Lieutenant Benjamin Gallop and twenty seamen, Pease left Boston Harbor to go after the pirate and his men.

Sailing southward, they reached Cape Cod the first week in October and were told that Pound had gone westward. The following Friday definite word reached Pease and Gallop, then off Woods Hole, that Pound was still at Tarpaulin Cove. All hands gave a cheer when the information was released, and the *Mary* set sail at once to meet the sea ruffians. Soon the pirate was seen in the distance, slowly sailing out of the cove. Hoisting the King's Jack, the Boston sloop approached the pirates, who then ran up a red flag on their mainmast. A terrific fight now ensued.

Captain Samuel Pease shouted across to the pirates to surrender in the name of the King of England, while Pound stood on the quarterdeck of his vessel flourishing his sword with great sweeping motions through the air and dared the others to come aboard. Gunfire now became heavy, the two ships engaging each other as fast as the weapons could be reloaded. Captain Pease shouted that quarter would be given if the pirates surrendered, but his words were met by curses and shouts of anger. At the height of the battle Captain Pease was seriously wounded and taken below. With renewed fury his men continued the conflict. Throwing their grapnels aboard the buccaneer craft, the Bostonians clambered over to the pirate vessel. A terrific hand-to-hand combat began.

It was one of the fiercest and bloodiest duels in the entire history of piracy, Pound and his followers seeming to fight with that strange fanaticism which typifies some defenders of a hopeless cause. Only when every pirate had either been killed or wounded did the contest end.

Thomas Pound was severely hurt in the side and arm. Pirate Thomas Johnson was shot in the jaw, and pirate Eleazer Buck had seven wounds in his arms, while his comrade John Siccadam had been shot in both legs. A bullet had entered the ear of pirate Richard Griffin, knocking his eye out on its passage through his head. William Warren was severely injured in the head. Every pirate was wounded, and six were killed: Henry Dipper, John Darby, John Hill, John Watkins, John Lord, and James Daniels. The Boston craft also suffered heavily in killed and wounded. Captain Samuel Pease of the *Mary* died of his wounds shortly afterwards, and was buried at Newport, Rhode Island.

That same night when the prisoners were all securely shackled, the victors sailed for Newport, where Captain Pease and several of the wounded were put ashore. The sloop *Mary* started for Boston with fourteen wounded pirates aboard, arriving October 18, 1689.

Boston's new stone jail awaited the arrival of Captain Pound and his crew. The walls were constructed four feet thick, with a fine, deep dungeon for dangerous men. Although no gold or silver had been taken by these unusual buccaneers, whose only purpose seems to have been to lure the government sloops or frigates out in chase of them, the appraiser made his usual summary of everything brought to Boston. He estimated that the value of the sloop and all on her amounted to something over 209 pounds. The fight had been a terrific one, as already indicated, with twelve of the fourteen wounded pirates in serious shape. The doctor was evidently very busy with the injured men, for his bill in administering aid and comfort to them came to the sizeable sum of twenty-one pounds, ten shillings.

Hawkins, the deserter at Cape Cod, had been the first pirate to reach Boston. Governor Bradstreet and his magistrates examined him on October 4, 1689. He was thrown back into jail. Tried again on January 9, 1690, Hawkins was found guilty. Shortly afterwards, Thomas Pound and the other wounded pirates were brought in. After a trial lasting several days, on January 17, Thomas Pound, Thomas Hawkins, Eleazer Buck, and Thomas Johnson, the limping privateer, were found guilty of felony, piracy, and murder, and were sentenced to be hanged.

As if the end of the trial were the signal for action, Waitstill Winthrop, one of the magistrates who had tried the pirates, suddenly decided that the verdict was not a fair one. Possibly the fact that he was a brother of Adam Winthrop, who married Thomas Hawkins' sister, might have had something to do with it.

Magistrate Winthrop visited numerous influential people of Boston to obtain their signatures on a petition for a pardon, and himself headed a committee including Samuel Sewall, which appeared before the governor. The old order, back in power under Governor Bradstreet, gave Hawkins, Buck, and Pound a respite.

It came near being too late, for by the time the governor had agreed to grant a respite, the condemned men had reached the gallows erected out over Boston Harbor. The order did not reach the North End until Thomas Hawkins was actually standing on the scaffolding, with the fatal hangman's noose adjusted around his neck. Just as the trap was to be sprung, the messenger reached the execution pier and stopped the hanging.

Thomas Johnson, the limping privateer, did not seem to have a single friend among the thousands of persons in the gathering. His bad record was well known in Boston. Still, there are those who believed that he was hanged to satisfy the crowd which had congregated on the waterfront.

Judge Sewall's ever-active conscience bothered him for helping to free Hawkins. In his diary the jurist says that some of those in the council "thought Hawkins, because he got out of the Combination before Pease was kill'd, might live; so I rashly sign'd, hoping so great an inconvenience would not have followed. Let not God impute Sin."

Less than a month later sentence of death was remitted on Thomas Hawkins, William Warren, Daniel Lander, Richard Griffin, John Siccadam, Eleazer Buck, and William Dunn, on payment of thirteen pounds, six shillings each. Four days later Thomas Pound was reprieved at the request of Epaphus Shrimpton and several women of quality among whom undoubtedly were Hawkins's sister, then socially prominent. So it proved that the limping privateer, Thomas Johnson, became the only pirate of all those who sailed with Pound to pay the extreme penalty on the Boston gallows. Having good family connections made the outcome safer in those days should one desire a-pirating-to-go.

After their narrow escape from the hangman's noose, the men remained in Boston until the following spring. Thomas Pound and Thomas Hawkins went aboard the frigate *Rose* in April 1690. Evidently Hawkins's desertion at Cape Cod had not affected his friendship with

Pound. On the twentieth of that month the *Rose* sailed from Nantasket for England. Thomas Hawkins, however, was never to reach England. The *Rose* fell in with a French vessel from Saint Malo, France, on May 24. The French ship fired a broadside into the English frigate, and both craft began a terrific engagement. Another English vessel came alongside and helped to defeat the French ship, but the battle lasted over two hours with heavy loss on both sides.

The *Rose* lost her mizzenmast, and her sails and rigging were torn and destroyed by the fire of the enemy. The French vessel fared even worse, for her ports were so raked that two or three of them were made into one in several places on her hull. Not less than one hundred Frenchmen were killed. Nevertheless the French captain was a quick sailor and escaped. Captain George himself was killed in the battle, while Hawkins also fell in the encounter. Pound, however, reached England safely, arriving at Falmouth where he communicated with Sir Edmund Andros, who had arrived in London. August 5, 1690, Captain Pound was appointed commander of the frigate *Sally Rose*. Later, when Andros became Governor of Virginia, the erstwhile pirate and his frigate were stationed off the Virginia coast. The arrangement was probably due to Sir Edmund's gratitude to the man who went through so much trouble for him back in the year 1689, when his escapades as a pirate almost caused his hanging from a Boston gibbet.

Some years later Captain Thomas Pound, pirate extraordinary and expert cartographer, retired to Isleworth, located near the outskirts of London, where he was accepted as a gentleman by all. In the year 1703 he died, loved and honored by his neighbors and associates in and around London. Though the whole truth of his strange experience as a pirate will probably never be revealed, it seems probable that his activities were not strictly in the piratical tradition.

It's said that when Sir Edmund Andros tried to escape from Boston and was captured, he was disguised in woman's clothing—his men's boots showed below the dress he wore and gave him away. After his years as governor of Virginia, Andros returned to England in 1698.

In 1691 in London Thomas Pound published an important "New Mapp of New England from Cape Codd to Cape Sables," which provided a basis for other charts for decades. The chart also was employed by Edward Rowe Snow when he searched for the treasure of pirate "Long Ben" Avery. Using a map he believed was drawn by Avery and Pound's chart, Snow searched unsuccessfully on Gallop's Island in Boston Harbor for Avery's hidden jewels. He did find an old dagger that he thought might have belonged to Avery.

CHAPTER 6

Thomas Tew of Newport, Aided by New York's Governor

Thomas Tew, grandson of the Richard Tew who settled at Newport in 1640, appeared at Bermuda in the year 1691, eager to purchase a share in the sloop *Amity*, which was owned by prominent men of Bermuda. He did not reveal his real plans for buying a share of the vessel, but bought a part-share in the sloop just as any other sailing master might have done. Thomas Tew was made the captain of the *Amity*. Obtaining a privateering commission, he enlisted a crew of volunteers for a voyage to the eastward.

Tew had already been a pirate, although his fellow-owners did not know this. A perusal of the Calendar of State Papers concerning England's relation with the West Indies for the year 1699 will reveal the statement of a man named Weaver, who said that it was "known to everyone that he [Tew] had before then [1691] been a pirate." Another sailor whose connections with Tew had been of long standing said that Tew was known to have done much "rambling." Nevertheless, as is often the case, those who should have been informed of Tew's background didn't find out until it was too late, and Tew sailed away from Bermuda in company with another privateer sloop, both bound for the west coast of Africa. Their orders stipulated the capture of the French factory of Goree, on the River Gambia.

When the two vessels were out of sight of land, a great storm arose. The other sloop sprung her mast, and rapidly fell behind. Two days afterwards the gale subsided and the disabled sloop was nowhere in sight. Thomas Tew took advantage of the situation to call all hands on deck. Without question, when many of the old timers filed out of the forecastle they guessed what was to follow, and they were not disappointed. Tew then made his speech.

> *You probably realize that the attack on the French factory will be of little value to the public and will give none of us any reward. There is not any prospect of booty. Speaking for myself, I took the commission for the sake of employment, so I am of the opinion we should turn our thoughts to bettering our condition. If so inclined I shall shape a course which will lead us to ease and plenty for the rest of our days.*

According to Johnson,* who wrote about the pirates more than two centuries ago, the men were all for Tew and his piratical plans, shouting, "A gold chain or a wooden leg—we'll stand by you."

In this manner the buccaneering career of Thomas Tew was resumed. Setting a course at once for the Cape of Good Hope, Tew rounded the Cape and some weeks later reached the Red Sea. As the *Amity* entered the Straits of Babelmandeb, a heavily laden Arabian ship hove in view, carrying three hundred soldiers who were guarding a treasure of gold. Tew surmised that the solders' resistance wound not be formidable against a bold attack. Ordering his men to battle stations, Tew sailed into the Arabian vessel. In spite of her overwhelming superiority in guns and men, the vessel struck her colors in short order. It was a rich prize. When the immense treasure was counted, every member of the pirate crew received a share of three thousand pounds sterling, while the powder captured was so bulky that much of it had to be thrown overboard.

Madagascar was the next objective of the pirates. Located in a pleasantly hot climate, the island offered such alluring possibilities to the quartermaster and twenty-three other members of Tew's crew that they decided to leave the ship then and there. Taking their individual treasures ashore, they bade farewell to their comrades. Captain Tew now began the long journey back to America.

Before losing sight of land, however, he fell in with another ship. Dreams of additional booty prompted him to hoist the Jolly Roger and

---

*As mentioned earlier, some scholars believe that Johnson was a pen name for Daniel Defoe.—*Ed.*

fire a gun to windward. The vessel proved to be the *Victorie*, which at once hove to and fired leeward, a favorite pirate recognition signal. Tew discovered that he had met the famous pirate, Captain Mission, who, it was known, had left France some time before fitted out as a privateer, frequently an intermediate step from merchant sailing to piracy. Mission had established a veritable island kingdom of pirates at Madagascar, which he called Libertatia. Certain acts of pirate Mission at his Utopian settlement compel us to admit that for some it did mean freedom.

Royally entertained aboard the *Victorie*, Tew was won over to the method and plans of his fascinating host. When it was suggested that he sail along with the *Victorie* for a visit to the pirate kingdom, he acquiesced. Following pirate custom, he consulted his crew, who proved to a man to be agreeable to this diversion.

The harbor of Libertatia was soon reached. As the two vessels slid in between the outer ledges of the bay, Captain Tew noticed with growing amazement that great forts guarded the approaches to Mission's island kingdom. Salute after salute came booming out to them from the strongholds ashore as they ran for the moorings. When Tew landed on the beach, the entire pirate company received him with great kindness and civility. The more we learn about this interesting piratical experiment, the more unusual it seems, for when Tew had met all of the other captains and officers ashore, he was invited to participate in a stately conference.

The conference was to decide the disposition of more than a hundred prisoners whom Mission had brought in as captives. Was the decision to be that they would draw and quarter every tenth man, or force half to become pirates and hang the others? Nothing so bloodthirsty was ever dreamed of in this piratical Utopia. The prisoners were examined and divided into two groups, it is true. Members of the first group were invited to join forces as fellow pirates, while those who for various reasons were not to become pirates were placed at work on the new pier, which was being built a half-mile from the mouth of the harbor!

Tew stayed on for a long time at Libertatia, until finally it was agreed that he sail out to capture slaving vessels then operating off the Guinea coast, freeing slaves so that he could bring them back to Libertatia to work with equal privileges with the other pirates. Evidently Mission wished to build up a strong, faithful, independent island empire free from classes and groups of oppressed or wronged individuals.

Captain Thomas Tew's crew when he sailed from the pirate haven consisted of two hundred men, a mixture of French, Portuguese, Africans, and Englishmen. Cruising around the Cape of Good Hope, he sighted a Dutch East Indiaman of eighteen guns, and soon captured her with the loss of but one man. There were several chests aboard bulging with English crowns, which Tew appropriated as booty. Nine willing Dutchmen were made members of his crew, while the others were set ashore in Soldinia Bay.

Cruising along the coast of Soldinia Bay, Tew captured an English ship that had aboard 240 slaves, some of whom the Negroes in Tew's crew recognized as relatives. When the slaves were told of the glorious and free life enjoyed by the pirates at Libertatia, they were all anxious to reach this happy land and join up with Captain Mission. As the Negroes accepted the new order of things, their handcuffs and leg-irons were knocked off, and they became free men. Arriving at Libertatia, the strangers were put to work on the construction of the pier inside the harbor.

Tew's next adventure was on a small sloop, the *Liberty*, which mounted eight guns. Accompanying him on this cruise was a strange character known as the schoolmaster, who commanded a sloop called the *Childhood*. Each of these pirate captains had one hundred men under him. Was this new venture a bloodcurdling voyage of plunder and pillage, with no quarter given, a cruise across the ocean highway to India to encounter adventure and seize rich booty? Decidedly not. These buccaneers were sent out from the pirate kingdom of Libertatia to chart and survey the treacherous coast of Madagascar, discovering and recording dangerous shoals and possible channels for future piratical fraternity. The sloops were gone four months on this humanitarian task, and returned to port with the job well done.

After his return, Tew told Mission that he believed trade should be established with America. He suggested that he would be glad to sail across the ocean to arrange for the purchase of a cargo of ship's stores, luxuries, and other commodities necessary for the comfort and enjoyment of the pirate kingdom of Libertatia. Captain Mission agreed to Tew's plan, and the *Amity* was made ready for the long journey around the Cape of Good Hope and across the broad Atlantic. Several American pirates who wished to return to their respective families at this time were allowed to sign on.

Tew set his course for the island of Bermuda. A bad gale that sprung his mast forced him off the course. After beating about for two weeks he decided to head for his home at Newport, Rhode Island, which he reached a week later. One might imagine that Tew would have feared to go ashore at his Newport home, but evidently a pirate's return was accepted as an ordinary occurrence. He was received with much respect on arriving ashore, especially when it was found out that he had been eminently prosperous.

Waiting to hear from him in Bermuda, however, were the five co-owners of the *Amity,* and included in their members was one of the Governor's Council! Tew at once sent a dispatch to them, asking for an agent to come to Newport to receive their shares of the *Amity's* trip. When Captain Starrs, the agent appointed by the Bermuda partners, sailed into Newport Harbor, he discovered that some of the money had been buried by Tew, while the rest was deposited in Boston. Substantial gains were made by all concerned in the venture, Governor's Councilman William Outerbridge becoming richer by over three thousand pounds. Tew was able to bank around eight thousand pounds for his efforts on the high seas. He brought so much Arabian gold into Newport that for a time these sizable coins, worth twice the value of Spanish dollars, were common not only in Newport but in New York as well!

Captain Tew journeyed to Boston to apply for a new privateering commission. He was refused. On his return to Newport, he obtained what he was after at the cost of five hundred pounds. Armed with his commission authorizing him to capture French ships, Tew went to New York, where he located one Frederick Phillips, who declared himself interested in a voyage to Madagascar. The ship *Frederick* was outfitted and made ready for sea, and Tew a few weeks later sailed with a full cargo for the port of Libertatia, the pirates' happy land. After a relatively uneventful journey, he reached the pirate's haven on the Madagascar coast.

Pleased with Tew's success, Captain Mission welcomed him heartily, and the rich cargo of New England merchandise was brought ashore, and distributed. After the welcome had worn off a little, Captain Mission suggested to Tew that a cruise to the Red Sea might prove lucrative to them both. For this purpose Mission furnished two large ships manned by 250 men each, and the voyage began.

Off the Arabian coast the captains, Tew and Mission, fell in with a ship of the Great Mogul, packed with 1,600 pilgrims on the way to Mecca, their Holy City. Although the Great Mogul's vessel carried more than one hundred guns, when the pirates sailed in against them they offered little effective resistance. In this short encounter not one of the buccaneers was killed. The pirates now boarded and examined their prize.

It seems that the lack of suitable women at the pirate Shangri-La was one of the few things that caused discontent among the pirates. When they encountered hundreds of desirable females on board the pilgrim vessel, certain ideas at once presented themselves. All women were forced to declare their marital status. The unmarried group were placed in one part of the ship, while the married women were congregated elsewhere. It was decided that about one hundred unmarried girls between twelve and eighteen years old could be accommodated without trouble back in Libertatia. And despite the pleas and entreaties of the Mecca-bound Mohammedans, the girls were removed to the pirate vessels.

The return journey to Libertatia began, with the pilgrim ship in company. On arrival at the Madagascar seaport, the pirates examined the pilgrims' ship's hold, where they located countless treasures in diamonds, rich silks, and gold. As the ship was not a good sailer, she was taken apart, and the hundred guns mounted in two batteries near the harbor's mouth. Affairs were now progressing so favorably that even the Swiss Family Robinson would have been envious. The prosperous pirate colony was by this time strongly fortified, and a pastoral scene was being developed in the rear of the village, where several score acres of land were cultivated. Three hundred head of sturdy black cattle were grazing on the rolling land nearby, and the great pier had been completed. Each pirate had chosen his own location for a home, which was built in such a satisfactory manner that it accommodated not one but two, three, or four of the wives of his particular choice.

One beautiful morning some months after Tew had returned from America, one of the pirate sloops came sailing into the harbor, chased by no less than five great ships of the Portuguese navy. It was a dangerous moment, but the pirates were equal to the occasion. Every cannon around the entire harbor system of fortifications was manned within a few precious minutes, and when the Portuguese ships drew abeam of the first fort, Tew was in command of every Englishman on the island and Mission in charge of the others.

All but one of the five warships safely ran past the outer system of fortifications. But when the Portuguese reached the inner harbor they received such a merciless pounding that two of the attackers were immediately sunk. Devastating fire was poured into the remaining vessels by the combined efforts of the shore batteries and the pirate ships in the harbor. A third vessel was boarded and taken, while the two remaining Portuguese men-of-war, realizing that the battle was lost, ran for the harbor's entrance to escape. They made it successfully, although they were badly damaged, and sailed away. It is said that this engagement became the subject of pirate conversation all over the world for years to come. The pirate stronghold on the Madagascar coast had defeated a fleet of the best ships of the Portuguese Navy!

Tew had acquitted himself well in the fight. As a reward, he was now made Admiral of the Fleet. Great dreams of a powerful piratical empire filled his mind. He suggested a voyage to the Indian Sea, to gather new recruits. The colony, thought Tew, was rich enough, but needed fresh blood. Leaving Libertatia on board the flagship *Victorie*, with three hundred of the toughest pirates manning his guns and yards, Tew decided to call on his old quartermaster, who had left the *Amity* to settle ashore on another part of the island. The quartermaster was pleased to see his old captain again, but declined as did the others in the colony to leave their idyllic settlement, where they were living in comfort and security, with plenty of their treasure still intact. But he asked Tew to stay for the afternoon, and had a feast prepared for the occasion. Meanwhile, a storm arose to churn the waters into a frightful gale, throwing the *Victorie* ashore on a rugged promontory near the settlement. All of the pirates aboard were drowned in full sight of Tew, who could give them no assistance.

This sudden change in the fortunes of the Newport pirate crew came as a shock to Thomas Tew, who was left without a ship and with no means of communicating with the home port. When weeks passed without word from buccaneer Tew, Captain Mission started a search for him. Two sloops sailed into the quartermaster's harbor some weeks later, to Tew's great happiness. His joy was short-lived, however, for while it was Captain Mission, the pirate leader had news of a tragic nature to give Tew. After Tew's departure with the three hundred men aboard the *Victorie*, another pirate vessel, the *Bijoux*, had also left the settlement with a large force of buccaneers aboard. Perhaps the camp had contained a spy, for in some way it became known to the natives that the pirate stronghold had been seriously weakened by the absence of the two ships. Seizing the opportunity, the natives secretly prepared to attack Libertatia.

The invasion of the buccaneer stronghold started in the dead of night. Men, women, and children were slaughtered without mercy, as the natives stormed in upon them. The weakened garrison proved no match for the determined Madagascars, who possibly had old scores to settle. Captain Mission, seeing the way the battle was going, fled to the waterfront, where he ran aboard a sloop at the pier. Hoisting sail, he and a small group hastily sailed out of the harbor. Another sloop later also got away, but only forty-five pirates survived the native onslaught. A substantial amount of diamonds and gold was brought away in spite of the speed of Mission's departure.

After the pirate captains commiserated with each other a sufficient time, Tew proposed a journey to America, where they could settle unmolested in either Newport or New York. But Mission claimed that he was a little homesick for his family in France, and would return to the continent before deciding. He gave Tew one of the sloops, however, and divided his diamonds and gold with the Newport pirate. The two parted company, Mission sailing away with a crew of fifteen, while Tew started from Madagascar with thirty-four Englishmen.

More trouble lay ahead. Running into a violent storm on the way to the Cape of Good Hope, Captain Mission's sloop went down within a short distance of Tew's vessel. The Newporter was unable to save his friend. It was such a terrific storm that not a single pirate could be saved from the raging seas, and Tew sailed off after futile efforts to help.

The rest of the journey around the Cape of Good Hope and across the Atlantic to America was more or less uneventful, the sloop arriving safely in Newport Harbor a few weeks later. Here Tew divided his gold and diamonds with the members of his crew, who, it has been said, hied themselves to Boston, where they appeared publicly on the streets of our sedate Athens of the New World. Tew, however, settled down quietly at Newport, where he lived without comment at his island home. Gradually others of his crew retired to Newport, one of them, Thomas Jones, marrying Penelope Goulden and settling in Rhode Island.

The other pirates, as was usual among seafaring men, soon squandered their wealth, and urged Tew to make further adventuresome trips for buccaneering gains. Tew was not anxious to go to sea again, but when other pirates joined their comrades in an appeal for action, Tew finally consented to plan another voyage.

A good friend of Thomas Tew was the governor of New York, Benjamin Fletcher. His honor was not averse to being seen with a notorious pirate on the streets of New York, nor did he mind dining with him at his palatial home. Of course, Tew had many dealings in New York, where he disposed of a large share of his uncut diamonds. Dow and Edmonds say that Governor Fletcher, like some other colonial governors, was always ready to turn "an honest penny," so when Tew presented himself at the governor's mansion to apply for a privateering commission to go on the voyage which his crew had urged, Governor Benjamin Fletcher readily consented—after the payment of three hundred pounds had been made, of course. This occurred on November 8, 1694.

"Tew appeared to me not only as a man of courage and activity, but of the greatest sense and remembrance of what he had seen of any seaman that I ever met with," said the governor later. "I wished in my mind to make him a sober man, and in particular to cure him of a vile habit of sweating." At the time of this statement Fletcher was being grilled as to his activity with Tew, and pretended that he had no idea that Tew was a pirate. "Captain Tew brought no ship into this port," said the governor. "He told me he had a sloop well manned and gave bond to fight the French at the mouth of Canada river, whereupon I gave him a commission and instructions accordingly. . . . It may be my misfortune, but not my crime, if they turn pirates," concluded the harassed leader of New York.

It was not characteristic of Tew to mince words, it seems, so the governor was probably trying to talk his way out of a bad situation. While outfitting the *Amity* in October 1694, the pirate had told a traveler that he plundered a ship of the Great Mogul the year before, receiving for his trouble twelve thousand pounds, in addition to the one thousand pounds that each crew member had for his share.

Sailing from Newport Harbor in the month of November 1694, Tew was shortly joined by two other vessels, one a sloop commanded by Captain Wake, an old pirate pardoned by King James, and the other a brigantine captained by Master Want, Tew's mate on his first trip. Others who made the voyage included Thomas Jones of Newport. Tew's fleet was further augmented by the appearance of Captain Glover in a ship from New York. By June 1695 the fleet had reached Liparau Island at the mouth of the Red Sea, where Tew joined the pirate armada of the great "Long Ben" Avery. A week later twenty-five Arab ships passed the pirate fleet in the dead of night. When Avery heard the news, he started in quick pursuit. Tew's *Amity*, unfortunately, could not keep up the fast sailing pace, so fell behind and was out of the entire affair. Avery soon came up with a Moorish ship, from which he took 60,000 pounds of gold and silver. Then another ship was sighted, overhauled, and captured, this time with 180,000 pounds to be divided.

Long Ben Avery taking an Arabian ship

Whether or not Captain Tew ever heard of the rich treasure taken from the other Moorish ships is not known, but he fell in with another one of the fleet some days later and attacked it. Perhaps his luck has turned, or his quiet life had made him and the crew soft, for when the Moors offered unexpected resistance to the Yankee pirates, Tew realized that he was face to face with defeat. Suddenly a shot carried away a portion of his stomach, and in the words of Captain Johnson, Tew "held his Bowels with his Hands some small Space; when he dropp'd, it struck such a Terror in his men, that they suffered themselves to be taken, without making Resistance."

And so Pirate Thomas Tew died, far from his native Newport, where he had planned to live in peace and comfort during his declining years.

———————————— ～ ————————————

Thomas Tew, a well-respected member of a prominent Newport family, had a wife and two daughters in that Rhode Island city. Prior to the voyage of the *Amity*, the question of whether Tew's activities had extended beyond legal privateering is debatable. He clearly found ways to justify his buccaneering, at least in his own mind. He reportedly assured the crew of the *Amity* that attacking the vessels of non-Christian infidels could not be classified as piracy.

According to Frank Sherry's *Raiders and Rebels: The Golden Age of Piracy*, as many as 1,500 pirates called Madagascar and nearby islands home in the decade following Tew's voyage to the Indian Ocean.

The most substantial account of Captain Mission and the Libertatia settlement is *A General History of the Pyrates* by Captain Charles Johnson, first published in 1724. As mentioned in earlier chapters, many scholars have attributed the work to *Robinson Crusoe* author Daniel Defoe, but this can't be known for certain. Some writers, such as Frank Sherry, have pointed out that there is no hard evidence that Captain Mission or Libertatia ever really existed, but there is no doubt that contemporaries feared the growth of a pirate state at Madagascar.

Whether Mission and Libertatia were real or fictional, the story of the "pirate utopia" remains compelling. Besides creating a society completely devoid of classes and racial prejudice (although obviously still highly sexist), Johnson (or Defoe) tells us that the pirates even created a new language made up of fragments of French, English, Portuguese, and Dutch.

In his 1969 book *True Tales and Curious Legends*, Snow wrote that in 1945 he was contacted by a descendant of Thomas Tew, Mrs. Johnson Sims of Philadelphia. Mrs. Sims enlisted Snow's help in finding Tew's treasure chest, which a relative had supposedly seen on Cape Cod around 1920. It was said that the chest was left in Chatham by Tew's grandson, then was sold to a collector. Acting on behalf of Mr. Sims, Snow tracked down the chest and bought it at considerable expense. Mrs. Sims then died and her heirs had no interest in the artifact, so Snow found himself the owner of a chest "with a beautiful Spanish filigree design" said to have been used by the famous Newport pirate.

Also in *True Tales and Curious Legends*, Snow related a colorful story passed onto him by Mrs. Sims from the "family papers." According to the story, Tew was shipwrecked at Maine's Boon Island along with his first mate Juan Carlos and a young Moorish woman they had taken prisoner. In this story Tew dies at the hands of the young woman, who shot him and then committed suicide on the island.

Carlos, leaving a treasure chest buried on Boon Island, was subsequently picked up by fishermen and taken to Portsmouth, New Hampshire. Carlos was said to have later retrieved the treasure chest, taking it to Concord, Massachusetts, where he buried it near the shores of White's Pond. Snow pointed out that in the entry in his *Journal* for November 5, 1854, Henry David Thoreau wrote about money-diggers who found pirate treasure in the area. Snow went on to report that the ghost of pirate Juan Carlos has been said to haunt Room 24 at the Colonial Inn in Concord.

CHAPTER 7

Captain Phillips,
Whose Head Was Pickled

John Phillips, whose head was brought to Boston in a pickle barrel, was a native of England. Working in the carpenter trade while a young man, he later resolved upon a seafaring life, shipping on a voyage to Newfoundland. His vessel was captured and the crew made prisoners by the pirate Anstis. Evidently Phillips was soon attracted to the life of a marine highwayman, because he signed pirate articles and became carpenter aboard Anstis's ship.

While sailing off Martinique, Anstis captured the ship *Irwin*, commanded by Captain Ross. Phillips' initiation into the brutal side of piracy could not have been more complete, for he witnessed aboard the *Irwin* one of the most fiendish occurrences ever recorded in the annals of piracy. A woman passenger aboard the *Irwin* was seized by a pirate and assaulted. Twenty other pirates in turn ravaged the girl in sight of the other captured persons on the *Irwin*. One of the latter, Colonel William Dolle of Monserat, forcibly intervened, whereupon he was terribly abused and severely wounded as well for his efforts to protect the unfortunate woman. Finally the pirates bent the poor girl's back until it snapped and then threw her overboard to her death.

A short time later the pirates decided to try for a pardon from the English government. The members of the buccaneer band sailed to the island of Tobago, where they drew up a round robin, signing their names in a circle so that no one signature headed the list. In this petition they appealed to the king for clemency, claiming to have been forced by the master pirate Bartholomew Roberts. They further claimed that they loathed and despised the mere thought of piracy, and their only reason for capturing vessels was to use them as a means of escape, and to obtain a pardon.

This unusual message was sent to England aboard a merchant vessel from Jamaica. Several of the braver pirates also shipped on the merchantman, including the principal character of this narrative, John Phillips. On reaching England, he went at once to some friends who lived in Devonshire. He was soon rudely awakened from his dream of clemency, when he heard that other pirates who had returned with him had been locked in the British jail. Hurrying to Topsham, he again shipped on a voyage for Newfoundland, this time under Captain Wadham.

When he had arrived safely on the American side of the Atlantic, Phillips jumped ship, and as the season was getting under way, became a Newfoundland fish splitter. At heart, he was still a dyed-in-the-wool pirate. Becoming better acquainted with his fellow fish splitters every day, he correctly evaluated the character of certain of the men. He chose an auspicious moment to sound them out. Would they care to exchange a fish-splitter's apron for the Jolly Roger? The answer was to his taste and a credit to his discernment. Sixteen of the men were in hearty accord with the succession.

At anchor in the harbor of Saint Peters, Newfoundland, lay a comfortable schooner belonging to William Minot of Boston. The pirates-to-be planned to seize the vessel on the night of August 29, 1723. But when the hour arrived for the venture, only four of the sixteen had summoned courage enough to make their appearance. Phillips was tired of fish splitting, and decided to attempt the venture in spite of reduced numbers. The five men appropriated and sailed the schooner from the harbor without trouble.

When safely away, the pirates drew up articles. This procedure was almost abandoned when it was found there was no Bible on board upon which the pirates could take oath. Finally one of the resourceful men found a hatchet, which was used instead of the Bible, and the ceremony continued. We include excerpts from the articles:

THE ARTICLES ON BOARD THE REVENGE

   1. Every Man shall obey Civil Command; the Captain shall have one full share and a half in all Prizes; the Master, Carpenter, Boatswain, and Gunner shall have one Share and quarter.

2. *If any Man shall offer to run away, or keep any Secret from the Company, he shall be maroon'd, with one Bottle of Powder, one Bottle of Water, one small Arm and Shot.*

3. *If any Man shall steal any Thing in the Company, or game to the Value of a Piece of Eight, he shall be maroon'd or shot.*

4. *If at any Time we should meet another Marooner that Man that shall sign his Articles without the Consent of our Company, shall suffer such Punishment as the Captain and Company shall think fit.*

5. *That Man that shall strike another whilst these Articles are in force, shall receive Moses' Law (that is, 4 Stripes lacking one) on the bare Back.*

6. *That Man that shall snap his Arms, or smoak Tobacco in the Hold, without a Cap to his Pipe, or carry a Candle lighted without a Lanthorn, shall suffer the same Punishment as in the former Article.*

7. *That Man that shall not keep his Arms clean, fit for an Engagement, or neglect his Business, shall be cut off from his Share, and suffer such other Punishment as the Captain and the Company shall think fit.*

8. *If any Man shall lose a Joint in Time of an Engagement, he shall have 400 Pieces of Eight, if a Limb, 800.*

9. *If at any Time we meet with a prudent Woman, that Man that offers to meddle with her, without her Consent, shall suffer present Death.*

Phillips was made captain, John Nutt the navigator, James Sparks the gunner, Thomas Fern carpenter, and William White, whose career ended later in Boston Harbor, became the single crew member. But it was not long before he had company, for the piratical cruise gathered ships and men. Some willingly joined the pirates; others had to be forced. Among the former was John Rose Archer. Archer had already served in illustrious company, for he had been with the great Blackbeard, as bloodthirsty a villain as ever hoisted the Jolly Roger. On account of his background of buccaneering bravery, Archer was made the ship's quartermaster.

September 5, 1723, was a busy day for the pirates. They captured several fishing vessels off Newfoundland and forced three men, Isaac Lassen, an Indian, John Parsons, and John Filmore, the great-grandfather of President Millard Fillmore. Later in the month Captain Furber and his schooner were taken. The Massachusetts Archives reveal that the next capture was a French vessel, from which the pirates removed thirteen pipes of wine, many supplies, and a large cannon. Two of the crew, Peter Taffrey and John Baptis, were forced at this time.

Early the next month an important capture was made. The buccaneers overtook the brigantine *Mary*, under Captain Moor, and a cargo worth five hundred pounds was transferred from the captured vessel. A few days later another brigantine fell to the pirates. This time a William Taylor joyously accepted membership in the crew as, according to his words, he was being taken to Virginia to be sold "and they met with these honest men and I listed to go with them." Just how honest Taylor eventually found the pirates is a question.

Ship after ship was captured as the pirates continued their profitable undertaking in the West Indies, but eventually their fortunes changed, and provisions ran low. When the meat rations were practically exhausted, they ran afoul of a French sloop from Martinique, mounting twelve guns. Ordinarily they would have sailed clear of this formidable opponent, but hunger made them reckless. Hoisting the black flag, Phillips ran alongside and shouted that unless immediate surrender was made, no quarter would be given. The French crew unexpectedly gave in at once. The buccaneers plundered the sloop and took four of her men, after which they allowed her to sail away.

By this time the bottom of the *Revenge* needed cleaning. To this end the ship was headed for the island of Tobago, where she was run up at high tide and careened. The pirates found bad news awaiting them here, learning that their old buccaneering associates had all been taken to Antigua and hanged. Even as the *Revenge* was having the heavy sea growth removed from her sides and bottom, the masts of a man-of-war became visible on the leeward side of the island. In hot haste the vessel was launched and at the flood of the tide she sailed from the harbor, leaving four Frenchmen on the beach.

For the next few days the pirates followed a northerly course, which brought the *Revenge* some distance to the south of Sandy Hook. The month was February 1724. They soon fell in with Captain Laws, master of a snow bound for Barbados. Fern, James Wood, William Taylor, and William Phillips (who should not be confused with Captain John Phillips) were sent aboard the snow and ordered to keep company with the *Revenge*. The two vessels pursued a southern course until latitude 21° was reached, whereupon Fern, who was disgruntled when Archer was made quartermaster, tried to run away with the snow. Captain Phillips was on the alert, however, and gave chase.

Drawing alongside, he ordered Fern aboard the *Revenge*. For reply Fern fired his pistol at Captain Phillips, missing him. A short skirmish ensued in which Wood was killed, William Phillips badly wounded in the leg, and the other two forced to surrender. As something had to be done at once for Phillips, the decision was made to amputate. Because of his experience in sawing, the carpenter was chosen to perform the operation. He went below and soon appeared on the deck with the largest saw he could find in the chest. Taking the painfully injured leg under his arm, he fell to work. Finally the leg dropped off the injured man's body. The task of sealing the wound was next. The carpenter heated his broadax white hot and seared the leg as best he could. Strangely enough, the operation proved a complete success, and William Phillips lived on to be tried as a pirate, condemned, and pardoned. Some time later a fishing schooner was captured. At the suggestion that Phillips be put aboard, the injured man demurred, fearing that he would be hanged upon reaching the mainland. He chose to convalesce with the pirates.

Within a short time the buccaneers seized a ship from London, from which they removed cannon and powder. An expert navigator, Henry Giles, was forced from this ship and came over to the *Revenge* with his "Books and Instruments." Since he was a man of parts, he was also placed in charge of the journal by Nutt, the sailing master.

Soon Fern again attempted escape, but this time Captain John Phillips promptly shot and killed him. Another person who tried to get away a little later was also summarily put to death. The rest of the forced men decided to be more cautious, having plans afoot, however, for eventually taking over the *Revenge*.

Two ships from Virginia were now captured, one of them in charge of another Captain John Phillips. The second ship was commanded by Captain Robert Mortimer, a young married man on his first trip as a master. Pirate Phillips went aboard Mortimer's ship. While there he heard of a mutiny aboard his own vessel. With quick decision Captain Mortimer seized this opportune moment to start a fight of his own. Grabbing a handspike, he hit Phillips on the head. The blow either lacked force or Phillips' head was singularly hard. He staggered back, drew his sword, and ran Mortimer through. At once two of the crew cut Mortimer to pieces. Mortimer's own men, frightened at the bloodshed, stood by without offering a hand to help their own captain.

Meanwhile two men were forced from the other ship, seaman Charles Ivemay and Edward Cheeseman, a carpenter, who was needed to take the place of Fern, killed by Phillips. As luck had it, John Filmore was rowing Cheeseman across to the *Revenge*. En route he found the opportunity to discuss certain plans with the carpenter, schemes which called for the eventual seizure of the *Revenge*. Cheeseman gave his heart and soul to the idea right there, and from that moment the perfection of details which brought final escape was effected.

Resuming the cruise, the pirates captured eleven vessels in rapid succession. William Lancy, who was captain of a fishing schooner, was brought aboard the *Revenge* and while there saw nine vessels overhauled and captured. One of the captains gave the pirate a merry chase, but was finally taken. Captain Phillips, enraged at this lack of consideration, ordered the unlucky commander, Dependence Ellery, aboard the *Revenge*, where he was prodded around the deck and made to dance and jump until he collapsed in a dead faint.

Now begins the voyage that ended in the death of Phillips. On April 14, 1724, Captain Andrew Haraden sailed from Annisquam for a trip aboard his new fishing boat, the *Squirrel*. The deck of the sloop was not quite finished. Leaving Ipswich Bay, the sloop fell in with another vessel, which was actually the pirate ship *Revenge*. Off the Isles of Shoals Captain Phillips sent a shot across the sloop's bow, and ran up a black flag with a skeleton on it. When Haraden saw that the situation was hopeless, he rowed across to the *Revenge* and surrendered. Phillips liked the lines of the trim sloop from Annisquam, and ordered all stores transferred to the *Squirrel*. The other fishermen were allowed to go aboard the *Revenge* and sail for home, but Haraden was forcibly detained on his own vessel, which now became the pirate flagship. Before long Cheeseman approached Haraden with ideas of escape, ideas in which Haraden was very interested.

Several of the forced men believed that the best time to capture the sloop was at night, but the presence of tall, husky John Nutt proved a stumbling block. The conspirators finally decided it would be too risky to try to take him without firearms. Cheeseman suggested a daylight attempt, when there would be less chance for confusion, and the conspirators agreed upon this plan. High noon on April 17, 1724, was chosen as the most appropriate time. The various tools of the carpenter could be placed around the unfinished deck, on which men were working, and then, at a given signal, the attack was to be made with the tools as weapons.

The initial moment arrived. Cheeseman brought out his brandy bottle, took a drink, and passed it to John Nutt, offering a toast, that they should all drink to their next meeting. Then Cheeseman and Nutt took a turn about the deck. Passing a broadax lying on the planks, Filmore casually picked it up. Holding it carelessly in his hand, he watched Cheeseman as the latter asked Nutt what he thought of the weather. Before Nutt could answer Cheeseman, Haraden winked knowingly at the other forced man, whereupon Cheeseman thrust a hand between the astonished Nutt's legs, grabbing the sailing master by the collar with the other hand. Striding across the deck with the struggling pirate, he threw Nutt over the side. But Nutt grabbed frantically at Cheeseman's coat sleeve, crying, "Lord, have mercy upon me! What are you trying to do, carpenter?"

Cheeseman answered that it was obvious what was happening, "For, Master, you are a dead man," he cried. Striking Nutt heavily on the arm, Cheeseman watched the pirate fall to his death in the sea.

Meantime there was plenty of action elsewhere on the sloop. When Filmore saw the sailing master being thrown to his death, he split the boatswain's head clear down to his neck in one mighty blow. Captain Phillips rushed on deck just in time to receive a terrific blow on the head from a mallet in the hands of Cheeseman. This broke the pirate's jaw, but Phillips leaped for his assailant. Haraden then sprang at the captain. Cheeseman, seeing Gunner Sparks trying to interfere, tripped him, causing him to fall into the way of the two Frenchmen, who hurled him into the sea.

Haraden now brought his trusty broadax down on the captain's head, killing him instantly. Cheeseman started toward the hold looking for John Rose Archer, the quartermaster. Encountering him in the runway, Cheeseman hit Archer two or three times with his mallet, but as he was about to finish him off, he heard someone shouting, "Stop!" It was Harry Giles, the young seaman who said that some of the pirates should be taken alive as evidence. Recognizing the wisdom of this, Cheeseman bound Archer and three other pirates hand and foot with ropes.

Captain Haraden was again in command of his sloop. While the *Squirrel* was running for Annisquam, the sailors cut the head from the body of Captain John Phillips and affixed it to the mast of the sloop.

Sailing up the bay, Captain Haraden ordered a gun fired to announce their happy homecoming. But in some way the gun went off prematurely, killing a French doctor on board. It is probable that the bodies of several of the pirates who had been killed in the struggle were taken ashore at Hangman's Island, in Annisquam Harbor.* Tradition, always a little at fault, had it that the men were hanged at the island, but as they were dead already, it seems likely that their bodies were strung up in chains to warn other pirates. There is no evidence on this point, however. The heads of Captain John Phillips and another pirate, Burrill by name, were brought to Boston in a pickle barrel.

Captain Andrew Haraden had now the not-too-easy task of proving his own innocence. The *Boston News-Letter* estimated the pirates' victims as three shallops, fifteen fishing vessels, three schooners, three brigantines, four sloops, and five ships—a total of thirty-three vessels which Phillips had captured in something less than eight months.

Haraden at once went to the "Harbor," as the present Gloucester was then called. There he made oath before Esquires Epes Sargent, swearing the details of his capture by the pirates and his eventual delivery. He then returned to the sloop to await investigation. Shortly afterward, on May 3, the four real pirates and the seven forced men were all locked up in the Boston jail.

The Court of Admiralty, with its customary pomp and ceremony, was held in Boston on May 12, 1724, to try the men accused of piracy. Lieutenant Governor William Dummer, erstwhile commander of the great fort at Castle Island, presided at the court held in what is now the Old State House. Skipper Haraden, who does not seem to have been brought to trial, gave important testimony as to the character of John Filmore and Edward Cheeseman, who were tried first. When Haraden told of the events of the 17th of April, in which Filmore and Cheeseman fought so effectively against the pirates, the court was visibly affected. Dummer ordered the room cleared, and the verdict of "not guilty" came as welcome news to the two accused men.

Later that day the court sat again but this time William Phillips,

---

*Snow is referring to what is now the western embankment of the railroad bridge over the Annisquam River—*Ed.*

whose leg had been sawed off by the energetic Fern, Henry Giles the navigator, Isaac Larsen, an Indian, and other pirates were brought to the bar. When it was revealed that Larsen had held Captain Phillips' arm when Haraden struck him with the adz, the court seemed favorably inclined toward the Indian. Filmore said that he had never seen Larsen guilty of piracy except when "they now and then obliged him to take a shirt or a pair of stockings when almost naked."

William Phillips, who had lost a leg, claimed to have been a forced man, but the evidence seemed to prove his guilt. William White, the only one left of the original five who captured the sloop at Newfoundland, was then brought in. Filmore, who had been at Newfoundland when the sloop was stolen, testified against him. Filmore said that White admitted he had been drunk when he joined up. William Taylor had so often been in conference with Captain Phillips that he was adjudged guilty. John Rose Archer, whose record was very bad because of his previous service with the great Blackbeard, was found guilty also, as were William Phillips and William White. The two Frenchmen were pardoned when it was shown that they had assisted in defeating the pirates. Phillips and Taylor were also reprieved, so there were only two pirates left in government custody when the date of execution, June 2, 1724, finally arrived. All others had been pardoned, for one reason or another.

Cotton Mather preached his usual sermon to the condemned men on May 31, 1724. According to Mather, both pirates had requested the sermon. Afterwards Mather conversed with the condemned men privately, and believed them truly repentant.

Previous to the springing of the trap both men gave substantial speeches of penitence.

Said Archer:

> *I greatly bewail my profanations of the Lord's Day, and my Disobedience to my Parents. And my Cursing and Swearing, and my blaspheming the Name of the glorious God. . . .*
>
> *But one Wickedness that has led me as much as any, to all the rest, has been my brutish Drunkenness. By strong Drink I have been heated and hardened into the Crimes that are now more bitter than Death unto me.*
>
> *I could wish that Masters of Vessels would not use their Men with so much Severity, as many of them do, which exposes us to great Temptations.*

William White followed with his parting message. Probably Cotton Mather had helped him compose the details.

> *I am now, with Sorrow, reaping the Fruits of my Disobedience to my Parents, who used their Endeavours to have me instructed in my Bible, and my Catechism. . . .*
>
> *But my Drunkenness has had a great Hand in bringing my Ruin upon me. I was drunk when I was enticed aboard the Pyrate.*

The usual large gathering of Boston people then watched the two men climb the ladder that led to the scaffold. At one end of the gallows the black pirate flag had been hung, the skeleton on it dancing in the wind as the men climbed the last rungs. The local paper said that the flag gave the whole affair "the sight dismal." At the signal the hangman sprung the trap and the two pirates were left hanging in the air. So died pirate John Rose Archer, aged twenty-seven, and pirate William White, aged twenty-two, between the rise and fall of the tide at the Charlestown Ferry in Boston. A few hours later their bodies were cut down, placed in an open boat, and taken over to Bird Island, whose low-lying flats were located between Noddle's Island and Governor's Island.

Down at Bird Island, meanwhile, Marshall Edward Stanbridge busily superintended the erection of a gibbet. Measurements had already been made of Archer's head, the local blacksmith turning out a wide iron band that would fit nicely. Other iron bands were made to go around Archer's chest, hips, and ankles, with chains connecting the various bands to keep them from slipping. On the arrival of the bodies at the island, that of White was quickly buried. Archer, however, who had been with Blackbeard, was hung in chains as an example for all to see. Incidentally, the iron bands and the chains, together with the hire of an extra man to help secure the bands and chains, cost the sum of twelve pounds, ten shillings.

So the body of Archer swung in the wind, its iron bands creaking rhythmically, a reminder of the awful fate awaiting pirates. Bostonians made excursions and trips out to Bird Island to see at close range the gruesome sight. One good citizen, Jeremiah Bumstead, a brazier by trade, took his wife and ten friends down the harbor six days after the execution to see the "pirate in Gibbits att Bird Island."

In later years Bird Island washed completely away. Today Bird Island, like the pirate who hung there, is only a memory.

———————————— ∾ ————————————

Snow mentions the Massachusetts Archives as a source for this chapter. All papers related to the pirates' trial in Boston are at the Archives, as is a bill for more than thirty-six pounds from the marshal for the costs of the execution and the gibbeting of Archer at Bird Island.

John Filmore (or Fillmore) of Wenham, Massachusetts, later wrote an account of his pirate encounter and his active role in the successful retaking of the *Squirrel*. The narrative was published in Suffield, Connecticut in 1802. One of the details claimed by Filmore is that on the night before the action he burned the soles of the feet of pirates Archer and White as they lay drunk, making it more difficult for them to fend for themselves the next day. For his trouble he was later awarded items that had belonged to Captain Phillips—a gun, a silver-hilted sword, and a tobacco box. John Filmore never returned to sea and had sixteen children through two marriages.

Captain Phillips' sword is said to have been wielded by Filmore's son, Nathaniel, during the French and Indian and Revolutionary Wars.

CHAPTER 8

Other New England Pirates

DIXIE BULL

Fortunately for the reader interested in pirate history, men like John Winthrop, William Bradford, and Captain Roger Clap were fond of writing about the daily occurrences of their times, for otherwise the first pirate in New England history, Dixie Bull, would be practically unknown to the modern generations.

What we have discovered about Dixie Bull is at best sketchy, but it has been established that he was living in London in 1631, one year after the settlement of Boston by the Puritans. In the fall of that year he arrived in Boston, in the colony of Massachusetts Bay, where he stayed for several months. It seems very probable that this young man was sent over to America by Sir Ferdinando Gorges. At least we know that he is mentioned with Gorges in a land grant at York, Maine. Coming from an extremely respectable family in England, he is called by Dow and Edmonds a man of "adventurous disposition." This should not necessarily condemn him. His disposition rapidly changed from adventurous to piratical, however, and all this came about because of the French.

Soon after reaching New England, Dixie Bull became a beaver trader and seemed to enjoy the life which involved bartering and associating with the Indians. Since his activities took him up and down the beautiful coast of Maine, he soon was known from Mount Desert Island to the shores of the Piscataqua River. A friend of the white settlers who had established themselves in various parts of the country, he also seemed to get along well with the Indians. The Pilgrim trading post at Penobscot Bay was one of his favorite visiting places.

This situation changed, however, as a result of a French shallop. The Pilgrim traders often journeyed inland from the trading post with their supplies of coats, blankets, biscuits, and the like, which they would exchange for beaver pelts and otter skins, leaving the settlement in the charge of a small group of men. One day, when they had left for the interior of Maine, a French shallop was seen approaching the shore. A man on the French vessel called to the Pilgrims in English, imitating the accent of a Scotchman. He explained that the shallop had just arrived from a long journey, and its passengers knew not where they were. Claiming that the vessel was leaking badly, he asked permission to bring her up on the beach at low tide for repairs.

The Pilgrims agreed, and the Frenchmen, after pulling their shallop up, went over to the trading post, where they found conditions ideal for their particular plans. There were only four men left at the post. Seeing the racks of guns and muskets on the walls, they examined them carefully, complimenting the Pilgrims all the time on their fine workmanship. Suddenly, however, the Frenchmen held up the four Pilgrims, using the trading post's own guns to accomplish their purpose. After rifling the post of some three or four hundred pounds' value in merchandise, they sailed away, telling the four unfortunate Pilgrims to inform their masters that gentlemen from the Island of Rhe had called.

Whether or not Dixie Bull knew of this depredation at the time is not known. Some time later, however, while he was sailing in Penobscot Bay, he sighted a French pinnace, which engaged him and captured his shallop, took all his supplies away, and left him destitute. This was in June 1632.

Without question, Dixie Bull tried manfully to get his revenge on the French pirates who had descended on both the Pilgrim trading post and his own little shallop. Organizing a small band of fifteen men of his own nationality, he sailed along the northeastern coastline, hoping to catch some French vessel and thus retrieve his losses. As the summer months waned and his own supplies grew smaller and smaller, Captain Bull realized that something would have to be done soon.

His next move was one which established him as the first New England pirate in history. Descending on the pinnaces and shallops of some defenseless English traders located nearby, Dixie Bull confiscated their supplies and forced several men from the traders' vessels to join his pirate band.

Thus reinforced, Captain Dixie Bull sailed brazenly into Pemaquid Harbor, where he looted the settlement at his leisure, because there was no opposition of any importance. Bull and his cohorts loaded aboard their shallop goods and merchandise to the value of more than five hundred pounds, leaving the inhabitants practically stunned, with the exception of a small group of armed men. These defenders sent a parting volley out toward the pirate ship just as the ruffians weighed anchor to sail off with their booty. One of the bullets scored a lucky hit, killing Captain Dixie Bull's second in command.

The death of the pirate caused a terrific reaction on his fellow sailors, as this was actually the first bloodshed which any of them had encountered. None had ever served before on any piratical voyages, and it was a long time before the effects of the incident wore off. Captain Roger Clap, who was commander at Castle Island for many years, interviewed several of the men a year later. Clap said that the pirates were so upset weeks afterwards that they were afraid of the very rattling of the ropes.

News of Dixie Bull's turning pirate reached Boston via a dispatch from Captain Walter Neal of Piscataqua, who wrote a letter to Governor John Winthrop, describing incidents that led to Bull's becoming a sea highwayman. An armed vessel with twenty men was sent up the coast to Piscataqua, now Portsmouth, New Hampshire, where it was joined by others from that settlement searching for pirate Bull. After the officials underwent much trouble in getting the expedition organized, the weather interfered. First it snowed, then came extreme cold, and finally contrary winds prevented the sailing. An interesting sidelight on the expedition is the fact that Samuel Maverick, mentioned years before in the York Deeds along with Dixie Bull, actually was the man chosen to outfit the expedition to capture him.

At last, late in November, the expedition was able to leave the seaport of Boston. A well-armed pinnace started up the coast with twenty of the strongest marines aboard. Reaching Pemaquid, the pinnace was joined by four other heavily armed vessels, one of which was from "Pascataquack." Weather conditions then interfered again, and the ships lay storm-bound in Pemaquid Harbor for the next three weeks.

Historians should take note of the fact that this force was the first hostile fleet ever outfitted in New England as well as the initial naval demonstration in the colonies.

But nothing ever came of the efforts of these brave men of New England. Week after week of searching went by, but they were unable to find Dixie Bull. Finally the fleet returned to Boston and Piscataqua, where the sailors were disbanded. Lieutenant Mason, leader of the expedition, was given ten pounds for his services, while the other expenses came to twenty-four pounds, seven shillings. When the month of February 1633 arrived, three deserters from Dixie Bull's pirate fleet reached their homes. Their opinion was that Dixie Bull had left American waters forever, going over to fight for the French. Writing in his journal two years later, Governor John Winthrop is of the same opinion. Captain Roger Clap of Dorchester, however, believed that Dixie Bull eventually reached England. His words follow:

> Bull got to England; but God destroyed this wretched man. Thus the Lord saved us at this time, from their wicked Device against us.

Bull was either executed or met a violent death on reaching England. Regardless of how he died, America never again to our knowledge saw the man who was destined to wear the mantle of New England's first pirate.

THE PIRATE OF DUNGEON ROCK

At sunset one summer's evening in 1658, a small pirate vessel anchored at the mouth of the Saugus River in Massachusetts. Four men, putting out in a boat, rowed up the river as far as they could, and made off into the woods. Several people observed the incident, and the news traveled over to Lynn and up to Boston.

By the next day, however, the vessel had vanished. On the walls of the Saugus Iron Works nearby, however, was a mysterious message asking the workers to perform a service. It said that if shackles, handcuffs, hatchets, and other ironmongery were made and left at a secret place in the woods, an amount of silver to the full value would be deposited in their place. The ironmongery was made and left at the designated place, and surely enough the next morning all the articles had been taken, and a rich sum of money secreted in the hiding place.

Some months later four men landed in similar fashion, making their way to the same pretty glen deep in the Lynn Woods. Near the great rocky ledge they built a rough dwelling place and sank a well into the earth. They even planted and tended a garden. The pirates seemed quite content in their wild, inaccessible location deep in the woods.

News reached the authorities, however, of these activities, and plans were made to apprehend the pirates. One fine day a British man-of-war appeared between Nahant and what is now Revere, anchoring close to the beach. A longboat full of British marines then rowed ashore. Here they were met by a guide, who soon jumped aboard, directing them up the Saugus River toward the pirate hideout.

Without warning the marines struck. All but one of the pirates was captured. Taken back to England, they were executed, to the best of our knowledge. The pirate who escaped, Captain Thomas Veale, fled deep into the woods to a high rock two miles farther north. Here he found a natural cavern, which began at the top of a high hill and extended more than a hundred feet into the earth. Today it is known as Dungeon Rock. Whether or not the pirates had buried their treasures in the depths of this huge rock probably will never be known, but many thousands of dollars have been spent here in an effort to find the alleged treasure.

Thomas Veale made his way into nearby Lynn and pretended to become a cobbler of shoes, but later left the scene to resume his piratical life. By 1685 he had a shallop with fourteen men aboard. While in New London Harbor, he was accused of piracy by Captain Daniel Staunton of Pennsylvania. Staunton appeared before the New London magistrate, demanding that Veale and his partner Harvey be arrested at once for piracy. The magistrate was uncertain about what he should do, and in the meantime Veale and Harvey escaped.

Veale lay in wait for shipping outside of New London Harbor. He attacked the ketch of Captain John Prentice, and, as both ketch and shallop manned guns, the two vessels kept up a running fight all the way to Boston Harbor. When Pirate Veale sighted Great Brewster Island, he veered off to the northward, probably running into his hideout up the Saugus River and dismasting his shallop.

The records in the Massachusetts Archives tell us of the excitement when Captain Prentice reached port. The court ordered the beating of drums to recruit forty men for the search for Veale and his crew. Evidently the pirate's fame was well known as forty men could not be found. It was common knowledge that Veale had a sizable treasure on board his shallop, for while in New London he had shown considerable wealth on the streets of that Connecticut town, offering John Wheeler fully three times the value for some carriage guns he desired.

The court then decided to announce "for their Incouragement . . . free plunder be offered to such as Voluntarily list themselves." If this plan failed to work, the men would be impressed. The forty men were finally recruited, and a parting message given to beware of "killing any of the enemy unnecessarily." After a voyage of several days, the expedition returned empty-handed. It is possible that Veale was hiding all the time at the Pirate Dungeon Rock in the Lynn Woods.

Thomas Veale was never caught, but a legend has come down through the years that a great earthquake closed the entrance to Dungeon Rock, walling him up alive there. The only recorded earthquake after Veale fled to the north from the vicinity of Boston's Brewster Islands did not occur until 1727; therefore if Veale was an active pirate in 1658, as stated by Alonzo Lewis in his *History of Lynn*, he must have been around ninety at the time of the 1727 quake that allegedly trapped him deep inside the cavern at Dungeon Rock.*

According to the legend, his skeleton was found years later when Hiram Marble moved to Lynn and began his excavations. Marble actually began digging in 1851, prompted by clairvoyant revelations of mediums in Charlton, Worcester County, Massachusetts. Marble dug unsuccessfully year after year. He erected a small but attractive home near the scene of his excavations, and his faith in the treasure was unusually persistent. One could tell that he was deriving real satisfaction and enjoyment from his undertaking. From time to time the mediums would produce messages from Captain Veale himself. The last one was, "Cheer up, Marble, we are with you and doing all we can."

But Marble never found the treasure. Assisted by his young son, who, it was said, was a more confirmed spiritualist than Hiram Marble himself, he spent the rest of his life digging in vain. His modest fortune of $1,500 was exhausted in 1855; from that time on he accepted the donations of visitors.

Some of the more philanthropic visitors, influenced by his kindness and faith, printed bonds in Hiram Marble's name, known as Dungeon Rock Bonds. For the sum of one dollar Hiram Marble issued these interesting documents, promising to pay the bearer one dollar WHEN ABLE. Marble was never able to redeem his pledges, dying in the year 1868, faithful to his dreams and spiritualistic advice to the end. Perhaps some medium can answer why this energetic, tireless man was not rewarded for his blind faith.

---

*Lewis wrote that the earthquake that entombed Veale took place in 1658.—*Ed.*

Illustration of Dungeon Rock, from Frank Leslie's Illustrated Newspaper, August 10, 1878 (courtesy of the Friends of Lynn Woods)

Dungeon Rock in Lynn Woods, Massachusetts (from In Lynn Woods with Pen and Camera, *by Nathan Hawkes, 1892)*

FIRST PIRATES HANGED IN BOSTON

A most interesting story of pirates who, perhaps, were the first ever hanged in Boston concerns Alexander Wilson, John Smith, and William Forrest. These men seized the ship *Antonio* off the Spanish coast in the year 1672. The *Antonio's* crew rebelled against the harshness of their captain and put him adrift in an open boat. Some of the ship's officers preferred to go with their captain in the longboat, which was provisioned.

Cotton Mather tells the story in his *History of Some Criminals Executed in the Land*. The pirates sailed the *Antonio* into Boston and went over to Charlestown, stopping at the home of Major Nicholas Shapleigh, at that time a prominent merchant. Shapleigh accepted certain goods from the pirate ship.

What might be called an Act of God then occurred. The captain of the *Antonio* came into Boston Harbor in the longboat, and after landing at Long Wharf, reported his strange voyage to the authorities, telling of the death of one of his officers by exposure. They informed him that the *Antonio* was also in port, and made haste to apprehend the three pirates. Brought back to Boston, the men faced their captain. Cotton Mather describes the scene:

> *The Countenance of the Master, was now become Terrible to the Rebellious Men, who, though they had Escaped the Sea, yet Vengeance would not suffer them to Live a Shore. At his Instance and Complain, they were Apprehended; and the Ringleaders of this Murderous Pyracy had sentence of Death Executed on them, in Boston.*

For receiving the pirate loot, Major Shapleigh was fined five hundred pounds. He pleaded poverty so the fine was reduced to three hundred pounds, which he paid.

The *Antonio* case excited so much comment that after proper consideration, a law against piracy was drawn up in General Court, October 15, 1673.

Eleven years later it also became a crime to entertain, harbor, or trade with "privateers, pyrates, or other offenders." The ranking official in each Massachusetts Bay Colony was empowered to issue warrants for the seizure of suspected pirates or privateers.

JOSEPH BRADISH

The date of the birth of Joseph Bradish was duly recorded at Cambridge, Massachusetts, as the 28th of November, 1672. Twenty-six years later he was aboard the hakeboat *Adventure* bound for the island of Borneo. While most of the passengers and crew were ashore at Polonais Island for water, Bradish and his associates aboard cut the cable and sailed away with the *Adventure*. As Joseph Bradish was the best artist, or navigator, aboard, he was chosen captain of the pirates.

After rounding the Cape of Good Hope, the ship's treasure was divided between the twenty-six pirates aboard, each receiving at that time over fifteen hundred Spanish dollars. Other riches and jewelry were divided later. The following spring, in March 1699, the *Adventure* arrived off the east end of Long Island. Captain Bradish went ashore at Nassau Island with most of his money and jewels. After an unsuccessful attempt to purchase a vessel in Rhode Island, Bradish finally purchased a small sloop that he came upon at sea, and departed. His men were put ashore along the coast, one here and one there, and said their farewells, going inland immediately. At last only Bradish and ten of his men were left. They finally agreed that the coast was clear and they could enter Boston. In this they were greatly mistaken, for as soon as they entered the great seaport, the authorities arrested them and threw them into the great stone jail. It was unknown to the officials, however, that Caleb Ray, the gaoler, was a relative of Bradish. After a few weeks plans were made to escape. It was the same jail in which Captain Kidd himself was confined a few weeks later. Fortunately for Bradish, he did not have to wear irons.

On the morning of June 25, Ray found the jail doors open, with Bradish and a one-eyed man, Tee Wetherly, both missing. Governor Bellomont was furious at the escape. He found that other pirates had escaped in the past, so ordered Ray dismissed at once. Governor Bellomont offered a reward of two hundred pieces of eight for the apprehension of Bradish and one hundred for Wetherly's capture. An Indian sachem named Essacambuit was in Boston at the time, and knew where Bradish was. Journeying at once to the area north of Saco, Maine, Essacambuit soon had the pirates captured and brought them safe to Fort Saco. By October 24 they were back in the Boston jail, where there was now no relative of Bradish to help them.

Bradish made the journey to London in the illustrious company of

Captain Kidd, who was also a prisoner on the man-of-war *Advice*. Bradish and Wetherly were later hanged at Hope-Point, London.

THE LAST PIRATES EXECUTED IN BOSTON

At ten o'clock on the morning of September 11, 1835, a lonely, terror-maddened pirate was taken from his cell at the Leverett Street jail in Boston to the scaffolding where he was to be hanged. Having feigned insanity to escape the death which befell the other members of his crew sometime before, Francisco Ruiz, declared sane by a medical board, stood on the platform with the hangman's noose around his neck, awaiting his fate. The signal was given and the trap sprung. In this manner the last pirate to be executed in Boston died, paying for his crime of three years earlier when the pirate schooner *Panda* captured the Salem brig *Mexican* on the high seas.

More than a century has slipped by since this episode in Boston history was enacted, but one of the men captured aboard the *Mexican* was still alive in 1906, living in Salem. He was Captain Thomas Fuller, then in his ninety-fourth year. Serving as cabin boy aboard the *Mexican* in his youth, Fuller had as shipmate one John Battis, who wrote an account of his experiences a few years after his capture and escape.

The story actually begins at Havana, Cuba, for it was in the summer of 1832 that we find the pirate yacht *Panda* lying at anchor in the harbor there. Her captain, Don Pedro Gibert, was a native of Spain and the son of a Spanish grandee. His mate, Don Bernardo De Soto, owner of the clipper-built schooner, had married a beautiful fifteen-year-old girl named Petrona Peyrara, who belonged to one of the first families in Spain.

Reputedly engaged in the slave trade, the officers and crew of the *Panda* were in reality pirates. Leaving Havana Harbor on the night of August 20, 1832 the *Panda* sailed the sea lanes until the evening of September 19, 1832, when the lookout at the masthead sighted a brig, the *Mexican* of Salem, sailing southward. The captain was notified at once and went into consultation with the mate, whereupon the carpenter, a thoroughly despicable individual, joined the pair. They decided to board the brig, take her money and cargo, put the crew below hatches where they would kill them, and destroy the vessel.

But the *Panda* was still a long distance from the brig, and it was not until the next day that the plan was carried out. Drawing closer to the

American stranger, Captain Gibert ordered the firing of a musket, and the brig *Mexican* hove to.

The *Mexican* had left Salem on August 29, commanded by Captain John G. Butman. Owned by Joseph Peabody, the brig carried a substantial treasure in silver, ten boxes of $2,000 apiece, with which the captain had planned to trade. Let us allow seaman John Battis, who later wrote the whole story of the encounter, tell us what happened, beginning with the events before sailing:

> It was suggested that we go after the cook, Ridgeley, who then boarded with a Mrs. Ranson, a colored woman living at Becket Street, so we set out to find him. He was at home but disinclined to go, as he wished to pass one more Sunday home. However, after some persuading he got ready, and we all started out of the gate together. A black hen was in the yard and as we came out the bird flew upon the fence, and flapping her wings, gave a loud crow. The cook was wild with terror, and insisted that something was going to happen, that such a sign meant harm. . . .
>
> At about ten o'clock we mustered all present and accounted for, and commenced to carry the specie, with which we were to purchase our return cargo, on board the brig. We carried aboard twenty thousand dollars in silver. . . . We also had about one hundred bags of saltpeter and one hundred chests of tea. The silver was stored in the "run" under the cabin floor, and there was not a man aboard but knew where the money was stored.
>
> . . . On account of the several acts of piracy previously committed on Salem ships, Captain Butman undoubtedly feared, or perhaps had a premonition of a like happening to his vessel, for the next day while aft at work on the main rigging, I heard the captain and first mate talking about pirates. The captain said he would fight a long while before he'd give his money up. They had a long talk together and he seemed to be very much worried. I think it was the next day after this conversation between Captain Butman and Mr. Reed that I was at the wheel steering when the captain came and spoke to me. He asked me how I felt about leaving home, and I replied that I felt the same as ever, "all right." I learned afterwards that he put this question to the rest of the crew.
>
> We sailed along without anything of note occurring until the night of the nineteenth of September. After supper we were all sitting

*together during the dog-watch (this being between six and eight
o'clock P.M.) when all seemed bent on telling pirate yarns, and of
course got more or less excited. I went below at twelve o'clock and at
four next morning my watch was called. Upon coming on deck the
first mate came forward and said that we must keep a sharp look-out
as there was a vessel 'round, and that she had crossed our stern and
gone to the leeward. I took a seat between the knightheads, and had
been sitting there but a few minutes when a vessel crossed our bows,
and went to the windward of us.*

*I was at the wheel when the captain came out of the cabin; he
looked toward the schooner, and as soon as he perceived her, he
reached and took his glass and went into the main-top. He came
down and closing his glass, said, "That is the very man I've been
looking for. I can count thirty men on his deck." . . .*

*Then the captain altered the brig's course, tacking to the westward,
keeping a little off from the wind to make good way through the water
to get clear of her if possible. After breakfast when we came on deck
the schooner was coming down on us under a full press of sail. I
noticed two kegs of powder alongside our two short carronades, the
only guns we had. Our means of defense, however, proved utterly
worthless, as the shot was a number of sizes too large for the gun.*

Just before the crew discovered that the cannons were worthless, the
pirate ship fired the musket shot, which we have already mentioned.
Hoisting the flag of Colombia, the schooner with its crew of ocean
marauders lay to about a half mile to the windward. Those aboard the
Mexican described her as a regular Baltimore clipper. Carrying thirty
men, the *Panda* had as armament a long thirty-two-pound swivel amid-
ships with two brass guns on each side, making five guns in all.

As she drew nearer, a pirate shouted across from the schooner
demanding to be told where the *Mexican* was from and what she carried for cargo. Captain Butman replied that his cargo consisted of tea
and saltpeter, and that he hailed from Salem. The same man then
ordered Captain Butman to get into a small boat with his papers and
row over. It was a tense scene as the captain prepared to leave his vessel. While the boat was made ready, Captain Butman shook hands with
the mate, Mr. Reed. and told him to do the best he could if he never saw
him again. Then he climbed in the boat with four of his men and pulled
away.

Reaching the gangway of the pirate schooner, the sailors were ordered to row to the forechains, where five heavily armed ruffians jumped into the boat. One of them called up to Captain Gibert, asking what should be done to the men and the brig.

"Dead cats don't meow,—have her thoroughly searched, and bring aboard all you can—you know what to do with them." One of the *Mexican*'s crew, Jack Ardissone by name, understood the Spanish captain's statement, and bursting into tears, told the other in broken English that it was all over.

Captain Butman and the five pirates then rowed back to the brig, where they all climbed aboard. It was soon discovered that the *Mexican* carried a load of silver dollars, and the crew were ordered to bring the money up on deck. As they started aft, one of them was tripped by the villainous carpenter of the *Panda*. This was the signal for an attack by the pirates on the entire crew of the *Mexican*. Armed with swords and clubs, the buccaneers unmercifully pummeled the men from Salem, beating one into unconsciousness. Murder, however, did not seem to be their aim, despite Captain Gibert's orders. Perhaps they were new at the game. Nevertheless no one was killed in the fight.

John Battis was struck with a long knife on the head, but he was wearing a heavy Scotch hat at the time, and the blow did little damage. The fight stopped almost as quickly as it had started, and those in the American crew still able to walk were sent on their interrupted journey for the boxes of silver dollars. The chests were soon piled high on the deck, whereupon the pirates signaled for the buccaneers aboard the *Panda* to send over the launch as the coins could not be carried in the smaller boat. The launch arrived, manned by sixteen ruffians who stowed the treasure of $20,000 and returned with the loot to the *Panda*.

After the launch had delivered the booty to the pirate schooner, twelve other men came back in her, went aboard the *Mexican*, and began searching for more treasure, hoping that there were additional boxes which the Americans had tried to secrete. Smashing a speaking trumpet over the head of the captain, they demanded money. John Battis and Jack Ardissone then made a run for the steerage, but they were going so fast they both toppled over into the hold, where Battis landed on Ardissone, breaking two of the latter's ribs. For some reason, the pirates did not follow. As there was no cargo below decks, the two men had a clean sweep from one end of the brig to the other.

Toward noontime it seemed to quiet down on deck, so Battis climbed
partway up the companion hatchway and cautiously raised his head to
the deck's level to determine what was going on. Just as he did so, a
cocked pistol was pressed against his skull, and he was ordered to come
up on deck. One pirate grabbed Battis by the collar and held him at
arm's length, as though he planned to knife him. Courageously Battis
looked the outlaw in the eye, and the reluctant buccaneer dropped the
knife. In fact, it seems as though none of the pirates except the captain
was anxious to kill anyone aboard the *Mexican*.

All the members of the crew were then ordered below, where they
could hear the marauders on deck destroying every part of running rigging they could find. The yards were tumbled down, and the cook's galley was filled with tar, rope-yard oakum, and the like, preparatory to
setting it afire. The aft companionway leading to the cabin was also
locked below. The pirates' plan, of course, was to burn the ship and
everyone aboard, whereas their captain had ordered them to kill all
hands before leaving the brig. Dreading the actual killing of the victims,
the pirates had decided to burn them alive instead and set fire to the
Mexican.

The pirates were seen leaving the brig about three o'clock that afternoon by Captain Butman, who was standing on the cabin table looking

Pirates robbing the brig Mexican *of Salem, Massachusetts (from* The Pirates Own Book,
1837; republished in 1924 by the Marine Research Society of Salem)

out through a small skylight which the pirates had forgotten to lock. As the smoke gathered and spread through the vessel, Captain Butman knelt in prayer for several moments, after which he told the crew to go forward and wait for him. The men obeyed. A few minutes later Captain Butman called his crew and ordered them to get water buckets to put out the fire. Drawing himself out of the cabin through the skylight, Captain Butman took one of the buckets filled with water which the crew, trapped below, handed to him, and crept along the rail toward the galley, or caboose, as it was called. Making sure to escape observation from the schooner, as it was still standing by, Captain Butman reached the galley and doused the fire, which was just breaking through the galley roof. He did not dare to extinguish the blaze entirely, however, as the pirates, who had started to sail away, would get suspicious and return.

Butman, with the fire under control, opened the aft companionway to let the crew come up on deck. Allowing the blaze to smolder so that the pirates would continue to sail away, Captain Butman ordered his men to examine the brig. It was found that all sails, halyards, and running gear were cut, and the headsails left dragging in the water. In spite of the great damage, before nightfall the brig was repaired and new sails were bent on the masts. All of the valuable instruments, including the compass, quadrant, and sextant, which had been safely hidden under a quantity of oakum, were now salvaged and put in place. Just before darkness came on, a strong northerly wind began to blow, which rapidly developed into a severe thunderstorm. Since the captain and the entire crew were anxious to escape as quickly as possible, they ran before the fury of the wind, not taking in a stitch of canvas. And well it was that they did. In the meantime the pirate captain, learning that his men had not made sure of the death of the Salem mariners before returning to their own vessel, ordered the *Panda* to cruise in the vicinity until they could again find the *Mexican* and murder every one on board. Thus the thunderstorm saved the Americans from death, for the pirates never caught them. On October 12, 1832, Baker's Island Light in outer Salem Harbor hove in sight and the *Mexican* soon reached Crowninshield's Wharf, where Captain Butman told his amazing story to a group of astonished listeners.

The ship's reporter from the *Essex Register* compiled a fine account of the entire episode, and the article was read everywhere with interest. Captain Hunt of the ship *Gleaner* sailed away from Salem Harbor shortly afterwards, a copy of the paper aboard his vessel. He spent much of his spare time memorizing the general appearance of the *Panda,* which was described in the paper. Running into the harbor of St. Thomas, Captain Hunt noticed a topsail schooner coming in the bay. As the vessel anchored a short distance away, Captain Hunt went below to obtain his copy of the *Register* and brought it up on deck, where he studied it carefully, glancing from time to time at the schooner. Later he obtained permission to go aboard the schooner on a pretext, and while there noticed two spars which he remembered had been on the *Mexican.* Hunt returned as soon as possible to his own vessel. He decided to run out of the harbor that night and search for an English man-of-war, where he could report his story. His visit aboard the pirate vessel, however, had excited suspicion, and just before dark the *Panda* hoisted sail and streaked out of the bay. As the schooner passed close to the *Gleaner,* a voice from the *Panda* shouted across to Captain Hunt that if he went to sea that night, every man aboard would have his throat cut before dawn.

Captain Hunt, deciding that discretion should be practiced, did not leave the harbor that night, but fortunately an English man-of-war appeared shortly, so that he was able to tell his story sooner than he had anticipated. The captain of the British frigate ordered an immediate search made, but the pirate schooner had escaped in the darkness. Every British warship was given a good description of the pirate vessel, however, and it was not long before she was sighted again.

The British warship *Curlew* was sailing off the African west coast when her master, Captain Trotter, received a description of the pirate schooner. He recalled that the lines were similar to a schooner he had recently noticed in the River Nazareth, and sailed at once for the vicinity. Anchoring off the mouth of the river, Captain Trotter took forty men and went upstream, reaching the *Panda* at daybreak. The pirate sentinel gave the alarm, however, and the alert buccaneers all went over the side and escaped ashore, where they hid in the swamps. The schooner was seized, but the accidental explosion of gunpowder aboard killed four men from the *Curlew* and ripped apart the *Panda* so that she soon sank, damaged beyond repair.

Fleeing inland, the pirates sought the protection of one of the native rulers in the vicinity, but when he heard that the might of the British Navy was interested in the pirates' apprehension, he released four of them at once. Five later turned up at Fernando Po, while seven others were captured back at St. Thomas, making a total of sixteen of the villains who were transported to England. After they had been in prison there for some time, it was decided that the pirates should be delivered into the custody of the American government, which should take such action as it saw fit.

With a high regard for the rightness of things, the captain of the British man-of-war *Savage,* who brought the sixteen pirates across the ocean, escorted the unhappy men into the very harbor from whence the *Mexican* had sailed on her fateful voyage. The people of Salem were so surprised and pleased at this admirable gesture of the British government that they decided to entertain the sailors from the *Savage* in a proper manner. As the War of 1812 had not been over for too many years, there was not a British flag in all Salem, and so the embarrassed reception committee went aboard the *Savage* and asked the English sailor for the loan of one of their own flags. The celebration thus was a complete success.

The sixteen Spanish pirates were escorted in carriages up to the town hall, where, in their heavy handcuffs, they created quite a stir. One of them, a seaman named Perez, made matters a little easier by turning state's evidence and confessing in full. The wretched men were found guilty of the crime of piracy, and as pirates against the United States were all moved to Boston and lodged in the Leverett Street Jail, awaiting trial in the federal courts.

The presence of such a large group of buccaneers created much excitement and comment. Cotton Mather, whose particular interest in such matters led him to visit and pray with the pirates while in jail, had long passed away, but another nameless person did visit the unfortunates at their Leverett Street Jail. He was a reporter from the *Boston Post,* and wrote in that esteemed newspaper for September 2, 1834 that having heard

> *a terrific description of the Spaniards now confined in Leverett Street jail on a charge of piracy, we availed ourselves of our right of entree and took a bird's eye glance at the monsters of the deep but were somewhat surprised to find them small and ordinary looking men, extremely civil and good natured, with a free dash of humor in their conversation and easy indifference to their situation. The first in importance as well as appearance is the Captain, Pedro Gibert, a Castilian 38 years old, and the son of a merchant. In appearance he*

*did not come quite up to our standard for the leader of a brave band
of buccaneers, although a pleasant and rather a handsome mariner.*

Manuel Delgardo became so unhappy in the Boston jail that he committed suicide by cutting his throat a short time after his arrival. Others in the condemned group also tried to end their own lives, but none was successful. They were held to await the case being called in the Boston Circuit Court.

On November 11, 1834, the trial began. Lawyers Hilliard and Child were chosen to represent the pirates, while Captain Butman and several of the crew of the *Mexican* were in court to testify against the Spaniards. Before long it was brought out that five of the sixteen were not aboard the *Panda* when the Salem brig was captured, so regardless of their subsequent careers, could not be tried for that particular crime. The five men were freed.

A dramatic incident was enacted in court during the trial when Thomas Fuller, called to the stand to identify Francisco Ruiz, became so

Thomas Fuller striking pirate Ruiz in court

enraged that he smashed the Spanish pirate across the shoulder with his fist. After a mild rebuke from the magistrate, the indignant Salem mariner apologized and sat down.

The case of First Mate Bernardo De Soto proved one of an interesting and complicated nature. It seems that in the year 1831 he had been master of his own ship, sailing from Havana, Cuba, and on the passage De Soto discovered the Salem ship *Minerva* on the rocks of one of the Bahama Islands. At great danger to himself he effected the rescue of no less than seventy-two persons, carrying them all safely to Havana. For this truly remarkable feat of bravery, De Soto had been awarded a beautiful silver cup by the grateful Americans. When this former act was brought to the attention of the proper people, it was suggested that a respite should be granted and the presiding judge readily acquiesced.

Meanwhile, the wife of pirate De Soto, whom the reader will recall was a member of one of the leading families of Corunna, was hastily summoned and crossed the ocean on the first ship, landing in New York. She was told to go at once to President Andrew Jackson in Washington. Enlisting the services of the Spanish ambassador, she quickly obtained the audience of the President of the United States. Andrew Jackson had already received word from Boston about the heroism of De Soto, and after due deliberation President Jackson announced the pardon of Bernardo De Soto. His grateful wife hurried to Boston with the news, and the pirate left the jail shortly afterwards, homeward bound.

No such happy news reached the other pirates, however, for the remaining six pirates were sentenced to be hanged in the rear of the Leverett Street Jail. They were Captain Don Pedro Gibert, Francisco Ruiz, the villainous carpenter, Manuel Boyga, seaman Castillo, Angel Garcia, and Juan Montenegro.

Judge Joseph Story sentenced the pirates to their death in the following words:

> *The sentence is that you and each of you, for the crime whereof you severally stand convicted, be severally decreed, taken, and adjudged to be pirates and felons, and that each of you be severally hung by the neck until you be severally dead. And that the marshal of this District of Massachusetts or his Deputy, do on peril of what may fall thereon, cause execution to be done upon you and each of you severally on the 11th day of March next ensuing, between the hours of 9 and 12 of the same day.*

When the day came for the execution, one of the pirates, Francisco Ruiz, had so successfully feigned insanity that he was given a reprieve until a board of sanity should decide his condition. The others mounted the scaffolding behind the Leverett Street Jail shortly after ten o'clock, where a Spanish priest followed them to receive their final confessions, but none of them expressed the desire for either penitence or confession. One pirate, Manuel Boyga, had succeeded in cutting himself with a sharp fragment of tin the night before, and was so weakened by loss of blood that he had to be carried and seated in a chair placed directly on the wooden framework of the drop, so that when the trap was sprung, he and the chair fell together. The others met their death in a brave manner.

Bernardo De Soto, who was pardoned by President Andrew Jackson, did not return to Spain to embarrass the parents of his dear wife, Petrona, whose efforts had saved his life. Instead, he sailed for the West Indies, where his ability soon earned him a berth on one of the vessels carrying passengers in those waters. One day, many years afterwards, Captain Nicholas Snell of Salem recognized the captain of a steamer operating between Havana and Matanzas as the same man who had been freed in the Boston courtroom over thirty years before. Introducing himself, Snell was greeted with great friendliness on the part of the former pirate, who recalled vividly the days when his life was in jeopardy at the Massachusetts capital.

DIXIE BULL In his 1959 book *Piracy, Mutiny and Murder*, Snow quotes a ballad he says was printed "probably in Boston by J. G. Hunt around 1825." The ballad, "The Slaying of Dixey Bull," begins:

> *Dixey Bull was a pirate bold,*
> *He swept our coast in search of gold,*
> *One hundred years have passed away*
> *Since he cast anchor in Bristol Bay.*

The (most likely fictitious) ballad goes on to describe a fisherman named Dan Curtis, "brave as a man can be," who challenged Bull to a swordfight. After an exciting battle on the shores of Maine's Beaver Island, Curtis ran his sword through Bull's chest, killing him: "Pirates, your flag and anchor pull; For Curtis killed your Dixey Bull."

Today the Beaver Island Yacht Club holds an annual "Dixie Bull Regatta" each August in honor of New England's first pirate. The eight-mile race begins and ends at Pemaquid Harbor, scene of Bull's first raid.

Dixie Bull is one of some sixty buccaneers one can learn about at the New England Pirate Museum in Salem, Massachusetts.

THE PIRATE OF DUNGEON ROCK For generations, residents of Lynn, Massachusetts, have been visiting mysterious Dungeon Rock and perpetuating its romantic myths. Dungeon Rock's legends are piled so high that it's difficult to determine if there's a kernel of truth buried somewhere. The chief source for the story is Alonzo Lewis' 1829 history of Lynn, which places the earthquake in 1658. There was in fact a strong earthquake in New England that year, but this obviously doesn't fit in with the known facts of Veale's piratical activity in 1685.

Saugus, Massachusetts, historian Richard Provenzano, author of the booklet *Pirates Glen and Dungeon Rock: The Evolution of a Legend*, has speculated that Lewis's inspiration for the story might have come in part from a section of Washington Irving's *Tales of a Traveller*, in which Captain Kidd's treasure is described as being buried on a ridge in the woods near Boston.

A recent photo of the stairs leading to Dungeon Rock in Lynn Woods, Massachusetts (photo by Jeremy D'Entremont)

The legend as it has been passed down also frequently includes the existence of a princess who became Veale's bride, sometimes said to have been entombed along with him in the cave.

In 1834, just a few years after Alonzo Lewis published his account of the Dungeon Rock story and long before Hiram Marble and his son Edwin began their years of fruitless toil in Lynn Woods, someone else in search of riches set off dynamite at the cave. They succeeded only in making access much more difficult.

A man named Jesse Hutchison spent some time digging at Dungeon Rock before the Marbles. Hutchison also was guided by mediums, and he gave up his unsuccessful search after a relatively brief time.

Hiram Marble died in 1868 at the age of sixty-five. His son Edwin continued the quest until his death in 1880. His sister for some years took visitors through the cave for a small fee. The Marbles had dug and blasted a tunnel about 150 feet deep over the course of almost thirty years. Edwin Marble is buried near Dungeon Rock.

The house Hiram Marble had built near the cave is long gone, but the stone stairs that he installed are still used by hikers and curiosity seekers. From time to time ghost hunters have visited the site, and some claim to have witnessed paranormal activity. The cave is open to the public during limited hours in summer, and near Halloween each year volunteers of the Friends of Lynn Woods provide tours of Dungeon Rock and information about its history on Dungeon Rock Day.

FIRST PIRATES HANGED IN BOSTON Nicholas Shapleigh may have claimed poverty in 1672, but records show that when he was killed by a falling mast as a vessel was being launched in Maine in 1682, his estate included land and mills, and also four African slaves and two Irish indentured servants. The town of Shapleigh, Maine, is named for him.

JOSEPH BRADISH Joseph Bradish has been omitted from many histories of piracy. But in *East Hampton History*, Jeannette Edwards Rattroy claimed that Bradish was a "much fiercer pirate than Captain Kidd." She continued, "Bradish was a bad lot, and his crew, from the description that has come down to us, fits in with the regulation pirate tales. One was pockmarked, another squint-eyed, another 'lamish of both legs,' another had a 'very downe looke.'"

In the book *Buried Treasures of the Atlantic Coast*, W. C. Jameson wrote that Bradish concealed a large treasure at Montauk Point at the eastern tip of Long Island, New York. This was learned from one of Bradish's crew by a jailor, according to Jameson. The details were said to be discovered years later in a journal discovered by a storekeeper who subsequently tried unsuccessfully to unearth the treasure. The whereabouts of the cache is now difficult to determine as storms and erosion have changed the contours of Montauk Point, according to the book.

THE LAST PIRATES EXECUTED IN BOSTON An account of the *Trial of the Spanish Twelve* was published in Boston in 1834, with day-by-day summations of the trial and the prisoners' testimonies, along with engraved portraits of each of the defendants. The volume is considered a rare collectible.

John Battis' account was published in Ralph D. Paine's 1923 book *Ships & Sailors of Old Salem*, and was reproduced in Philip Gosse's *The History of Piracy*. Gosse wrote, "With the hanging of the crew of the *Panda*, piracy as a real menace to the shipping in American waters may be said to have ended."

Part II

Chesapeake Bay to Florida

CHAPTER 9

Captain George Lowther

Captain George Lowther is the first in a series of as bloodcurdling villains as ever sailed the waters off the Atlantic Coast. He trained the infamous Low, who in turn aided and abetted two other marauders of the sea, Francis Spriggs and Charles Harris.

Early in 1721 George Lowther sailed down the Thames River from London, bound for the Gambia River aboard the ship *Gambia Castle*. Serving in his capacity as second mate, he soon noticed that Captain Charles Russell had a group of passengers aboard, soldiers under John Massey, who were going to garrison a fort near the Gambia River.

The *Gambia Castle* reached its destination safely, and the soldiers were put ashore under the leadership of Massey. However, trouble started a short time later. The merchants and traders, normally expected to victual the garrison, were very meager in their daily allotments of food, so after a few days of such hardship, Massey's indignation mounted to the point of rebellion. Boldly he declared that he had brought his soldiers all the way from England with the understanding that they were to be treated in a handsome manner with plenty of food and provisions, and if the population did not change its attitude, then he would have to "be under the necessity of consulting for himself."

At that time the governor of the colony was sick and was taken aboard the *Gambia Castle*, where accommodations were better suited to his recovery. Lowther, with the governor aboard, began to think of capturing the ship, as he felt the temporary conditions would make the ship's seizure less difficult. He had struck up a friendship with soldier Massey, and now became openly belligerent to Captain Russell, who ordered him punished by the other sailors. This they refused to do. Lowther soon sought the ear of Massey, telling him of his humiliation at the hands of Russell in front of the crew, mentioning the fact that the crew had stuck by him. Massey listened carefully, for by this time he was sick of the whole business. The merchants ashore had not added to the rations for the soldiers, nor were they planning to do so. As a result of their talk, the two men agreed to seize the ship at the earliest opportunity.

This was accomplished in a clever manner. When the time came for mutiny, Lowther sent word ashore to Massey by messenger that he should repair on board at once. The officer realized that the moment for action was at hand. Massey stepped out into the barracks and spoke to the soldiers, who because of their ill treatment were ready for almost anything. "You that have a mind to go to England, now is the time," Massey told his men. Most of them agreed on the impulse of the moment to join him. Massey sent a message out to the chief mate that the King of Barro was coming aboard for dinner.

As the governor of the colony was then ashore with Captain Russell, the chief mate was perplexed at the message, and consulted with Lowther about it. Lowther recognized it at once as a signal that Massey was bringing his soldiers aboard, and, seizing the chief mate, had him confined below, while the crew made preparations for sailing. That afternoon Massey and his soldiers came aboard the *Gambia Castle,* bringing with them the governor's son, almost all the stores ashore, and the guns from the local fort. When he learned what was transpiring, Captain Charles Russell rushed down to the shore and called out to the ship, offering them whatever terms they wished if he could only be allowed aboard again. George Lowther scornfully refused Russell's terms, but he did put ashore in a small boat the governor's son and three others who decided against a sea voyage at just that time.

The *Gambia Castle* then sailed out of the harbor, and soon the shores near the Gambia River were but a thin line on the horizon. The seriousness of the situation made the men silent, for they were just beginning to realize that there was no turning back. Lowther perhaps understood what their thoughts might be, for shortly afterwards he took definite action. Calling all hands aft, the pirate announced that the time had come to make their plans for the future.

"Men, it is folly to return to England," exclaimed Captain Lowther, "for by seizing this ship we have been guilty of an offense, the penalty for which is hanging, as you all know. I for one, do not propose to chance such a fate. If you do not accept my proposal please set me ashore at some safe place. However, my proposal is that we should seek our fortunes on the high seas as other brave men have done before us." Needless to say, the men accepted Lowther's plan at once.

The ship was stripped flush fore and aft with the cabins knocked down, and the name *Happy Delivery* was bestowed on the old *Gambia Castle*. Eight articles were drawn up and sworn to over a Bible, after which every member of the crew was given a chance to sign his name. A fitting idea of a pirate's mind two hundred years ago can be gained by study of the following eight articles which Lowther offered to his men.

1. *The Captain is to have two full shares; the Master is to have one Share and a half; the Doctor, Mate, Gunner, and Boatswain, one Share and a quarter.*

2. *He that shall be found guilty of taking any unlawful Weapon on Board the Privateer, or any Prize, by us taken, so as to strike or abuse one another, in any regard, shall suffer what Punishment the Captain and Majority of the Company shall think fit.*

3. *He that shall be found Guilty of Cowardice, in the Time of engagement, shall suffer what Punishment the Captain and Majority shall think fit.*

4. *If any Gold, Jewels, Silver, & c. be found on Board of any Prize or Prizes, to the Value of a Piece of Eight, and the Finder do not deliver it to the Quarter-Master, in the Space of 24 Hours, he shall suffer what punishment the Captain and Majority shall think fit.*

5. *He that is found Guilty of Gaming, or Defrauding another to the Value of a Shilling, shall suffer what Punishment the Captain and Majority of the Company shall think fit.*

6. *He that shall have the Misfortune to lose a Limb, in Time of Engagement, shall have the Sum of one hundred and fifty Pounds Sterling, and remain with the Company as long as he shall think fit.*

7. *Good Quarters to be given when call'd for.*

8. *He that sees a Sail first, shall have the best Pistol, or Small-Arm, on Board her.*

On June 20, 1721, a week after articles had been signed, the *Happy Delivery* fell in with the brigantine *Charles* of Boston, Massachusetts. After ransacking the brigantine in a thorough manner, removing all articles of value, the pirates allowed the *Charles* to sail away. Not a single person aboard the Boston brigantine had been injured in any way, nor was the vessel herself damaged. Later Lowther captured a Spanish pirate, which had a short time before overtaken and looted a ship from Bristol, England. Lowther impressed the British seamen and set the Spaniards adrift in a launch, after burning both the Bristol ship and the Spanish vessel.

On reaching Hispaniola, Captain George Lowther sighted and approached a French vessel, which had a cargo of wine and brandy. Pretending that he was a merchant who desired to purchase certain wines and brandies of the Frenchman's ample stock, he went on board to view the liquors. Lowther then carried his deception further by offering a price for the greater part of the cargo, which the Frenchman refused. This annoyed the buccaneer a trifle, so he stepped closer to the French captain, and whispered in his ear that they were going to take all the cargo anyway without paying anything. The terror-stricken Frenchman then collapsed, and Lowther ordered the immediate removal of thirty casks of brandy, five hogsheads of wine, and other valuable goods in the cargo. As the Frenchman had given in so easily, Lowther gave him five pounds pounds for his trouble.

The French settlements appealed to the mind of Officer Massey, whose rank was never divulged. He told Captain Lowther that he was anxious to go ashore and pillage the villages along the water's edge. Lowther admonished him, claiming that such a plan would result in death and disaster, for only at sea was a pirate successful. "Stay in our own field of activity," were Lowther's words of advice to the soldier, and a majority of the crew agreed with him. Most of the soldiers, nevertheless, were still under Massey's command, and the army leader from that time on made himself objectionable. He picked quarrel after quarrel with Lowther as the weeks went by, with the crew and soldiers frequently testing their swords against each other on the deck.

Captain George Lowther realized that this state of affairs could not possibly continue. When a small sloop was taken soon afterwards, Massey expressed his desire to be allowed to take her over. Lowther, who by this time was getting very tired of Massey's continual quarreling, readily agreed. Massey found ten of the soldiers willing to sail with him, and soon Lowther and his followers were alone on the high seas.

False news of Lowther's capture by the British man-of-war *Feversham* was received in London, and Captain Charles Russell, from whom Lowther had stolen his vessel, started for Barbados to testify against the pirate. Russell had his long journey for nothing, however. When he arrived in Barbados there were no pirates awaiting him, for their capture had been merely a rumor.

Meanwhile Captain George Lowther had taken a small sloop, which he ordered to accompany him. A short time later he careened both vessels at a small island. Part of the time the pirates spent with certain of the native Indian women, who did not object to engaging in amorous activities with the English pirates. Finally, when the ships were ready the pirates sailed away for the Bay of Honduras, arriving there in the last week of 1721. Here it was that Lowther fell in with Captain Ned Low of Boston, and the two evil spirits joined forces. Shortly afterwards, they embarked on a vicious career of buccaneering and murder. Their various adventures while sailing together are described elsewhere in this volume. It is said that Edward Low was a quick and willing pupil of his pirate teacher, George Lowther.

Finally Low and Lowther came to the parting of their respective ways. On the night of May 28, 1722, Captain George Lowther, in company with Charles Harris, a pirate who had become his lieutenant, sailed for the waters around New York and Long Island. A few days later he fell in with the ship *Mary Galley*, homeward bound for Boston. Lowther removed a barrel and thirteen hogsheads of rum, five barrels of sugar, and several cases of pepper, together with six Negroes. All of the passengers were robbed of their entire wealth, but the *Mary Galley* was allowed to proceed on her way the following morning.

The next destination of the pirates was the upper waters of Chesapeake Bay, where they captured a large sloop. Anchoring the same evening not too far from shore, the pirates were heard beating their drums all night long, according to the reports of the excited populace of that region. Word was rapidly passed up and down the shores, and all shipping in the region was brought to an immediate standstill.

A well-aimed dig at the majesty of the British Empire was made at this time by Benjamin Franklin's brother, James, in the pages of Boston's *New England Courant*. Commenting on the absence of any men-of-war in the vicinity of Chesapeake Bay, where the bold pirate George Lowther was then known to be, Franklin's newspaper printed the following on August 6, 1722:

Captain George Lowther awaiting the careening of his vessel, shown in the background

Philadelphia, July 26. On Sunday the 22d arrived a small sloop, Jonathan Swain, Master, from Cape May, by whom we have Advice, That a Pyrate Brigantine and Sloop have been cruising on and off both our Capes for above Three Weeks. . . . They were both seen on Thursday last cruising about their old Station, not fearing disturbance from the Men of War, who, by dear experience, we know, love Trading better than Fighting.

Leaving Chesapeake Bay, Lowther approached the shore of South Carolina, where he overtook a ship that had just sailed from the Carolinas bound for England. It was the *Amy*, commanded by Captain Gwatkins, who was not afraid of pirates or anything else. When Lowther, thinking he would scare Gwatkins, hoisted the Jolly Roger, Gwatkins let go a broadside that did great damage aboard Lowther's ship. The pirate then tried to escape. Running aground on the Carolina coast, Lowther ordered all his men to take their arms and go ashore, where they could scatter if defeated. Captain Gwatkins sailed as close as he dared to the beach, and filling one of his boats with armed men, jumped in the midst of them. His sailors resolutely rowed toward the stranded sloop, intending to burn it. An unlucky shot from the shore hit Gwatkins as the men were approaching the pirate craft, wounding him fatally, whereupon his mate took charge and returned to the *Amy*. Because of the death of his captain, the mate abandoned the fight and hoisted sail, leaving the pirate to roam the seas and plunder at will.

It had been a narrow escape for Lowther, who rowed out to his sloop the moment the *Amy* sailed away. As many in his pirate crew had either been killed or wounded, Lowther thought it wise to pull in at one of North Carolina's many inlets. There he rested his men who were not hurt and gave the wounded a chance to recover.

Winter caught them, however, before they were prepared to go to sea again, so they remained at their North Carolina inlet throughout the winter months, hunting the great black cattle which roamed through the underbrush there, capturing hogs and other animals whenever they could for their food. When the weather grew extremely cold, they went back aboard the sloop.

With the first signs of spring, Captain George Lowther told his men a voyage to the fishing grounds off Newfoundland was in order. The next day the sloop left the inlet and proceeded out to sea. Lowther's first victim was the schooner *Swift*, which was captured with forty barrels of salt beef. In the pages of the *Boston Gazette* of the period we read that three men were forced from the crew of the *Swift*, Andrew and Henry Hunter and Jonathan Deloe. Several other vessels were taken shortly afterwards. On July 5, 1723, Captain Lowther fell in with the brigantine *John and Elizabeth*, and forced two men from her, after removing stores from the cargo.

The merchants and sailors of New England were now so thoroughly frightened that they were overcautious. Almost every master sighting a sail in the distance would run away from it, and time after time two honest captains meeting far at sea would turn and run at once. In the pages of the *Boston News-Letter* for August 22 we read of a sloop with a white bottom, having eight gun ports, which anchored off Block Island and sent a small boat ashore. The men asked for a pilot and provisions, going over to Captain Rea's establishment, where they paid for some sheep with silver money. It was believed that Lowther, the pirate, had made the visit, until two weeks later when the true story became known. The sloop had been a London vessel, commanded by Captain Rupert Wappen, and had actually carried a dozen or so chests of silver, but she was not a pirate nor had Captain Lowther been aboard. Other reports came thick and fast regarding Lowther's whereabouts, but they were all false.

Oblivious of the excitement which he was causing up and down the Atlantic coast, Captain George Lowther actually had sailed for the West Indies, where he captured a vessel loaded with provisions from Martinique. Lowther followed this capture by taking the *Princess*, commanded by Captain Wickstead. A short time later he decided the *Happy Delivery* needed careening, for the vegetation had grown to such an extent on the bottom of the ship that her speed was too slow.

Blanco Island was chosen as an ideal location for this work, and Lowther ran the *Happy Delivery* up on the beach at high tide, sending the guns, sails, and supplies ashore.

Captain George Lowther, however, had careened his last ship. Just as the men started to work on scraping the bottom of the *Happy Delivery*, the lookout sighted another sloop sailing along just off the cove. It was the armed sloop *Eagle*, commanded by Walter Moore, who was bound for Comena. Having chanced to sail close to Blanco, Moore noticed a vessel careened on the beach. He passed in close enough to determine what type of ship it might be. Firing a shot of inquiry which forced Lowther to show some sort of flag, Moore awaited an answer. Lowther was desperate. As the tide was out, he was hopelessly trapped, but decided to try a ruse. Running the flag of Saint George up to the topmast head, Lowther hoped this would satisfy the armed sloop, but it did not. Captain Moore became more and more curious, and chose to come in closer.

Lowther observed the action. Determined to sell his liberty dearly, he opened fire with his guns from the shore as the *Eagle* neared the beach. The organized fire from the *Eagle* proved too much for Lowther, however, and his men either surrendered or broke and ran for the woods. The tide was sweeping in all the time, and at high water Captain Moore was able to go aboard the *Happy Delivery*, and soon had her anchored off in deep water. He organized a searching party of twenty-five armed men; by nightfall sixteen buccaneers had been taken in the dragnet, but Captain Lowther was not among them. The pirate had succeeded in eluding the searching party completely.

Captain Walter Moore sailed away from Blanco with sixteen prisoners and the *Happy Delivery* in company. A Spanish sloop was sent to capture the rest of the pirates shortly afterwards. Four more men were eventually captured, all of whom became slaves for the rest of their lives. Lowther, however, still managed to escape.

When the sloop *Eagle* finally arrived at St. Christopher's, a Court of Vice-Admiralty for the pirates was ordered convened on March 11, 1724. Fourteen men were tried for piracy. Two others had either died of wounds or were freed. Eleven were found guilty. Two of the condemned pirates were afterwards pardoned. Nine days later the unpardoned pirates were hanged from a gallows erected between the rise and fall of the tidal waters at St. Christopher's. Although Lowther was not captured and hanged, he did not escape, for another vessel touched at Blanco Island a few weeks later. A searching party sent to capture him found the pirate leader lying beside his discharged pistol, dead, it is said, by his own hand. It is believed that in desperation he finally committed suicide. Such was the strange finish of Captain George Lowther, who among his other villainous achievements trained the despicable Edward Low of Boston, Massachusetts.

In *Raiders and Rebels: The Golden Age of Piracy*, Frank Sherry wrote of George Lowther's penchant for sadistic torture, employed ostensibly to learn the location of treasure from captives. One of his favorite methods, wrote Sherry, "was to place burning hempen matches between the fingers of his captives and to allow them to sear the flesh to the bone."

It's interesting to note the similarities in the various examples of pirate articles that have survived. Lowther's articles, like those of John Phillips and Bartholomew Roberts, included a sort of insurance for pirates injured in battle. Also common in pirate articles—but missing from Lowther's—were provisions to elect a captain or remove him as necessary. Rules such as this were probably established more out of desire to prevent conflict than any notions of a just society.

The island off Venezuela where Lowther died, Blanco Island, is commonly known today as La Blanquilla and is named for its white sand beaches.

In his 1953 book *True Tales of Pirates and Their Gold*, Snow stated that Lowther made a last desperate effort to elude those in his pursuit. Lowther and his crew, wrote Snow, sailed up from the West Indies into the Rio Grande River all the way to the area that is now Alamosa, Colorado. The pirates encountered Spanish explorers who told them of a cave where "fabulous amounts of gold" had been hidden. The Spaniards had been unable to find the cave, which they said was marked with a large Maltese cross at the entrance.

The pirates subsequently found the cave, which provided evidence of some prior civilization in the area—but there was no gold in sight. After hiding their own treasure in a part of the cave, Lowther and his pirates were attacked by mysterious strangers who killed three of the men. Lowther and one other man recovered and returned to sea. It was after he returned to La Blanquilla that Lowther committed suicide, wrote Snow. The surviving pirate from Lowther's crew returned to England and recounted the tale, and it was included in an 1813 edition of the *General History of the Pyrates*. According to Snow, many people have since entered the Colorado cave described in this story but none have found gold, although interesting artifacts such as tools and fragments of Spanish armor have been discovered there.

CHAPTER 10

Captain Edward Low, the Infamous Buccaneer

On August 12, 1714, the Reverend Mr. Benjamin Wadsworth of the Old Brick Church in Boston united Edward Low and Eliza Marble in marriage. After this almost momentary meeting, the careers of the two men had widely divergent paths. The Reverend Mr. Benjamin Wadsworth later became president of Harvard College. Low, a year or so after his marriage, began his career as a pirate, in which profession he gradually sank to deeds so infamous and depraved that he was finally abandoned in an open boat by his own men.

Born in the parish of Westminster, Ned Low was the younger brother of the notorious Low hanged as a highwayman at Tyburn. Ned went to sea at an early age. On one of his visits ashore in Boston he became so attracted to the town that he decided to establish himself there, and obtained employment at a shipyard. Shortly after this, his marriage to Eliza Marble took place. At that time he made a definite effort to be an honest man, living quietly at home with his wife whom he dearly loved.

The first child of the Lows died soon after birth. The next baby, a girl, lived, but her mother died. Probably Eliza Low's death was responsible for Low's subsequent behavior, for it was shortly afterwards that he became quarrelsome at the shipyard and was discharged. The death of his young wife and then the loss of his job when he had been leading an honest life was such cruel fortune that he now seemed anxious to revenge himself on all humanity.

Unable to obtain employment elsewhere in Boston, Low shipped aboard a sloop bound for Honduras. As he displayed unusual ability, he was detailed to go ashore with the armed crew whose business it was to steal logwood from Spanish territory. The loading went on uneventfully until, one day, the logboat reached the sloop just as dinner was ready and appetizing odors were filling the air about the sloop. The captain ordered the men to make another trip before they could have their dinner. This was too much for Low, who was hungry and tired after a long day. Working himself into a frenzy, he discharged his musket at the captain. Low then jumped aboard the small boat and rowed ashore with the rest of the twelve men aboard.

On the beach the men all gathered around Low to make plans for the future. The thirteen men agreed to become pirates, with Edward Low as their captain. A black flag was fashioned and hoisted aloft. The next day the pirates fell upon a small ship, which they easily captured. Then Low set a course for the Grand Caymans Islands, a pirate rendezvous near Jamaica. Here they encountered Captain George Lowther, a well-known buccaneer. After a few days spent fitting out the vessel, Low joined forces with Lowther, the latter assuming the title of captain of the fleet, with Low as lieutenant. They finally decided to sink Low's smaller vessel, and the whole company sailed away aboard the *Happy Delivery*, Lowther's larger craft.

The first ship that the pirates encountered, the *Greyhound*, was commanded by a Yankee captain, Benjamin Edwards of Boston, who exchanged shot for shot until he realized his hopeless position, and surrendered. Five of Edwards's crew were impressed. Seven other Boston vessels suffered the same fate as the *Greyhound* primarily because Lowther hated all men from New England, where the hanging of pirates was becoming a habit. Lowther captured a fine sloop from Newport and turned it over to Ned Low as his personal command. Next a Jamaican sloop was seized and given to Charles Harris, one of the forced men from the *Greyhound*, who had shown much piratical promise after his capture. With these three ships and a small sloop as a tender, the sea marauders started once more on their voyage of plunder and pillaging.

The pirate fleet sailed for Port Mayo at Matique, where good careening grounds were available, the ships' bottoms being badly in need of scraping. Setting up a small colony ashore, they placed their plunder in tents erected near the beach.

One day, as the pirates were working scraping the bottom of the *Happy Delivery*, a band of natives, with blood-curdling yells rending the air, suddenly swooped in upon them from the forest!

Taken at a disadvantage, the men retreated to the sloops lying at anchor, near the shore, leaving their stores on the beach to be plundered by the enemy. This disaster naturally caused no little bitterness among the pirates. Quarreling and recrimination flamed among them. Hungry and discouraged, they up-anchored and sailed away. After such a disastrous defeat, the pirates planned to consolidate all the stores aboard one ship. Lowther was in command of the largest sloop, which he had named the *Ranger*. It was such a staunch craft, with ten guns and eight swivels, that the pirates chose it to remain afloat, while all the other sloops were scuttled because of the emergency. Low and his infamous company of one hundred sea brigands then sailed away.

Several weeks went by with no other vessel sighted. They finally overtook a small brigantine near the island of Discade, in the West Indies. Going aboard the vessel, they plundered and sank it. The pirates felt better after the capture, for the affair revived their flagging spirits. Sailing for the Bahamas, the buccaneers fell in with and captured the brigantine *Rebecca*, homeward bound for Boston. There were five women and eighteen men aboard, but all eventually reached home safely after being transferred some time later to another captured vessel.

It was shortly after this that Lowther and Low fell apart. Evidently Lowther had been steadily growing tired of the dissatisfied attitude and senseless cruelties of his lieutenant. Low was given the *Rebecca* and a crew of forty on the afternoon of May 28, 1722. Captain Lowther, having taught his pupil the lesson of cruelty on the high seas only too well, sailed away from Ned Low of Boston forever.

Captain Low now began a voyage to New England waters. Arriving off Block Island early in June 1722, he fell in with a sloop from New Jersey, which he boarded and plundered. Later in the day he captured a Newport sloop commanded by James Cahoon. Disabling the sloop, Low then stood away to the southeast, in an attempt to flee the vicinity.

Cahoon reached Block Island that same midnight, however, and a whaleboat arrived in Newport Harbor the next morning with the terrifying news that a pirate ship was off the coast. All Newport was aroused. The governor of Rhode Island ordered drums beaten around town for volunteers to fight the sea rovers, and the excitement in Newport reached fever intensity.

Two of the best sloops in Newport were outfitted and prepared for battle. Captain John Headlund was chosen to be master of the first sloop of ten guns and eighty men. Captain John Brown commanded the other sloop, which had six guns and sixty men. The sloops were under weigh before sunset the same day, at which time the pirate ship was still visible from the heights of Block Island. But a wind which sprang up allowed the buccaneer to escape from his pursuers, and the men of Newport returned home without their prey.

When news of Pirate Low's being off the coast of New England reached Boston, the drums were beaten for a muster, and over a hundred volunteers left Boston Harbor under Captain Peter Papillion to hunt him down. Although he was unable to catch Low, Papillion did overtake the brigantine *Rebecca*, which Low had abandoned in the charge of homeward-bound Marblehead sailors. The fittings and goods on the *Rebecca* were sold at Captain Long's house in Charlestown.

Captain Low had actually sailed to Buzzards Bay, where his men went ashore on No Man's Land to steal sheep for food and to replenish the water supply. The plan at that time was to sail for the Bahamas. But Low changed his mind, and sailed north until he reached Roseway, near what is now Shelburne, Nova Scotia. A fishing fleet of thirteen vessels lay at anchor. Suspecting nothing, the fishermen would allow a boat from Low's vessel to approach. Once aboard a schooner, Low's men would draw cutlasses and pistols from under their clothes and force the fishermen to surrender. One by one the freebooters visited the entire thirteen vessels in this manner, thoroughly plundering the helpless fishermen of all usable material.

Captain Low took special interest in one particular schooner, the *Mary*, owned by Joseph Dolliber of Marblehead. Choosing the *Mary* for his new flagship, he renamed her the *Fancy*, transferring his own men and supplies to her decks. All the fishermen except ten were allowed to go aboard Low's old brigantine, and a short time later they sailed for Boston.

Low's adventures for the period immediately following are told in detail in Philip Ashton's narrative, also in this volume, so we shall pick up the story after Ashton, a fishing lad from Marblehead, escaped to the island of Bonaco [usually spelled Bonacca—*Ed.*]. This took place on March 9, 1723, during the period when Low was ashore on Roatan Island.*

---

*Ashton escaped to Roatan on March 9, 1723, and went to Bonacca the following year.—*Ed.*

Captain Edward Low of Boston, "the most infamous pirate of all"

Running into a terrible storm, Low barely weathered the blow. After the winds subsided he came across a great ship badly crippled, having lost all her masts in the hurricane. Low removed a thousand pounds' worth of gold and silver from the disabled vessel. This same hurricane, it may be noted, caused terrific damage at Port Royal. The cannon of Fort Charles on the island were washed into the sea, while at least four hundred persons lost their lives. The gale wrecked forty vessels in the harbor.

On August 3, Low sailed into St. Michael's Road, capturing seven vessels without resistance. One of them, the pink *Rose*, was a former man-of-war, and could easily have won over the pirate craft with any show of strength. But there was such terror attached to the name of Low that no opposition was offered. Quick to appreciate the advantages of the *Rose*, Low assumed command of her, giving Charles Harris the captaincy of the schooner.

In a short time Captain Harris fell in with a galley commanded by Captain Wright, who resisted the pirates in a short skirmish. This so enraged Harris that he allowed the pirates to parade around the decks of the defeated galley, cutting and slashing the prisoners at will. The Portuguese captives, including two Roman Catholic friars, were triced up at each arm of the foreyard, but before they died Harris had them cut down again. When they had recovered their senses, they were again trussed up aloft and the process repeated until death spared them further torture.

Captain Low happened to be aboard at the time, and in the mixup one of the pirates slashed him across the lower jaw, laying bare his teeth. Low complained bitterly about the way the surgeon sewed his jaw up. Enraged, the surgeon smashed him across the mouth, bidding him to sew up his own chops. As the surgeon was a necessary member of the ship's company, Low accepted the affront in silence.

Following this fracas, the two pirate leaders steered for Madeira. At this port they seized an old man from a fishing boat and sent his companions ashore for water. When the water was duly delivered, the hostage was released, bedecked in stolen finery as a show of the pirate's generosity. Later, while off the Cape Verde Islands, the *Liverpool Merchant* and the *King Sagamore* were captured. For some perverse reason the buccaneers put ashore Captain Andrew Scott completely naked. About this time Nicholas Merritt of Marblehead, together with other forced men who were thoroughly disgusted at Low's cruel antics, escaped from his control by sailing away in a small trading sloop which had been captured a short time before. When they ran into the Azores for needed provisions, the crew members were made prisoners and thrown into jail. But several, including Merritt, escaped and eventually reached America.

After careening his vessels at the island of Bonavista, Low sailed for St. Nicholas for water. At the southeastern end of the island Captain George Roberts and his sloop *Margaret* fell prey to the pirate fleet. (Roberts later wrote of his experience in *The Four Voyages of Capt. George Roberts*, published at London in 1726.)*

Brought into Low's cabin by one of the other pirates, Roberts was welcomed by Commodore Low himself, who apologized, with fine irony, no doubt, for taking Roberts' ship. Roberts answered grimly that it was still in Low's power to let him go. Low argued that he was but one man out of many; all business of that nature had to be done in public, and by a majority of votes. Neither he nor the others wished to meet with vessels of their own nations, but when it happened, it could not be avoided. As the pirates were gentlemen who depended on Dame Fortune, they could not be ungrateful to her. After a long discussion which settled nothing, Roberts was allowed to leave the cabin.

The subsequent ten days or more, about which Captain Roberts discourses at length in his journal, give us much insight into the minds and reactions of pirates on the high seas, and for anyone desiring a real running account of the life of a pirate, nothing has been written which illustrates better the thoughts and actions of the buccaneers of two hundred years ago.

The next morning after the capture Captain Roberts turned out at eight o'clock and went up on deck. While taking a walk around the boat, he was met by a man who asked if the captain remembered him. Roberts disclaimed ever having seen the fellow before, whereupon the man gave him further information.

"I once belonged to you, and sailed with you when you were Commander of the *Susannah* in the year 1718," said the pirate.

Two others, who were also under him on the same voyage, later came up to Captain Roberts, expressing their sorrow that he had fallen among thieves, and promising to give him substantial presents of silk and linen before he departed if he was permitted to leave the ship. The three men then glanced around as if to see if other pirates were listening. Satisfied

---

*Many experts believe that this work was written by Daniel Defoe.—*Ed.*

that they were indeed alone with the captain, they told him to be very careful, as Roberts' mate had divulged information that Roberts was an expert pilot familiar with the coast of Brazil, whereas not one sailor of the whole pirate fleet had any nautical knowledge of Brazilian waters. They further charged him with the need for utmost secrecy, for it would mean certain death to them were it known they had so spoken.

Later in the day Captain Low came up on deck, and asked Roberts if his bed had been comfortable. Roberts replied that everything had been satisfactory, and stated that he was obliged for the care which had been taken. Low nodded and ordered the consultation flag run up. This flag was a strange one, a green silk emblem on which the yellow figure of a man blowing a trumpet had been sewn. Shortly afterwards boats came from the other vessels of the fleet, and soon the deck was filled with pirates. Captain Low invited them to dinner and a conference in the cabin. The motley crowd poured down the hatchways into the cabin, and those who could not squeeze into the crowded compartment went below into the steerage.

When the pirates had finished eating, Captain Low asked Roberts if he happened to be married, and if so did he have any children. Roberts answered that not only was he married, but that he had five children when he left home, and possibly had six by then, "one being on the Stocks when I came from Home." Then came further inquiries about his wife, whether she was well provided for or not. Roberts replied that he had left her in rather indifferent circumstances, and if the present trip turned out poorly, the wife and children might suffer for bread. Low, whose own child was then living in Boston, turned to pirate Russel and said, "It will not do, Russel."

Russel asked Low what the trouble was, and Low replied that they could not take Captain Roberts, who was needed at home. Russel said that self-preservation was the first law of nature, and necessity has no law. Then Low said that it would never be with his consent. The time came for the vote, all the pirates leaving the cabin. Roberts was told to stay below and await the verdict.

Two hours later the pirates returned. It seems that Russel had been very bitter against Roberts, but most of the others wished to let him sail away. Russel interviewed Roberts then as to what would happen should he be allowed to leave. He would be short-handed; they would allow him no supplies; he had lost his cargo and money. How could Roberts hope to sail under those circumstances? Roberts answered him question for question in such a masterly fashion that he excited the admiration of the crew, and nothing was settled that day.

The next day, in the forenoon, Captain Russel returned. His conversation soon indicated that he was attempting a new tack to win his point. He told Roberts he knew him to be a man of great understanding, and wished him well. Then he said that the only way out would be to sink the Roberts sloop, and then have Roberts join the pirate company until their next capture, at which time Roberts would be given the new vessel and a crew, and could sail away.

Roberts told Russel that his kind offer could not be accepted, and gave his reasons. If the owners of the vessel should hear of it, he would have to make restitution, or he might even be hanged as a pirate. Russel retorted that they, the pirates, would give Roberts a bill of sale for the vessel and cargo, which would settle the difficulty. Roberts admitted

Snow's 1944 edition of this book identifies this illustration as Russel and Roberts, but The Pirates Own Book *identifies it as "Low presenting a Pistol and a Bowl of Punch," explaining that Ned Low captured Captain Graves of Virginia and offered him a drink of punch. When Graves refused, Low cocked his pistol and said, "Either take one or the other."*

that this might absolve him, but even if he received thousands of pounds in wealth, he would not be at peace with his conscience. By this time a small group of the pirates had gathered around to hear the argument, and one of them said that Roberts would do well at preaching sermons, and would make a good chaplain. Others, however, quickly decided that they could do without "Godliness to be preach'd there: That pirates had no God but their Money, nor Savior but their Arms." A silence then fell over the buccaneers gathered on the deck, after which Captain Jack Russel replied to Low's remarks.

"I suppose you think, that all the Claim we have to the Ships and Goods that we take, is by an Act of Violence, and therefore unjust?"

"I could not express my Conceptions of it better or fuller," answered Roberts, "but hope that neither you nor Captain Loe will be offended at my taking so much Liberty."

At this clever retort, the crew agreed that they were enjoying to the utmost the arguments of the two men, Russel and Roberts, and thought they were very well matched. One of them added that Captain Russel seldom met with a man that could stand up to him. The arguments continued throughout the day, and still nothing was settled. Finally Captain Low got up and called the gathering to him.

"Gentlemen, the Master, I must needs say, has spoke nothing but what is very reasonable, and I think he ought to have his Sloop. What do you say, Gentlemen?" Almost every man agreed with him, several of them suggesting that a small amount should be presented to him before he went aboard his vessel. Russel, boiling mad at the turn of events, determined secretly to kill Roberts.

Approaching Low, Russel suggested that as the pirates had voted to return the sloop to Roberts, he would like to take the captain over to his own vessel, where he could treat him to a sneaker of punch before his departure. Low, suspecting nothing, assented, and Roberts had perforce to accept the offer, although he said in his book, "I had rather stay'd with Loe." But Russel overwhelmed him with kindness, and seemed so solicitous that Roberts felt that perhaps all would be well. Roberts and Russel left at once for the latter's vessel.

After a sumptuous repast a bowl of punch was set on the table. Captain Jack Russel took a bumper, and drank the first toast of the evening, which was called "Success to our undertaking." Roberts, not daring to refuse, drank with the rest. The next health was announced, "To the King of France." The third toast gave Russel the opportunity for which he waited. It was started as "to the King of England." By the time it had gone halfway around the table, however, the pirates were saying "the aforesaid health," and when it came Roberts' turn, he cried out, "To the aforesaid health."

"What health is that?" shouted Russel, becoming angry.

"Why," answered Roberts, "The King of England's health."

"Who is the King of England?" countered Russel.

"He that wears the crown is certainly king while he keeps it," answered the perplexed Roberts, wondering what it was that Russel, who was working himself into a rage, was getting at. "King George at present wears it," concluded Roberts.

At this remark Russel, who considered it was high time to shoot Roberts, whipped out his pistol. But the gunner grabbed Russel and disarmed him. Russel then shouted out that the Pretender was the real King of England, and it was a sin to allow such a traitorous dog to live. With those words he grabbed another pistol from his holster and cocked it instantly. Fortunately, just as he fired, a pirate struck the gun out of Russel's hand, so that the charge went off without doing any damage.

The gunner announced that Roberts had not been to blame, and that Russel had acted in a hasty manner. Russel, still furious, began to argue with the other pirates, but they were all against him. The result was that Russel, by vote of the other pirates, had all his firearms and weapons taken away for the time being. Sensing the danger that Roberts was in, the master, the gunner, and five or six others decided to sit up all night with the poor man, to prevent Russel or his cronies from finishing the plan of murder.

The next morning Roberts was rowed back to Low's ship, where the gunner and the steward told Low the whole story of the night's events. While Low was hearing of the affair, Russel had gone to the first mate of Roberts' old ship, and by four o'clock that afternoon, had talked the man into becoming a pirate. Then Russel rowed over to Low's ship, and confronted Low and Roberts. He was ready to play his next card.

"The mate of the sloop is willing to enter with us as a Volunteer," said Russel, whereupon Low asked what they should do, as the captain could not sail away without the mate.

"Zounds!" exclaimed Russel, "the mate is a lusty young brisk Man, and has been upon the Account before, and told me but even now."

Low retorted that to give Roberts his sloop without hands was to give him a lingering death. Russel came back by declaring that he only spoke for the good of the whole company; the rest could do as they pleased. He was the acknowledged quartermaster, duly elected, and would enter the mate then and there, and had a pistol ready for any who opposed him. As the pirate law was very clear on that particular point, the other pirates, after a little complaining, admitted that Russel's plan would have to be carried out. Russel, realizing that he had won, now turned to Roberts.

"Master," said Russel, "the Company has decreed you your Sloop and you shall have her; you shall have your two Boys, and that is all: You shall have neither Provisions, nor any Thing else, more than as she now is. And, I hear, there are some of the Company design to make a Gathering for you; but that also I forbid, by the Authority of my Place."

Captain Roberts stoutly objected to being placed on his sloop under such impossible conditions, and started to discuss the situation, but Captain Low gave him the wink, and Roberts subsided. Later that afternoon Low called to Roberts, explaining that whatever he had said to Russel, the latter would have taken it "edgeways."

Further discussion of Roberts' case ensued. Russel said he was ready to take Roberts aboard his vessel, as his duty as quartermaster allowed. He would see that Roberts was placed aboard his sloop. As soon as Roberts reached Russel's vessel, the pirate reiterated to the unhappy captain that he was to be placed aboard the sloop without food or drink. At ten that night he called the sloop's boat over, and asked the occupants if they had cleared the sloop of everything as he had ordered. They answered in the affirmative. Then Russel inquired about the sails, and when he found the mainsail was still on the sloop, ordered it removed, as he did not wish Roberts to have any sails whatever.

"Damn it," said one of his men, "Then you must turn the Man adrift in the Sloop without a Mainsail."

"Pish," said Russel, "The same miraculous Power that is to bring him Provisions, can also bring him a Sail."

"If he be such a mighty Conjurer," said one, "how the Devil was it that he did not conjure himself clear of us?"

The gunner seems to have been a pretty fair sort, judging from the reasoning which he used in the following statements:

> *If any of you were at Tyburn, or any other Place to be executed, as many better and stouter Men than some of you, have been, and the*

Spectators, or Jack Catch should make a Droll and May-game of you, you would think them a very hard-hearted, as well as inconsiderate Sort of People. . . . Take care, Russel, you have not this to answer for one Day . . . and I tell you, John Russel, if ever such Cases as these be any more practis'd, my Endeavor shall be to leave this Company as soon as I possibly can.

Two sailors then stepped into the boat and rowed Captain Roberts over to his sloop. Halfway across he met the schooner's boat, with his two boys aboard, and they were all transferred to the sloop in short order.

After a long and tedious voyage of considerable hardship, in which improvised methods were necessary to sail the ill-manned sloop, Captain George Roberts finally reached land in a starving condition. It is believed that the pirates, without Russel's knowledge, had smuggled aboard a few meager provisions.

In spite of Roberts' glowing account of Low's genial nature, the Boston pirate was actually one of the most horrible buccaneers of the deep. Roberts was lucky to encounter the bloodthirsty leader in a pleasant mood. In addition, Low knew that Roberts had a wife and children at home. This appeared to make a difference to this Jekyll-Hyde pirate, Edward Low of Boston.

With Roberts out of sight and mind, Low now began a campaign of terror and brutal deeds which have seldom been equaled in piratical annals. After leaving Captain Roberts, he started for the Brazilian coast. But no victims could be found, so the fleet sailed northward. Finally reaching the Triangles, near the island of Surinam, the pirates careened and scraped the vessels. The pink was lost at this time as is told in Philip Ashton's story.

Shortly afterwards the buccaneers captured a French sloop. Low then assumed command of the sloop, putting Captain Spriggs in charge of the schooner. After capturing several vessels, they fell in with an extremely rich prize, the *Nostra Signiora de Victoria*, from Portugal. As the treasure which Low knew had been on the ship could not be found, he tortured some of the sailors until they revealed what had happened to it. The day they had been taken, the Portuguese captain had placed the entire treasure worth $50,000 in a money bag, which he suspended out of a cabin window. When the pirates climbed aboard his ship, the captain cut the rope and the treasure fell into the sea.

The fury of Low at this discovery was almost unbelievable. He had the poor man lashed to the mast, whereupon Low drew his cutlass and slashed off the captain's lips with quick, decisive strokes. Broiling the severed members of the man's face, he then compelled the Portuguese mate to turn cannibal and eat them while hot from the fire. After this bit of horrible torture, the pirates murdered in cold blood every officer and sailor from the *Nostra Signiora de Victoria*. It had been a bloody day for Captain Low and his men.

Low seems to have developed an overwhelming hatred for New England men, for not only was Boston a port where many pirates were hanged, but Low himself had once been discharged from a position which he held in that town. His treatment of Yankees grew more and more severe. When, however, he seized a Spanish vessel that had in

The Portuguese captain cutting away the money bag

turn captured several New England ships, and even then had their captains confined below decks, Low ordered his crew to eliminate the entire Spanish company. The buccaneers waded into the helpless Spaniards, cutting them to pieces with poleaxes and cutlasses, and shooting those who jumped over the side. Several Spanish sailors managed to escape and swim ashore, although severely wounded. Some days later Low's men were walking on the beach, when one of the wretched Spanish sailors, crawling out of the bushes, asked for quarter.

"God damn you, I will give you quarters presently," said the pirate, and he shoved the end of his musket down the throat of the helpless Spaniard, pulling the trigger. An illustration of the scene is included in these pages.

Later the American captains were released and allowed to sail for home, after having promised not to reveal they had met Low. In the pages of the *American Weekly Mercury*, however, we read the whole account in detail.

With Low so close to New York, the man-of-war *Greyhound* was dispatched to catch this bloody rover of the seas. She sighted him in the early morning hours of June 10, 1723. The battle that followed was a fierce one. Finally the sloop and the schooner began to edge away, with the *Greyhound* in hot pursuit. After a running fight, which lasted two hours, the pirates got out their boats in the dying wind, and began to row their vessels away from the heavier man-of-war. But the *Greyhound*, employing the same tactics, came up with them around two-thirty that afternoon. When the mainmast of the schooner was shot away, Low decided that he had had enough, and sailed away, leaving his friend Captain Harris and his crew to be captured aboard the schooner. This cowardly action hurt Low's reputation aboard his own vessel, and he soon realized it. Captain Edward Low decided that the next victim he met should suffer for his loss of face.

Two days later he fell in with a whaling sloop from Nantucket, about eighty miles off the island. One of the whaleboats was some distance from the sloop, and the men rowed hastily over to another vessel in the vicinity and escaped. The whaler was boarded. Nathan Skiff, the captain, was found to be an unmarried man, so Captain Low had him stripped and severely beaten on the deck, after which his ears were slashed off. Then he was shot through the head and his sloop scuttled. The story of the incident was brought ashore by the whalers, who had reached land in a small boat, and the tale subsequently was printed in

Crew member of Captain Low's company killing a wounded Spaniard who had asked for quarter

the *Boston News-Letter*. Incidentally, the pages of the *News-Letter* of this period often mention the exploits of the infamous Captain Low.

Two days following the whaling incident, Low captured another vessel, a fisherman off Block Island. The poor captain was dragged aboard, and other pirates held the victim while Low cut and slashed at him with his cutlass, finally decapitating him. The same day two more whaling sloops were taken, and the master of one craft was brought aboard. Low, gone berserk by now, pounced on him. He stabbed the captain's chest and cut a hole, pulling out the man's heart, which he roasted over a grill. The captain's mate was made to turn cannibal and eat the heart. The other whaling captain was taken aboard. Captain Low cut off his ears, had them roasted, and sprinkled them with salt and pepper, after which his crew were forced to eat their own captain's ears.

And so it went, down through the pages of Captain Low's subsequent career. We need not dwell on any more of his sadistic adventures. Enough has been told of his fiendish methods. His style of torture changed slightly as his tastes varied. There was a period when he would hang those he captured. At other times various new forms of torture were suggested, approved, and inflicted.

When the fall of 1723 came, Captain Ned Low of Boston was cruising in the Atlantic. At that time the fleet included Captain Low's own *Merry Christmas*, which had been captured the previous July, and the ship *Delight* in command of Captain Spriggs. A short time later Captain Spriggs deserted and went on his own account.

We cannot state with any degree of certainty exactly how and when Low met his fate, but we read in the pages of the *Boston News-Letter* that he captured a ship called the *Squirrel* in January 1724. The following May sailors arriving at St. Lucia reported they had been taken by Low, who at that time had only thirty pirates in his crew. A French warship was dispatched to capture him, and discovered Low and three others of his group adrift in an open boat. Low had murdered his quartermaster, and the crew arose against him and cast him adrift without food or provisions. The French captain quickly brought Low into the harbor at Martinique, where the pirate was tried by the French court along with his companions. They were adjudged guilty and hanged on the gallows.

There are many who do not believe the story that Low was set adrift, but confirmation is present in a most unusual manner. In the Massachusetts State House in Boston, buried for years under huge stacks of similar documents, can be found a statement of one Jonathan Barlow, a sailor who was with Captain Ned Low aboard the *Merry Christmas*. It confirms the abandoning of Low on the high seas by his own crew, so it is reasonable to assume that the story of his hanging in Martinique is a true one.

———————— ∿ ————————

Ned Low as a boy was a petty thief and gamester in the area around the House of Commons in Westminster, England. He "was always ready to attack any one who might catch him cheating or attempt to relieve him of his ill-gotten gains," wrote George Francis Dow and John Henry Edmonds in *The Pirates of the New England Coast*. Low's highwayman brother mentioned by Snow had a similarly early start. At the age of seven he was carried around the streets in a basket on the back of a porter, and would snatch hats and wigs from passersby. He moved on to larger prey after outgrowing the basket.

Snow mentions Low's jaw being sliced open and the botched surgery that followed. This left Low with a permanent evil grin, it's said—a face to match his personality.

Most pirates welcomed people of all races into their crews, but Low was an exception. He would trick black sailors into signing articles and invite them on board, where they would be clamped in irons and subsequently sold into slavery.

The book *The Four Voyages of Capt. George Roberts* is now considered by many to be the work of *Robinson Crusoe* author Daniel Defoe. In *Under the Black Flag*, historian David Cordingly wrote that while the book may be entirely fictitious, "the nautical detail is so authentic that it seems likely it was based on interviews with former pirates or . . . was based on real events." While the events in the book can't be taken for fact, it is regarded as an important, detailed portrait of life on a pirate ship.

Edward Rowe Snow was an avid treasure hunter, and he once found what might have been a portion of a treasure buried by the crew of Ned Low. In 1947 Snow purchased a mysterious map, but it wasn't until five years later that he put the pieces together and came to believe that he possessed a treasure map of Nova Scotia's Isle Haute drawn by Low himself, or possibly one of his subordinates. The map was examined by experts and was found to have been drawn on seventeenth-century paper.

In June 1952, armed with his map and metal detector, Snow set out for Isle Haute and made arrangements to stay at the lighthouse. Snow wrote of his approach to Isle Haute in his book *True Tales of Pirates and Their Gold*. "Almost

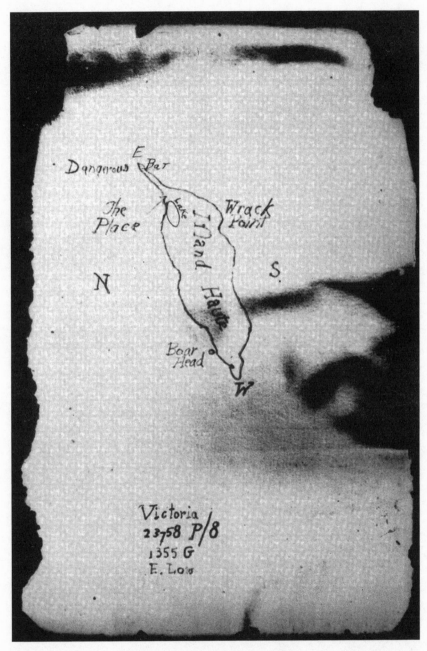

Edward Rowe Snow owned this map and believed it to be pirate Edward Low's treasure map of Isle Haute, Nova Scotia. (From Snow's True Tales of Pirates and Their Gold, *1957)*

nothing can equal the thrill of sailing out to sea on the way to a romantic island which one has never visited. When this thrill was combined with the knowledge that pirates had buried treasure on the island to which we were sailing, my excitement knew no bounds."

Soon after he arrived, Snow's metal detector picked up a strong reading at the edge of a previously dug pit. By himself as the sun was setting, Snow dug with a pick for twenty minutes when he suddenly uncovered the ribs of a human skeleton.

"On my next swing with the pick," he wrote, "the sharp point caught on something in the ground. The earth tore away and I saw it was a human skull which rolled across my feet! Completely losing my nerve, I scrambled out of the pit, grabbed the lantern, and started walking rapidly toward the lighthouse far away on the top of the island cliff." The next morning Snow returned to finish his digging, and he found several coins in the area around the skeleton. The Spanish and Portuguese coins were well over two hundred years old.

Before returning to Massachusetts, Snow was interviewed by the Royal Canadian Mounted Police. When it was determined that part of his modest treasure find was gold, the coins had to be left "in the efficient care of the Bank of Nova Scotia." A short time later Snow was able to obtain a license to export the coins. *Life Magazine* ran a feature on the Isle Haute "Red Taped Pirate Gold" on July 21, 1952.

Snow believed that the bulk of Low's treasure might have been found long before he reached Isle Haute's shores. Note to present-day treasure hunters: Searching for treasure anywhere in Nova Scotia now requires a license under the Treasure Trove Act, and violators can face heavy fines. And visiting Isle Haute at all requires the permission of the Canadian Coast Guard.

CHAPTER 11

Captain Francis Spriggs, Active off Florida's Coast

When Captain Lowther sailed down the Thames from London in March 1721 aboard the *Gambia Castle*, one of his more lively crew members was Francis Farrington Spriggs. Later, when Captain Low joined forces with Lowther, Spriggs and Low became good friends, and when the two captains separated the following year, Spriggs chose Low as the man he wished to follow.

We tell elsewhere the story of the battle between the *Greyhound* and the pirates, in which Captain Low escaped while Captain Harris was captured. In that encounter, Francis Spriggs was back at his favorite post of quartermaster on Low's vessel. Toward the end of the year 1723, Low took another vessel, the ship *Delight*, off the Guinea coast, and in a short time he put Spriggs in charge of her with a crew of sixty men. In spite of this promotion, Spriggs was then nursing a grudge. A member of the pirate crew had without reason murdered a prisoner in cold blood and a debate ensued. Spriggs believed the pirate should be executed as a penalty, while Ned Low did not feel that the buccaneer deserved this punishment. This led from a heated discussion to open animosity. The quarrel, instead of being forgotten, became more pronounced, and two nights later Spriggs sailed away forever from Captain Low.

The following day all hands of the renegade crew were called together to elect a new captain. They chose Francis Spriggs. The buccaneers made an emblem quite similar to that which Low fluttered to the breeze whenever overtaking a ship, consisting of a white skeleton holding an arrow in one hand and an hour glass in the other. After the election and sewing of the new flag, the pirates hoisted the standard to the masthead and fired a salute of guns. Then they sailed for the West Indies, keeping on the alert for ships to rob and sink.

A Portuguese vessel, which hove into sight a short time later, didn't have a chance against the newly organized band and capitulated at once. The pirates were able to obtain some valuable merchandise from the cargo. Not satisfied with their loot, they decided to have some games with the captured crew. One of the little antics in which they indulged was called "sweating." A group of pirates would take one of the captives between decks around the mizzenmast. Several candles on the mast six feet up threw an eerie light on the scene. A circle of pirates gathered about four feet from the mizzenmast, and the captive was forced to run around the mast again and again, while the pirates, armed with various types of sharp instruments, all the way from penknives to six-foot pikes, prodded the man. Accompanied by raucous laughter and songs, the game reached its height after ten or twelve minutes of torment for the victim, who was exhausted by this time. Captive after captive was thus abused. When the pirates tired of their sport, the Portuguese crew members were thrown into an open boat with a limited amount of provisions and set adrift.

Having seized two other vessels, Captain Spriggs, on March 22, 1724, came up with the ship *Jolly Bachelor,* in command of Captain Hawkins, near the island of Roatan. Since her cargo of logwood did not appeal to the outlaws, they removed what they could of the stores and ammunition before practically wrecking the ship. In a short time the ruffians were knocking down the cabins, smashing the windows, and cutting the cables. The two mates were forced to join the pirate crew, and then the *Jolly Bachelor* was allowed to proceed. Burridge, the first mate, finally signed articles with Captain Spriggs.

On March 27, the sloop *Endeavor,* from Newport, Rhode Island, was captured, and the mate, Dixey Gross by name, said he did not wish to go with the pirates. He was then told he should have his discharge, which would be written on his body at once; every pirate aboard gave him ten lashes on his bare back.

Six days later the pirates sighted another vessel. After drawing within cannon range, the sea marauders fired a broadside into her. The vessel proved to be the same one which they had captured on March 22, the *Jolly Bachelor*. This strange occurrence made the pirates so angry that they boarded the ship and began to slash right and left with their swords and cutlasses. They started for poor Captain Hawkins with the intention of killing him, but his old mate Burridge rushed aboard and pleaded for his former commander, thus saving Hawkins' life.

The *Jolly Bachelor* was soon ablaze. Later that evening luckless Captain Hawkins was forced to eat a dish of assorted candles. After this unpleasant meal, the captain was thrown and pushed about the cabin until he was a mass of bruises, whereupon he was allowed to join the other prisoners forward. On April 4, Spriggs reached the island of Roatan, which Philip Ashton, whose story is told elsewhere, had left several days before. There Spriggs marooned the following men: Captain Hawkins, his boatswain, Captain Samuel Pike, Dixey Gross, Simon Fullmore, an old man whose name was not known, and James Nelley, one of Spriggs's pirates who was causing trouble. As soon as an ancient musket and a supply of powder and ball were brought ashore for the unfortunate men, Spriggs sailed away. In a relatively short time the marooned victims were rescued by Captain Jones of the *Merriam* and taken to Jamaica.

Spriggs was now forced to clean his ship's bottom. After the task was completed, he decided to settle an old score. In his mind all this time was revenge on Captain Walter Moore of St. Christopher, who had caught and defeated his old friend Captain George Lowther, later causing his death. Making great sweeps across the seas where Moore usually sailed, one day he encountered what he believed to be Moore's vessel, the sloop *Eagle*. The craft actually proved to be a French man-of-war, which turned and gave chase at once. In the excitement the Frenchman lost her main topmast, allowing Spriggs to escape.

Captain Francis Farrington Spriggs now believed the waters around Bermuda would be more favorable for his activities, and sailed northward. Late in April he fell in with a New York schooner commanded by Captain William Richardson, who came into Boston Harbor the following month with the serious news that Spriggs was on his way up the coast, planning to sink or burn every sloop, schooner, or ship anywhere north of Philadelphia. Because of the threatening danger, His Majesty's ship *Sea Horse*, in command of Captain Durrell, sailed at once in search of Francis F. Spriggs.

Meanwhile, Spriggs was continuing his course into northern waters. On May 2, 1724, he captured the brigantine *Daniel*, bound for Boston, forcing two sailors to join his crew. This was done, according to the local

Boston paper, "notwithstanding their importunate Prayers and Tears to him to dismiss them." Spriggs told Master John Hopkins of the *Daniel* that he was after Captain Solgard, who had captured Charles Harris, Spriggs's dearly beloved fellow pirate later hanged at Newport. Indications are, however, that Spriggs never reached New England, for we hear from him next on June 4 near St. Christopher, where he captured a small sloop commanded by Nicholas Trot. As the cargo was practically valueless to the pirates, they treated the crew shamefully, hoisting them aloft to the main and fore tops, and then letting go the ropes so that the men came crashing down on the deck. After amusing themselves by this strange torture for a time, they allowed the crippled and bruised sailors to get back aboard their sloop as best they could and sail off.

A short while later Captain Spriggs captured a fine ship from Rhode Island, which had as part of her cargo some splendid horses on their way to St. Christopher's. The pirates abused these animals to the utmost, riding them backwards and forwards across the deck, and galloping fore and aft, while they shouted like devils all the time. So frantic did the horses become that in their frenzy they threw their buccaneer riders, forcing the pirates to give up what they considered an interesting pastime. The sea ruffians then turned their attention to the ship's crew. The usual tortures were applied to the unfortunate sailors, who were whipped and cut in a horrible manner. The pirates explained that the absence of boots and spurs for proper horsemanship was responsible for their punishing the sailors.

Appearing off Jamaica, Spriggs attracted the attention of two British warships in the harbor of Port Royal. James Wyndham, the captain of one man-of-war, the *Diamond*, had spent much time studying the career of the notorious Spriggs, and so rightly figured the pirate leader would sail for the Bay of Honduras. Proceeding from Jamaica with all sails set, Captain Wyndham caught Spriggs in the very act of plundering a fleet of logwood vessels then loading. Captain Spriggs, realizing that he was trapped, ordered the gunners to fire at the man-of-war, but after a few broadsides had been exchanged, thought of a method of escape. A short distance away were some dangerous shoals, which Spriggs's vessel was able to clear, while the *Diamond* could not sail over them. The pirate leader therefore ordered every buccaneer to the sweeps, and they rowed across the shoals to freedom, the heavier man-of-war *Diamond* helpless to maneuver in chase. The fire from the British warship had killed six pirates and wounded an equal number, however.

The Bahama Channel soon attracted the attention of the captain, who was now in company with Captain Shipton, a bold rogue of ill repute. After capturing a sloop loaded with slaves, he fell in with Captain Richard Durffie, bound for Newport. When he proposed to load Durffie's vessel with Negroes, he met with the other's objections that their lack of provisions would make them all starve to death, so Spriggs put only a dozen slaves aboard the Newport-bound vessel and let Durffie sail away.

Off the western end of Cuba, Captain James Wyndham was still trying to locate Spriggs and his companion, when one day he observed two sails on the horizon. They were the pirate marauders, who also recognized Wyndham's man-of-war, and so parted company. Heading at once for Florida, the frightened Shipton drove his sloop with such recklessness that it soon smashed aground and was wrecked. Few of his seventy men escaped. Some of the buccaneers were captured by the Indians ashore while others surrendered to the sailors from the warship. It is actually on record that cannibalistic Indians killed and ate sixteen of Shipton's pirates, while forty-nine others were taken aboard the *Diamond*. The sailors aboard the man-of-war were able to secure two thousand pounds in gold from the pirates they captured.

Spriggs, who seemed to bear a charmed life, escaped again. Returning to the Florida coast, he located ten pirates, including Shipton, who had managed to escape. Spriggs took the buccaneers back to his old haunts in the Bay of Honduras before the end of 1724, and together with Shipton, who had assumed command of a large dugout canoe, again hit the logwood vessels loading in the Bay. They made seizure after seizure until the captured craft numbered sixteen. Boston men seem to have been the particular victims of Spriggs' activities, but as more vessels from Boston than from any other port were getting logwood, it is only natural that they would be captured with greater frequency.

One day Shipton overcame the crew aboard the Boston ship *Mary and John*, commanded by Captain Thomas Glen who had as his first mate Matthew Perry. Glen was placed aboard another vessel.

Spriggs, anxious to sail away for a rendezvous at the usual pirate headquarters on Roatan Island, told Shipton to follow him after arranging for a crew aboard the newly captured *Mary and John*. Because Shipton was short-handed, however, he placed Mate Perry back aboard his own ship, the *Mary and John*, with two other forced men, Nicholas Simmons and Jonathan Barlow, to serve as crew. Three buccaneers went aboard to guard the forced men. Making a survey of the situation, the pirates decided to tie the hands of Matthew Perry, the mate, but still allow him to give advice on the sailing of the ship. It was then arranged that Simmons would be acting master and navigator.

Simmons, although he agreed to be master and navigator, had ideas of his own as well. As soon as they were out of sight of land, he untied the hands of Perry, and together they formed plans to seize the ship from the buccaneers. Jonathan Barlow handed Perry a pistol. Thus there were three armed pirates against three forced men. Perry, hearing one of the pirates rummaging in the steerage, started to shoot him, but at the critical moment his pistol missed fire. At the sound of the click, the pirate jumped around and faced the mate, and Perry discovered to his horror that the pirate carried no less than four pistols in his belt. Drawing one, the buccaneer fired at close range, but his pistol also missed fire. Simmons then rushed up and fired point-blank at the sea rover, killing him instantly, whereupon he shouted, "In the name of God and His Majesty King George, let us go on with our design."

Barlow, meanwhile, had been busy on his own account, having succeeded in killing the second pirate. The third desperado surrendered without offering the slightest opposition. Heading the *Mary and John* for northern seas, the three happy mariners brought the ship into Newport several weeks later. The account of the adventures of the *Mary and John* was published in both the *Boston News-Letter* and the *New England Courant* in February 1725.

It would be pleasing to tell of the subsequent hanging of Spriggs and Shipton, but truth compels a less satisfactory ending. Very little is known about these sea marauders after they sailed for the rendezvous at the island of Roatan. Four months later a report was brought into New York Harbor that Spriggs had increased his fleet to five vessels. The following month a Captain MacKarty sailed into Boston Harbor with the news that Spriggs had seized a South Carolina pink. The buccaneer at that time was sailing a vessel mounting twelve guns and shipping thirty-five men. MacKarty brought a warning that Spriggs was behaving inhumanly with all his prisoners and was threatening again to sail up to New England. He never carried out his threat.

Over a year later the *New England Courant* published the news that Captain Francis Farrington Spriggs and Captain Shipton had both been marooned by their own men and were later captured by the "Musketoo Indians."

Spriggs' quartermaster, Philip Lyne, then started on a piratical cruise by himself, capturing vessels off Newfoundland and in the Eastern Atlantic waters. In October 1725 two sloops from Curacao, falling in with pirate Lyne, fought a terrific battle with the buccaneer, in which all but five pirates were killed before Lyne surrendered. Brought into Curacao, Lyne and his four companions were given a short trial and then hanged by the Dutch Government. The fate of Spriggs, however, will always be a mystery.

Spriggs seems to have been an exceptional seaman. Descriptions of him are not as vivid as those of Ned Low, but Spriggs certainly cut his own wide swath of prodigious mayhem from Rhode Island to Jamaica to Africa. His final fate remains unknown.

In his own fairly brief but spectacular pirate career, Philip Lyne is said to have killed thirty-seven masters of vessels. A particularly gruesome account of the executions of Lyne and his cohorts appeared in the *Boston Gazette* on March 28, 1726, and is quoted in David Cordingly's *Under the Black Flag.* The men had been wounded but nobody bothered to treat their injuries, so they "were very offensive, and stunk as they went along, particularly Line the commander, who had one eye shot out, which with part of his nose, hung down on his face."

CHAPTER 12

Charles Harris,
Hanged with His Crew at Newport

Pirate Charles Harris, the subject of this chapter, was navigator aboard the ship *Greyhound* in 1722. Captain George Lowther, whose career we discuss elsewhere, captured the Boston-owned *Greyhound* on January 10 of that year, while the ship was homeward bound under her commander, Captain Edwards. Edwards had fought desperately for more than two hours, but finding further resistance useless, had surrendered his ship, crew, and cargo. Coming aboard, the pirates, who were expecting to discover rich treasures, were disappointed to find a mere load of logwood. Exasperated, the buccaneers vented their wrath on members of the crew, suspending two of the unfortunate sailors from the mainmast and unmercifully lashing them. The *Greyhound* was set afire, and the captain and crew removed to Lowther's ship, the *Happy Delivery*.

Aboard the pirate craft, Lowther extended them the usual invitation to join up, ordering mugs of rum given to all hands. The artist, or navigator, first mate Charles Harris, was forced to join the pirate crew, as were four seamen. Captain Edwards and the other captured men who refused to join were permitted to sail for home aboard another logwood vessel.

Charles Harris evidently enjoyed the free and easy life aboard the pirate ship. Less than a week later he unqualifiedly signed articles as a full-fledged member of the ship's company, under the insistent urgings of Captain George Lowther. The pirate captain decided Harris was well fitted for his new tasks, for a few days later he was so pleased with his accomplishments that he awarded him the command of a new Jamaica sloop. Of course, the former Captain Edward Low, mate of the *Happy Delivery*, had already been handed the captaincy of another captured vessel, but that episode is described in the chapter about Low.

For more than a year following his promotion, Captain Charles Harris cut a ruthless path of piracy wherever he chanced to sail. Then he disappeared from sight for a period of five months. Perhaps he went ashore or became ill; in any case the contemporary sources are silent as to his whereabouts at this particular time. In May 1723, however, he reappeared off South Carolina as captain of the sloop *Ranger*. Here, in company with Low, Harris helped capture three ships in quick succession. Some weeks earlier, Captain Low had sliced off the right ear of a certain Captain John Welland, whose vessel had been overtaken. While the encounter was at its height, another vessel sailed right into the clutches of the pirates, and Captain Welland, together with his crew, was allowed to board the second vessel commanded by Captain Estwick of Piscataqua, New Hampshire. The outraged Welland reached Portsmouth aboard the Estwick ship, and later gave valuable testimony against Harris at his trial at Newport.

When Harris, still cruising in company with Low, reached a position off Long Island, New York, he sighted a large ship bearing down upon him. As the ship drew nearer, Harris noticed that it was bristling with guns, and accordingly prepared his sloop for battle, as did his fellow pirates on board the other vessel. The time was four-thirty in the morning, June 10, 1723. The ship then tacked and stood to the south, whereupon Low and Harris gave chase. At eight o'clock Harris opened fire, followed at once by Low, but the stranger returned shot for shot. The black flags of piracy, now hoisted on the two sloops, were hastily pulled down half an hour later when it was realized that the ship was a man-of-war, the *Greyhound*, commanded by a man who had sworn to capture the two pirates. His name was Captain Peter Solgard.

The sea rovers sent a "bloody" flag aloft, signifying that they were not planning to board, and managed to keep a mile away, but the man-of-war slowly gained in pursuit. Exchange of fire continued at a brisk rate for half an hour. The wind dropped and then died away completely, giving the pirates an opportunity to escape. Resorting to their oars, they rowed steadily away. Captain Solgard soon discovered what the pirates were doing, and ordered eighty-six sailors to man the *Greyhound*'s oars. With this added help, the man-of-war gradually crept up on the pirates again so that by two-thirty in the afternoon she was close enough to place herself between the sloops.

Captain Peter Solgard of the *Greyhound* then concentrated his fire on the sloop commanded by Harris, allowing Low to escape. Shot after shot raked buccaneer Harris' craft. The mainsail was first to fall, after which the sloop was gradually reduced to a helpless hulk. At four o'clock Captain Harris saw that further fighting was useless and surrendered, asking for quarter. One pirate suggested that they all blow themselves up, but Harris refused this solution of their troubles, whereupon the pirate committed suicide. An hour later all the pirates had been brought aboard the *Greyhound* as prisoners, and the pursuit of Captain Low began. Darkness fell before the man of-war could overtake Low, so once again this villain succeeded in making good his escape.

It was perhaps one of the most joyous days in the history of Rhode Island when the *Greyhound* arrived in port with forty-eight pirates aboard. Of these, thirty outlaws were brought ashore, and escorted under heavy guard to the Newport jail. Several of the pirates had died as a result of the engagement, eight were wounded, and seven were held aboard the *Greyhound*, which continued to search for Low and his sloop.

The seven pirates who were kept aboard the *Greyhound* while she was out hunting for Low were brought back to Newport July 11. They were Captain Charles Harris himself, 25 years old, of London; Joseph Libbey, 21 years old, of Marblehead; and the following five persons, whose homes were not known: Thomas Hazell, 50; John Bright, 25; Patrick Cunningham, 25; John Fletcher, 17; and Thomas Child, 15 years old.

When the news was circulated that more than thirty pirates were in jail there, Newport became the center of interest in all New England. The probability of a mass hanging attracted the attention of citizens from as far off as New York and Maine. How pirate-conscious Cotton Mather could have stayed away from Newport at this time is incomprehensible to me.

The Honorable William Dummer soon arrived from Boston with many members of His Majesty's Council, and Governor Cranston of Rhode Island, accompanied by several local judges, met with the Boston group at the town house. Thus the Court of Admiralty was organized on July 10, 1723, and then adjourned until the morning of the next day. Two alleged pirates were freed without further action. The other buccaneers, headed by Harris, were brought into court to be arraigned.

Captain Solgard of the *Greyhound* was among the first to appear against the pirates and his testimony was particularly damning, especially when he told of the fight with the two sloops. Captain Welland, who had lost his ear, then took the stand, and by the time he had finished, it was clear what the verdict was going to be. Nevertheless, every man among the pirates pleaded not guilty, claiming he had been forced. Fourteen of them were ordered for trial at that same session.

At this time the Advocate General addressed the Court. His speech included a definition of piracy and a pirate, with reference to the Roman emperors and His Majesty's dominions. He then called several men who gave important testimony, including Captain John Welland, Peter Solgard, Edward Smith, and William Marsh. In summing up the case after their testimony, the Advocate General mentioned, among other things, that the plea of being forced should be ignored, for unless it were, no pirate would ever be convicted, as they would all claim they were forced. He ended by asking for a conviction. His wish was granted with two exceptions, John Wilson and Henry Barnes. All the others were sentenced to be hanged.

The next group of pirates then appeared at court. Captain Welland was able to recognize six of them, while carpenter John Mudd testified that he well remembered one of the buccaneers whose name was Joseph Sound, for Sound had cut the very buttons off his sleeves at the time of Mudd's capture. Benjamin Weekham of Newport recognized William Blades and John Waters as two of the pirates at the time he was taken in the Bay of Honduras. William Marsh testified that John Brown, "the tallest" (as distinguished from John Brown "the shortest," also a pirate) told him that he had willingly joined up, as he had "rather be in a tight vessel than a leaky one." And so it went throughout the trial, the pirates either betraying each other or being accused by other maritime men.

The youthfulness of four of the pirates was of interest. John Brown, "the shortest," Thomas Jones, and John Fletcher were only seventeen years old, while Thomas Child was a boy of fifteen when brought to the bar. While none of the four was eventually hanged, the fact that they were brought to trial is a sad commentary on conditions of that particular age.

An Indian, Thomas Mumford by name, testified that while fishing off Nantucket, he had been captured with five other Indians, two of whom were hanged by Low at Cape Sables. Mumford was released. The pirate doctor John Kencate presented a problem to the court, but the Advocate General decided that if "he received part of their plunder, was not under a constant durance, did at any time approve, or join'd in their villanies, his guilt is at least equal to the rest." Captain Welland then testified in favor of the doctor, saying that the medical man "seem'd not to rejoice when he was taken but solitary, and he was inform'd on board he was a forced man, and that he had never signed the articles." Others spoke in the doctor's behalf, and finally it was decided that Dr. John Kencate, formerly chirurgion [surgeon] of the *Sycamore Galley*, could walk out of the Newport town house a free man.

Such was not the fate of the next two men brought in, Thomas Powell and John Libbey, whose records spoke against them. Powell was the gunner on board the *Ranger*, while Libbey, according to the statement of Thomas Jones, was "a stirring, active man among them, and used to go aboard vessels to plunder." John Wilson's testimony claimed that on the Sabbath Day before the *Greyhound* captured them, Powell expressed the strange wish that he and Wilson could both go ashore stark naked. Mumford, the Indian, attempted to testify in Powell's case, but could not be understood. Finally an interpreter was found, Abissai Folger, who said that Mumford had seen Powell "shoot a Negro, but never a white man." The Indian also admitted that he had seen Libbey steal a pair of stockings from a captured vessel.

Powell then testified that he had been captured by Lowther in the Bay of Honduras, and from Lowther had gone over to Low. Libbey claimed that he had been a forced man, and actually had a newspaper advertisement to prove it! The ad turned out to be a waste of money however, for Libbey was sentenced to be hanged along with gunner Powell.

The next group of pirates reluctantly filed into the unfriendly atmosphere of the courtroom. One of them, John Bright by name, was the drummer who beat the drum "upon the round house in the engagement." Captain Welland spoke on behalf of one Patrick Cunningham, who had brought him water when he lay bleeding from the wounds inflicted by the vicious Captain Ned Low. Cunningham and John Brown "the shortest" were recommended for remission, but John Bright and the other two were sentenced to hang. Thus ended the greatest pirate trial in New England history.

The local ministers made frequent visitations to the Newport jail. In a pamphlet published at Boston after the affair was over, one of the ministers noted that while the pirates were in prison, "most seemed willing to be advised about the affairs of their souls." John Brown, "the tallest," wrote out a warning to the younger generation, part of which I quote below:

> *It was with the greatest Reluctancy and Horror of Mind and Con-*
> *science, I was compelled to go with them . . . and I can say my Heart*
> *and Mind never joined in those horrid Robberies, Conflagrations and*
> *Cruelties committed.*

John Fitz-Gerald, the Irish lad from Limerick County, composed a poem that expressed his feelings at the time. We quote a few lines:

> *To mortal Men that daily live in Wickedness and Sin;*
> *This dying Counsel I do give, hoping you will begin*
> *To serve the Lord in Time of Youth his Precepts for to keep;*
> *To serve him so in Spirit and Truth, that you may mercy reap.*
>
> *In Youthful blooming Years was I, when I that Practice took;*
> *Of perpetrating Piracy, for filthy gain did look.*
> *To Wickedness we all were bent, our Lusts for to fulfil;*
> *To rob at Sea was our Intent, and perpetrate all Ill.*
>
> *I pray the Lord preserve you all and keep you from this End;*
> *O let Fitz-Gerald's great downfall unto your welfare tend.*
> *I to the Lord my Soul bequeath, accept thereof I pray,*
> *My Body to the Earth bequeath, dear Friend, adieu for aye.*

The entire countryside around New England was deeply stirred by the news that the greatest mass execution ever staged in the vicinity was about to take place. The gibbets were erected, in the usual fashion, between the rise and fall of the tide, at Gravelly Point, Newport, and the drop was tested for the gruesome occasion. On the morning of July 19, 1723, every person who was able began what was almost a pilgrimage across the open fields to Gravelly Point, and those fortunate enough to obtain boats were early on the scene to reach one of the best vantage points. When the pirates arrived at the scaffolding, most of them spoke of their wrongdoings, cautioning the youngsters of the populace who had gathered at the scene of execution to avoid the sins which would lead to a pirate's death on the gallows.

In a postscript to the *New England Courant* for July 22, 1723, we learn that Mr. Bass went to pray with the pirates on the scaffolding, while the Reverend Mr. Clapp [usually spelled Clap—*Ed.*] concluded with a short exhortation to them.

Then, at high noon, the solemn and terrifying business of executing twenty-six pirates began. Before one o'clock every last reprobate and scourge of the sea had been hanged and was dead. Newport, however, did not follow the Boston and London custom of hanging the bodies in chains after death, for the buccaneers were cut down and unceremoniously buried on Goat or Fort Island down the bay.

Their black flag, with the emblem of death holding the hourglass in one hand and a dart in the other, was fluttering from one corner of the gallows. This was fitting justice, for many of the forced men had often heard the pirates exclaim:

This flag is our Old Roger, and we shall live under it and die under it.

The 1723 executions in Newport took place at the height of the authorities' war on piracy. Between 1716 and 1726, more than four hundred pirates in all were hanged in the colonies.

We learn from *A General History of the Pyrates* that Peter Solgard was honored by the mayor of New York City, Robert Walter, for "so noble and faithful a Discharge of his Duty." Solgard's service "not only eased this City and Province of a very great Trouble," read a resolution, "but of a very considerable Expense."

Snow wrote in *True Tales of Pirates and Their Gold* (1953) that some of the men who assisted in the executions obtained the pirates' treasure chest containing thousands of gold doubloons and pieces of eight. The chest was smuggled ashore, wrote Snow, and buried "under four feet of sand and gravel along the overhanging cliffs of Newport." The conspirators then somehow managed to lose the map indicating where they had buried the chest, and a subsequent storm changed the contours of the beach. The chest was apparently lost forever.

But in 1949, wrote Snow, "two young ladies were strolling along the shore under the overhanging cliffs" at Newport. The waves had washed away part of a cliff, and "as the girls came closer, there, exposed to their gaze, was a treasure chest!" Unfortunately, the young women were unable to move or open the heavy chest. Later, when one of them returned, the chest had disappeared, possibly buried again by shifting sands. Snow believed that the chest remained to be rediscovered at the base of the Newport cliffs.

PART III

NEW YORK, PHILADELPHIA, AND SOUTHWARD

CHAPTER 13

Captain William Kidd,
"The Innocentest of Them All"

Captain Kidd's name has echoed down the corridors of time as a flaming symbol of the blood-and-thunder buccaneer, the sinister figure digging at midnight on a lonely beach where fabulous treasure chests of gold lie buried.

Discount all stories of this nature which you may have heard, and prepare yourself for a surprise. The actual facts in the life of William Kidd of Dundee, Scotland, New York, and Wapping-on-the-Thames prove that this adventurer of the high seas had a comparatively mild career, judged by standards of the period.

There appears to be little doubt that Kidd's father was a minister, the Reverend Mr. John Kidd, a Puritan. This good man, because of his religious convictions, had undergone the terrible torture by the boot, in which the victim's foot is squeezed and twisted until it is hopelessly out of shape.

William Kidd was born at Dundee in 1654, as nearly as we can tell, and followed the sea as a young man. By 1689 he was in command of a privateer and had settled in New York. For his services in connection with the arrival of Governor Slaughter, the assembly granted him £150. His certificate of marriage, issued in 1691, mentions him as William Kidd, gentleman.

Kidd for some reason returned to London in 1695. Recognized as an outstanding mariner, he was hired to command a privateering scheme developed by a group of prominent Englishmen. This organization, composed of the leaders of English political life, included no less a person than the king himself, who, of course, chose to remain in the background. Shareholders were Richard Coote, Earl of Bellomont; Sir John Russell, First Lord of the Admiralty; Sir John Somers, Lord Keeper of the Great Seal; the Duke of Shrewsbury, Secretary of State; and the Earl of Romney, Master-General of the Ordnance. It was agreed that King William, in permitting the expedition, was to receive one-tenth of the profits from the voyage. William III had contracted to advance £3,000 himself, but found a convenient excuse to reconsider when the time came.

Paine in his *Book of Buried Treasure* describes the Earl of Bellomont, Richard Coote, as an "ambitious and energetic Irishman." In appointing him Royal Governor of New York and Massachusetts in 1697, King William was especially anxious that Bellomont stamp out the piracy then rampant along the New York and New England coasts. On the other hand, the privateering cruise was nothing but a sort of robbery on the high seas from ships of enemy nations and pirates in general. So important was this expedition which Kidd was appointed to lead, that the document authorizing it was issued under the Great Seal of England. Kidd was nominated for the post by Robert Livingston, an influential Englishman who was familiar with qualifications of the various sea captains and knew of Kidd's notable exploits as a privateersman.

Although the venture was announced to the public as a cruise to suppress pirates, the real purpose was to obtain the "Goods, Merchandise, Treasure and other Things which shall be taken from the said pirates." An idea of the type of man desired can be found in the articles drawn up at the time of sailing. They specified that if no prizes were taken, there would be no pay, regardless of the time Kidd remained away from port. A prospective crew member with a wife and family depending on him would have hesitated a long time before signing such articles, and naturally only privateer-minded seamen or pirates would be attracted to such an assignment. Kidd himself, although feeling it an honor to be chosen, was not anxious to lead the expedition. He viewed the plan, it is said, without undue enthusiasm.

A prosperous ship captain with a fine home and family in New York, Kidd thought that the idea of sailing the high seas with a bloodthirsty share-and-share-alike crew was scarcely an enticing prospect. But other men, especially Lord Bellomont, worked on his sympathies, so that

Kidd eventually capitulated to the fine talk of his social superiors. He was offered about three shares in forty of whatever treasure he captured on the high seas.

Kidd's privateering commission should interest the reader. Excerpts are as follows:

> *WILLIAM REX*
>
> *WILLIAM THE THIRD, by the Grace of God, King of England, Scotland, France, and Ireland, Defender of the Faith, etc. To our trusty and well beloved Captain William Kidd, commander of the ship, Adventure Galley, or to any other, the commander of the same for the time being, greeting:*
>
> *Whereas, we are informed that Captain Thomas Tew, John Ireland, Capt. Thomas Wake, and Capt. William Maize . . . have associated themselves with divers other wicked and ill-disposed persons, and do, against the law of nations, commit many and great piracies, robberies, and depredations on the seas upon the parts of America and in other parts. . . . Now, know ye, that we being desirous to prevent the aforesaid mischief . . . do hereby give and grant to the said William Kidd (to whom our Commissioners for exercising the office of Lord High Admiral of England have granted a commission as a private man-of-war, bearing date the 11th day of December, 1695) . . . full power and authority to apprehend, seize, and take into your custody, as well the said . . . pirates, freebooters, and sea rovers, being either our subjects or of other nations associated with them. . . .*
>
> *In witness whereof, we have caused our Great Seal of England to be affixed to these presents. Given at our Court in Kensington, the 26th day of January, 1696, in the seventh Year of our reign.*

The terms of the agreement finally allotted to the king one-tenth of all proceeds from the voyage. After Captain Kidd and Livingston had been paid, the bulk of the remainder of what the underwriters hoped would be a substantial fortune was to go to Bellomont, Somers, Orford, Romney, and Shrewsbury.

The vessel chosen was a sturdy one. Outfitted with thirty-four guns, the 287-ton *Adventure Galley* was made ready for sea at Plymouth, England. As only the adventuresome sailor with no home ties or the out-and-out privateersman could afford to go on such a trip, by the time Kidd had recruited seventy rough and ready seamen, he had exhausted all available men of that type. Therefore he sailed for New York in April 1696 to complete his task.

As Kidd was anxious to sail, he recruited all types of characters, with no questions asked. Finally 155 daring lads were aboard. The *Adventure Galley* weighed anchor and sailed down the Hudson with her course set for the West Indies.

Evidently word of the expedition had been spread abroad. The Spanish Main was singularly free of pirates. After several months spent in futile cruising, Kidd recrossed the Atlantic, rounded the Horn, and made harbor in Madagascar. Three-quarters of a year had passed, and the stores were running low. The motley gathering aboard the privateer was grumbling and growling. No prizes, no pay, and they had spent nine dreary months at sea!

Matters shortly became worse. Kidd learned with dismay that the Madagascar pirates had intelligence of his arrival. He must learn their whereabouts! While cruising with that object in view, fate relented. Word came to him of a shipwrecked French vessel in a Malabar port. Crowding on canvas, Kidd ran for the scene of the disaster. The wreck was sighted, and on the distant beach the white gleam of tents told its story.

Crowding his boats with armed buccaneers, Kidd went ashore. The helpless Frenchmen were promptly subdued and their supplies and a moderate amount of gold appropriated. With this loot Kidd was enabled to restock his vessel. With the renewal of hope, the murmurs of his crew subsided.

But more trouble beset the expedition. While touching at Mehila Island, the crew went ashore. Within a short time fifty of the crew fell ill of some mysterious malady and died. Hastening from this fatal spot, Kidd encountered a small native craft from Aden during the summer of 1697. This boat he plundered of a few bales of coffee and pepper. Tidings of the exploit brought two Portuguese men-of-war from Aden to capture Kidd and his men. But for the episode, let us read Kidd's own story, taken from the Public Record Office in London:

> *The next morning September 23, 1697 about break of day saw the said two Men of War standing for the said Gally . . . the Commodore of the said Men of War kept dogging the said Gally all Night, waiting an Opportunity to board the same, and in the morning, without speaking a word, fired 6 great guns at the Gally. . . . The Fight continued all*

day and the Narrator had eleven men wounded; The other Portuguese
Men of War lay some distance off, and could not come up with the
Gally, being calm, else would have likewise assaulted the same.

It may be assumed that Kidd ran with all the canvas he could crowd
on the vessel from this not too pleasant encounter. At any rate, he is
reported, shortly after this event, closing in upon the *Loyal Captaine*,
which was bound for Surat under the command of Captain How [or
Howe—*Ed.*]. By some means Kidd's crew learned that rich Armenians
and Greeks were aboard with precious stones and other valuables.
Their cupidity was aroused. Gunner William Moore urged taking the
vessel by trickery. Kidd, however, demurred, and allowed the *Loyal
Captaine* to sail away to safety, knowing that it would be piracy if the
vessel were captured. Moore was enraged and did not forgive Kidd for
letting the rich treasure slip away. In revenge he started trouble that
resulted in a near-mutiny among the crew.

Two weeks later the incident occurred for which Kidd was later
hanged. The gunner, William Moore, ringleader of the troublemakers,
was talking with Kidd while sharpening a chisel on the grindstone. Evidently Kidd had been mulling over the incident of the near-mutiny.

"How could you have put me in a way to take this ship and been
clear?" asked Kidd.

"Sir," said Moore, "I never spoke such a word, nor thought such a
thing."

"You are a lousy dog," growled Kidd, angrily.

"If I am a lousy dog, you have made me so. You have brought me to
ruin and many more," answered Moore in a surly tone.

This remark infuriated Kidd. He seized a wooden bucket encircled
with iron hoops and smashed it to pieces against Moore's head. The
gunner fell heavily to the deck. He was taken below by the ship's surgeon and the next day died without recovering consciousness. Although
this was a severe punishment for crossing his commands, many another
captain of that period in history has been guilty of as brutal treatment of
his crew for insubordination without being hanged for it.

Captain William Kidd gradually came to suspect that the Arab ships of
the Great Mogul were deceiving him with an extra set of flags. Whenever he overtook one of the Moorish vessels, it would be flying the
British standards. To counter this subterfuge he resorted to another—flying the French flag at his mast. The next Arab he encountered had the

French standards flying, and Kidd triumphantly boarded the ship, demanding the French pass which all Moorish vessels needed to prove their alliance. When it was produced, Kidd seized the vessel in the name of King William. As the Arabs were operating under French protection, and England and France were to the best of his knowledge at war, the capture seemed perfectly legal. Kidd's privateering orders plainly authorized him to seize the ship.

After confiscating the cargo, Kidd burned and sank the prize. Since it was in November 1697, the capture actually took place after the Treaty of Ryswick, but the news of the peace did not reach the Indian Ocean until April the following year.

Another ship of the Great Mogul's fleet, the *Quedah Merchant*, which Captain Kidd seized by the same ruse in February 1698, was his most important capture. About $500,000 worth of rare silks, silver plate, jewels, and gold was found aboard the vessel. Kidd was so pleased with the *Quedah Merchant* that he decided to make it his flagship, and abandoned the *Adventure Galley*. Launched at Deptford in 1695, the *Galley* had not stood the years well. The French passes from the two vessels Kidd carefully preserved for the future.*

Arriving at the port of St. Mary, Captain Kidd found the notorious pirate Robert Culliford in the harbor aboard the frigate *Mocha*.† According to the terms of his commission Kidd was in duty bound to attack Culliford's frigate. But his crew refused to obey his commands and he was forced to desist.

Not only did the crew refuse to attack the pirates, but ninety-five of them actually deserted Kidd and went over to Culliford. This fact, more than any other, should convince us that Kidd was not a pirate at heart, since his crew of blackguards were willing to desert him for a man whose record was infamous and bloodthirsty. Discouraged by the turn matters had taken, Kidd decided to sail for American waters with the booty from the *Quedah Merchant*.

Reaching Snake Island in the West Indies April 1, 1699, Kidd anchored in the harbor and went ashore. He found to his dismay that

---

*It's believed that Kidd and his crew stripped and burned the *Adventure Galley* later, after most of Kidd's crew had joined up with Robert Culliford.—*Ed.*

†A decade earlier, Culliford had been a member of Kidd's crew and had stolen Kidd's ship *Blessed William* in the harbor at Nevis.—*Ed.*

the people would not deal with him because he had been officially declared a pirate. Kidd knew not where to turn. He went to the Island of Nevis hoping to find a friendly reception, but was unwelcome. From Nevis he ran to St. Thomas, where all the inhabitants turned against him. Antigua, his next port of call, was equally hostile. Kidd's dilemma was serious. He learned that other more notorious and murderous highwaymen of the sea had been given amnesty, but his name was bracketed with that of the great "Long Ben" Avery, the despoiler of Arabian ships. They were the only two buccaneers still denied amnesty by the 1698 Act of Grace.

Like a hunted animal, Captain William Kidd sailed from port to port. Because of the proclamation, no one would accept his friendship. Finally, he approached an English trader, Henry Bolton, by name, who agreed to help him, especially when Kidd showed him his royal commission with the Great Seal of England firmly affixed. Bolton also noticed the signatures of Lord Bellomont and the Earl of Orford. Captain Kidd explained that he was desperately worried about the whole situation, and asked Bolton to get him a small sloop on which he could sail to New York and contact Bellomont. Kidd stated that he was certain that there was some strange misunderstanding which he could easily correct with Bolton's assistance. After an exchange of goods in which Kidd obtained the sloop *St. Antonio* for merchandise and supplies, Kidd asked Bolton for additional assistance. The following is from Bolton's statement, made at a later date:

> *Capt. Kidd took several Goods out of his ship, and put them on Board the Sloope I sould him and left his owne ship in the River Higuey and desired me to doe him all the service I could in selling and disposeing of the Goods left on Board of the said ship for Account of the Owners of the* Adventure Galley. *. . . . That Capt. Kidd at his going to New Yorke promised to return himselfe or send some other persons in two Moneths to bring Necssaryes for refitting his said ship. . . .*

Captain Kidd took leave of Bolton and sailed for New York to contact Lord Bellomont. Perhaps Bolton gave him some good advice, or Kidd himself may have formed careful plans, but we know that when Kidd arrived at Lewes, Delaware, he had decided upon his course of action. Although many adventuresome souls like to think his journey up the coast was a treasure-burying campaign, nothing could be further from the truth. Of course, pirate James Gillam [or Gilliam—*Ed.*] was set ashore with his sea chest, which probably contained some gold, but no other treasure was brought to the mainland at this time.

After purchasing many needed supplies in Delaware Bay, Captain Kidd sailed around Long Island, entering Long Island Sound from the eastward, where he anchored in Oyster Bay. His wife and children joined him aboard ship at this time. Uncertain of his reception by Lord Bellomont, Kidd decided to deal with the governor from a distance, and sent for James Emmott of New York, a leading maritime lawyer, to come aboard the sloop. Emmott informed Kidd that Bellomont was in Boston. Kidd at once sailed for Narragansett Bay where James Emmott was put ashore in a small boat. He carried with him the two French passes, which figured so prominently at a later date.

Emmott hired a horse and set out for Boston. The last rays of the evening sun were fading in the west, when in the distance, the lawyer sighted the spires and rooftops of the great town of Boston. But dusk had settled when he clattered across Boston Neck. A short time later he drew bridle at the Blue Anchor Tavern (located where the *Boston Globe*

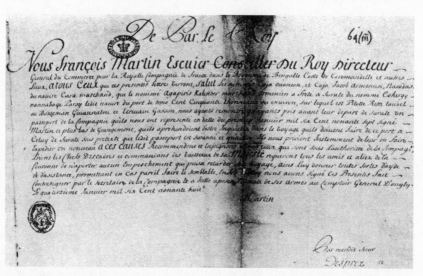

The French pass of the Quedah Merchant. *Captain William Kidd took the above pass from the master of the* Quedah Merchant. *As the presence of the pass proved the captured vessel legitimate privateering prey, Kidd turned it over to Bellomont on his return to Boston. The pass, together with that of another vessel Kidd captured, was purposely hidden by unknown parties. Two centuries after Kidd was hanged, they were found in the public record office in London by Ralph D. Paine. Thus Kidd died an innocent man.*

building stands today). Having supped, he inquired where he could find Lord Bellomont. Bellomont, he learned, was staying at the Province House nearby. Soon afterwards, Emmott sounded the door knocker of that official residence.

Governor Bellomont admitted him to an audience at once. Emmott told Bellomont that he represented Kidd, and informed the Lord that Kidd had returned to New England. The exact location of the vessel he withheld. Bellomont was intensely interested in Kidd's adventures, especially that which pertained to the large treasure, but he feared to act according to his desires because of the English political situation and the declaration of Kidd's piracy. While Emmott was talking, Bellomont's mind was undoubtedly busy wondering what course he should pursue. His final decision was to betray the man who was awaiting his word off the Narragansett shore. He would make Kidd the victim of the whole venture.

Sometime after midnight he sat down and wrote Kidd a letter, but shortly tore it up. Time and again during the next few days he wrote and rewrote his message. Finally he finished a draft which was clever enough to fool Captain Kidd completely. This letter brought the alleged pirate hurrying to Boston. Bellomont's letter is interesting:

> *[June 19, 1699]*
> *Captain Kidd:*
> *Mr. Emmott came to me last Tuesday night late, telling me he came from you, but was shy of telling me where he parted with you, nor did I press him to it. . . . He proposed to me from you that I would grant you a pardon. I answered that I had never granted one yet, and that I had set myself a safe rule not to grant a pardon to anybody whatsoever without the King's express leave or command. . . .*
>
> *Mr. Emmott delivered me two French passes taken on board the two ships which your men rifled, which passes I have in my custody and I am apt to believe they will be a good Article to justifie you. . . . Mr. Emmott also told me that you had to about the value of 10,000 pounds in the Sloop with you, and that you had left a Ship somewhere off the coast of Hispaniola in which there was to the Value of 30,000 pounds more which you had left in safe hands. . . .*
>
> *I have advised with his Majesty's Council and showed them this letter this afternoon, and they are of opinion that if your case be so clear as you (or Mr. Emmott for you) have said, that you may safely*

> *come hither. . . . I make no manner of doubt but to obtain the King's*
> *pardon for you. . . .*
>
> *I assure you on my word and on my honor I will performe nicely*
> *what I have now promised. . . .*
>   YOUR HUMBLE SERVANT

Unfortunately for Kidd, he was without suspicion of Bellomont's duplicity. Bellomont sent Duncan Campbell, Boston postmaster, to accompany Emmott on his return to the pirate ship. The two men reached Kidd a few days later. To Bellomont's letter Kidd wrote in reply:

> *June 24th, 1699*
> *May it please your Excellencie:*
> *I am honor'd with your Lordship's kind letter of ye 19th., current by*
> *Mr. Campbell which came to my hands this day, for which I return my*
> *most hearty thanks. I cannot but blame myself for not writing your*
> *Lordship before this time, knowing it was my duty, but the clamorous*
> *and false stories that has been reported of me made me fearful of writ-*
> *ing or coming into any harbor till I could hear from your Lordship. . . .*
>
> *A Sheet of paper will not contain what may be said of the care I*
> *took to preserve the Owners' interest and to come home to clear up my*
> *own Innocency. I do further declare and protest that I never did in the*
> *least act Contrary to the King's Commission, nor to the Reputation of*
> *my honorable Owners, and doubt not but I shall be able to make my*
> *Innocency appear, or else I had no need to come to these parts of the*
> *world. . . .*
>   WM. KIDD

Although it appears from Kidd's tone that he believed completely in Lord Bellomont's honesty, his actions indicated that he was still determined to leave part of the treasure behind when he started for Boston. It was on Gardiner's Island that he put ashore most of the booty.

Gardiner's Island, formerly known as the Isle of Wight,* is located at the eastern end of Long Island Sound. More than three thousand acres

---

*It was called this by Lion Gardiner, who bought it from the Montauk Indians for "a large black dog, a Gun & ammunition, some rum, and a few Dutch blankets."—*Ed.*

of wooded land present a fine view to the visitor. At the time of Kidd's adventures, John Gardiner lived on the island. One day late in June he noticed a strange sloop anchored offshore, and on rowing out to it, met Captain Kidd.

Kidd had aboard the sloop two Negro boys and one Negro girl, whom he asked the owner of the island to take ashore and keep for him until he returned from Boston. The privateer rewarded Gardiner for his kindness with several bales of goods. The grateful islander in turn sent out six sheep and a barrel of cider. Kidd fired a four-gun salute as he sailed away. Three days later he returned with a request that Gardiner store a chest and a box of gold and several other bales of goods for him. Besides these articles, Kidd put ashore a small amount of gold dust, and presented the islander with a bag of sugar.

Kidd, having received another friendly message from Bellomont, set sail for Boston. After an uneventful trip around Cape Cod, Captain William Kidd sighted the beacon at Greater Brewster Island, July 1, 1699, later coming up the Narrows to pass Nix's Mate Island, where the bodies of buccaneers were often hung in chains. That evening he lodged with his friend, Postmaster Campbell. The treasure he brought with him he secreted in his room at Campbell's house (located near the present corner of Washington and Water Streets in Boston).

The famous captain spent most of the following week strolling around the streets of Boston town, visiting here and there, frequenting the taproom of the Blue Anchor Tavern, and acquainting himself with the wharves and piers of the waterfront. His supposed security, however, was merely a wishful dream, for Bellomont suddenly gave orders for Kidd's arrest. Cornered at his lodgings, Kidd drew his sword.* When he was pinioned unexpectedly from behind, he was forced to surrender. In this manner, Captain William Kidd, gentleman, learned of his betrayal at the hands of his own partner, Richard Coote, the Earl of Bellomont.

Kidd was taken at first to the home of the jailer, but later was removed to the stone jail, where the City Hall annex stands today. The authorities made a systematic search of his lodgings, discovering six bags of gold and one handkerchief filled with the yellow metal. Some personal belongings of Mrs. Kidd were also taken at this time. These were later returned, it is said.

---

*Kidd was arrested at the home of Peter Sergeant, one of Boston's wealthiest citizens, in the presence of the Earl of Bellomont.—*Ed.*

Captain William Kidd in his dungeon cell at Boston's stone jail. The jail's thick walls had not prevented the escape of two pirates some weeks before—hence Kidd's heavy chains.

On board Kidd's ship when it returned to America was one James Gillam, a notorious pirate, who had killed Captain Edgecomb of the *Mocha* frigate. Lord Bellomont was especially anxious to locate Gillam. By some ruse and a bit of luck he finally secured him. Bellomont, though a deceiver and a man who lightly broke his word to William Kidd, was, we must admit, an astute detective when it came to tracking down pirates. Here are his words describing the capture:

> BOSTON *the 29 November 99.*
>
> *My Lords*
>
> *I gave your Lordships an account in my Letter of the 24th of last moneth by the last ship that went hence for England, of my taking Joseph Bradish and Tee Wetherley, the two Pyrates that had escape from the Goal of this town; and I then also writ that I hoped in a little time to be able to send your Lordships the news of my taking James Gill [am] the Pyrat that killed Captain Edgecomb, Commander of the* Mocha *frigat for the East India Company. . . . I have been so lucky as to take James Gillam, and he is now in Irons in the Goal of this town. My taking of Gillam was so very accidentall that I cannot forbear giving your Lordships a narrative of it, and one would believe there was a strange fatality in that m[an's] Stars. . . . I examined Captain Knot . . . and then he told me of Francis Dole in Charlestown, and that he believed Gillam would be found there. I sent half a dousin men immediately over the water to Charlestown and Knot with them. . . . Two of the men went through a field behind Dole's house, and . . . met a man in the dark (for it was ten o'clock at night) . . . and it happened as oddly as luckily to be Gillam, he had been treating young women some few miles off in the Country, and was returning at night to his Landlord Dole's house, and so was met with. I examined him, but he denied everything, even that he came with Kidd from Madagascar, or ever saw him in his life. . . . He is the most impudent hardened V[illai]n I ever saw in my whole life. . . . Cuthbert informs that being lately in the East India Company's service . . . Gillam had killed Captain Edgecomb with his own hand, that he had served the Mogul, turned Mohametan and was Circumcised. I had him searched by a [su]rgeon and also by a Jew in the town to know if he were Circumcised, and they have both declared on oath that he is. . . . Four pound weight of gold brought from Gardiner's Island which I formerly acquainted your Lordships*

of, and all the Jewels, belonged to Gillam, as Mr. Gardiner's Letter to Mr. Dummer . . . will prove. . . .

We have advice that Burk an Irishman a Pyrat that committed severall robberies . . . is drowned with all his ship's company. . . . It is said he perished in the hurrican that was in those Seas. . . .

Your Lordships most humble and obedient Servant
BELLOMONT

It was impossible at this time to hang a pirate in Boston since the British Admiralty rules specified that the court must sit in London. Bellomont wrote to the Lords of Trade and Plantations, July 26, 1699, asking their advice as to the disposal of the Kidd case. The verdict was that Kidd should be sent to England. February 16, 1700, Kidd and the other pirates sailed from Boston Harbor for the last time, bound for England and their doom.

Meanwhile, the Great Mogul had complained to the East India Company of the capture of the *Quedah Merchant,* and in turn the East India Company complained to Parliament. When the Tories discovered that the Whig cabinet of Lord Somers had backed Kidd, they made the most of it, speaking lengthily in Parliament and publishing pamphlets and newspaper articles by the score. Embarrassed by this turn of events, the Whig government of Somers solemnly repudiated the unfortunate captain.

It was as a result of this controversy that Lord Bellomont had been notified that if Kidd landed in America he should be arrested at once. This explains, in a measure, his singular treatment of Kidd. The pirate, in this way, came to be tried by the very government that was being criticized for allowing Kidd to conduct privateering operations on the high seas.

Unluckily for Kidd, the alleged pirate, he arrived in England just as the opposition party was discussing the possible removal from office of his partner John Somers, Lord Chancellor of England. Kidd's case became a political issue. As if this were not enough, his capture of two ships belonging to the Great Mogul had antagonized the powerful East India Company. Kidd freely admitted taking the two vessels, but rightly claimed that existence of the two French passes gave him full privileges of attack and capture. The only trouble was that the two French passes which Kidd willingly surrendered to Bellomont were being purposely concealed by those who found such a course politically expedient. So Captain William Kidd became the scapegoat, as was intended. The passes came to light two hundred years later through the remarkable research work of Ralph D. Paine and one is reproduced in this volume [see page 176].

Some of the testimony at Kidd's trial may be of interest to the reader. He was in jail more than a year before the trial was finally called. All his efforts to find the passes failed. To make matters worse, Lord Bellomont had died in far away Boston. Kidd now realized that whatever hope he may have had was futile.

The crown was aware that it might be difficult to prove Kidd a pirate. Therefore it was decided to try him first for the killing of William Moore, the gunner. An imposing array of legal talent confronted Captain Kidd at the trial, but he was allowed no counsel at all. Although Kidd pleaded not guilty to the charge of murder, others in his crew, in order to save their own lives, testified against him, and were freed. Kidd was convicted of the murder. After they were certain of his eventual death, the Court, deciding there was nothing to lose, proceeded to try him for piracy. Kidd's remarks at the time are of interest:

> It is hard that the life of one of the King's subjects should be taken away upon the perjured oaths of such villians as these. Because I would not yield to their wishes and turn pirate, they now endeavor to prove that I was one. Bradingham [the ship's doctor, who testified against Kidd] is saving his life to take mine.

The crown next proved that Kidd captured the two ships belonging to the Great Mogul. Again Kidd insisted that the two French passes be produced. Again they failed to materialize. In spite of the testimony of several leading mariners of the day, who spoke of the sterling character of Kidd, the jury found the privateer guilty of piracy. Six in his crew were to hang with him. Before the sentence was read to him, Captain William Kidd made a final statement.

> My Lords, it is a very hard judgment. For my part, I am the innocentest of them all, only I have been sworn against by perjured persons.

Execution Dock at Wapping-on-the-Thames has long since disappeared from the waterfront of London, but I visited the ancient Pirates' Stairs while there in 1942. It was down these same stairs that William Kidd took his last long walk on the morning of May 23, 1701.

The usual procession preceded the actual execution. The deputy marshal, carrying the silver oar, emblem of the Admiralty, walked ahead of
the doomed men on their way to the gallows.

Following his execution by hanging *infra fluxum et refluxam maris* at
Wapping, Kidd's body was cut down and soaked with tar for preserv-
ing purposes. The remains then were thrown into an open boat and
rowed up to the shore near Tilbury Fort. Here the body of Kidd was
suspended in chains to warn other sailors of the price exacted for piracy
on the high seas.

What has caused the legend of Captain Kidd as a bloodthirsty pirate
and burier of buccaneering riches to reach such huge proportions down
through the years? Two men are more to blame than any others. They
are Lord Thomas Macaulay and Governor Fletcher of New York.

Lord Macaulay in his *History of England* makes several erroneous statements in his story of the period. Macaulay confuses privateering and
piracy, for he definitely places Kidd in the latter group. In fairness to
Macaulay, his account of Kidd is written in one of his posthumously
published chapters of his monumental history, which he never had a
chance to correct. His words follow:

> *Kidd, having burned his ship and dismissed most of his men . . .*
> *who easily found berths in the sloops of other pirates, returned to New*
> *York with the means, as he flattered himself, of making his peace and*
> *living in splendor.*

Of course, Kidd never burned his ship. His men deserted him; he did
not dismiss them. Writing from the Whig viewpoint, Macaulay naturally tried to whitewash the Whig cabinet responsible for the Kidd
episode. Macaulay had plenty of data available, for there are many ref-
erences to Kidd in Luttrell's notes taken in the years 1699 to 1700. Thus
we see that Macaulay must be at least partially blamed for perpetuating
the Kidd legend. On the other side of the Atlantic, Governor Fletcher of
New York, with a keen interest in pirate ventures, was filled with lively
concern when the British leaders hired Kidd to clean out all the buccaneer nests on the Atlantic. Replaced by Bellomont, Fletcher did everything in his power to discredit Kidd and his expedition. While Kidd was
in New York, Fletcher contrived to blacken his character as much as he
could, and rumors derived from this source spread through the
provinces. The Kidd legend was further extended by the articles that

The body of William Kidd hanging in chains near Tilbury Fort, England. Kidd was executed at Wapping-on-the-Thames on May 23, 1701.

Kidd posted in New York. A similar procedure was used by the dyed-in-the-wool pirates, when they required new candidates to sign their articles. The reader will find striking resemblance between the articles which Kidd posted and pirate articles, quoted elsewhere in this volume. The following are typical:

3. *If any man should Loose a Joynt in ye said service, he should have a hundred pieces of 8.*

4. *If any man shipps himself aboard yet said shipe and should offer to go away from her, he shall suffer what punishment ye Capt. and ye Quarter-Master shall think fitt, and shall have no share.*

Another reason for the popular misconceptions of Captain Kidd's career is the following poem, which shall end the story:

My name is Captain Kidd, who has sailed, who has sailed,
My name is Captain Kidd, who has sailed.
My name is Captain Kidd, What the laws did still forbid
Unluckily I did while I sailed, while I sailed.

Upon the ocean wide, when I sailed, when I sailed.
Upon the ocean wide, when I sailed
Upon the ocean wide, I robbed on every side
With most ambitious pride, when I sailed.

Farewell the ocean main, we must die, we must die
Farewell the ocean main, we must die;
Farewell the ocean main, the coast of France or Spain
We ne'er shall see again; we must die.

It has been repeated in many books that William Kidd was the son of a minister, but it is now believed that he was the son of a Dundee sailor who died when William was five. Much of his early life still remains a mystery.

The *Loyal Captaine* was a ship of the English East India Company. Ten days after the *Adventure Galley*'s encounter with the *Loyal Captaine*, a Dutch ship was encountered. Again William Moore and others on the crew wanted to take the ship, but Kidd refused on the grounds that Holland was an ally of England.

This aggravated the already precarious situation that led to Moore's being killed by Kidd.

The *Quedah Merchant* was an Indian-owned ship operated by a group of Armenian merchants with a mostly Indian crew. According to Richard Zacks in *The Pirate Hunter: The True Story of Captain Kidd*, when Kidd learned that the English East India Company was also involved with the *Quedah Merchant*, he considered returning it to its owners. But he decided against this, fearing more unrest in his crew and believing it was a legal capture as it had a French pass. The ship was renamed the *Adventure Prize* after its capture by Kidd.

When Captain Kidd left on his fateful privateering voyage aboard the *Adventure Galley*, he left his wife Sarah and three-year-old daughter, also named Sarah. Richard Zacks has written that the captain "loved Sarah deeply." The family was briefly reunited shortly before Kidd's arrest in Boston. After Kidd's death, Sarah wed her fourth husband, merchant Christopher Rousby. Their fourth child was named William.

In February 2000, underwater explorer Barry Clifford of *Whydah* fame announced that, after a two-plus-years search sponsored by the Discovery Channel, he had located what he believed to be the remains of Kidd's ship *Adventure Galley* at Ile Sainte Marie off the northeast coast of Madagascar. The island was an important pirate base for close to forty years. Some, like Richard Zacks, questioned whether it could really be Kidd's ship, since the *Adventure Galley* was believed to have been stripped and burned: it seemed like nothing of substance could still remain. But Clifford claimed that seventeenth-century Chinese pottery and a metal oarlock helped identify the remains.

The search for the *Adventure Galley* is detailed in Clifford's book *Return to Treasure Island and the Search for Captain Kidd* as well as in a Discovery Channel documentary, *Quest for Captain Kidd*. Clifford's team also located another pirate vessel called the *Fiery Dragon* in the vicinity. Project archaeologist Dr. John de Bry believes that both sites, which are close together, have been correctly identified. The identification of the *Adventure Galley* is based largely on the fact that the remains are of an English ship of consistent size with a dating of approximately 1690 to 1720.

Says the project's historian, Ken Kinkor, "We have a great deal of work remaining. I am inclined to think that the ID for the *Fiery Dragon* will only be strengthened by such work. I'm not so sure in the case of the *Adventure Galley*. This is because, as Zacks points out, the *Adventure Galley* was so thoroughly stripped before she was fired. There is simply not nearly as much evidence on the site to argue one way or another. But based on what we've gotten thus far, we believe that these identifications are satisfactory." At this writing in the fall of 2003, the team plans to return to the site soon.

There's scarcely a rock along the east coast, particularly from Nova Scotia to New England, New York, and New Jersey, that isn't claimed by someone to conceal the legendary treasure of Captain Kidd. Most of the treasure confiscated after Kidd's arrest went to the British Admiralty. Some of it in turn ended

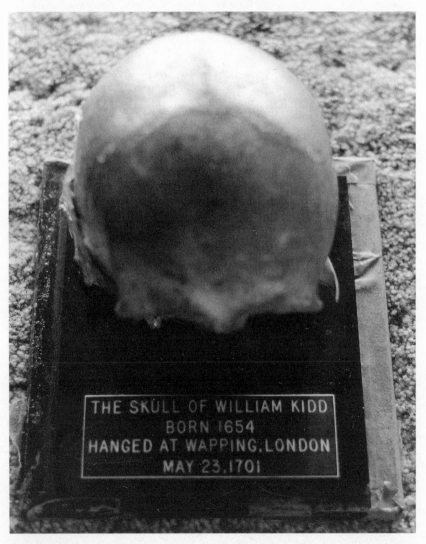

This skull, said to be that of Captain Kidd, was one of many pirate-related artifacts collected by Edward Rowe Snow over the years. (Photo by Jeremy D'Entremont)

up helping to pay for the new Greenwich Hospital for old and disabled sea-men, designed by Christopher Wren. The bottom line is that Kidd apparently returned with far less treasure than expected, and as Richard Zacks has said, the "English government got almost all of it and the rest was embezzled—not buried." Of course there is disagreement among scholars and treasure seekers, and for some the hunt continues.

In an article called "I'm Not Afraid of Capt. Kidd!" in the February 1966 issue of *Yankee* magazine, Snow announced that he had added the skull of William Kidd to his impressive collection of pirate artifacts. "Whenever an item in this category is available," he wrote, "I have often attempted to obtain—and some-times have succeeded in obtaining—the actual relics, much to my wife Anna-Myrle's unhappiness."

Snow wrote that the official gallows watcher, John Hill, swore that he would now allow anyone to steal Kidd's skull—a common practice—during the months the body was hung in a prominent location near Wapping-on-the-Thames. But according to Snow, it was apparently Hill himself who stole the skull. It was then taken to one of the Channel Islands off France, where it was secreted until around 1920, when it was offered to collector Hubert Palmer. Palmer refused it on the grounds that it was evil, and he said that anyone who ever obtained the skull would be placed under a "piratical curse." Snow pooh-poohed the notion of a curse—for one thing, Kidd was a privateer and not a true pirate, he believed.

During the German invasion of France, the skull's owner buried it for safe-keeping, wrote Snow. Then in 1952 it was smuggled out of France. It eventu-ally reached Red Bank, New Jersey, "where it was made known to a small group of those who enjoy pirate swords, treasure chests, guns, and the like." Snow readily admitted that the pedigree of the skull was impossible to prove.

Not too long after he wrote the *Yankee* article decrying the pirate curse, E. R. Snow's daughter, Dolly Bicknell, remembers, "Several bad things happened to him, and then his car was stolen with the skull inside it." A friend helped locate the skull and arrange its safe return. "The person who had stolen it was having second thoughts," recalls Dolly, "and bad things were happening to him—he was glad to be rid of it!"

CHAPTER 14

Blackbeard, Alias Teach, the Most Ferocious Pirate

Returning from the muddy airfields of North Africa early in the spring of 1943, I was one of several Army Air Corps patients aboard the British hospital ship *Amarapoora*, bound for the famous city of Bristol. So many seafaring adventurers and pirates had hailed from Bristol in the old buccaneering days that I was especially anxious to see this fascinating seaport. After a three months' period of fretful convalescence, I was finally given permission to visit the wharves and piers of the ancient metropolis, and the career of one bold adventurer who had sailed from Bristol kept forcing its way to the front of my mind. His name was Edward Teach, or Thatch.

Edward Teach, alias Blackbeard, was born in Bristol, England, although the exact location of his birthplace is unknown. Going to sea at an early age, Teach did not attract attention until the year 1716, when he was serving under pirate Benjamin Thornigold [sometimes spelled *Hornigold* or variously; see page 4—*Ed.*]. Early in 1717 Captain Thornigold, with Teach aboard, sailed from New Providence in the West Indies for the American mainland, capturing several vessels in rapid succession, including a Havana sloop with 120 barrels of flour and a ship loaded with wine from Bermuda. Next a craft from Madeira, loaded with a rich cargo of silks and bullion was intercepted and robbed, after which the vessel was allowed to proceed to her South Carolina destination.

Their next capture was a large French Guineaman, bound for Martinique. By this time Edward Teach had shown such energy and leadership that he asked Captain Thornigold if he could take charge of the latest capture. Thornigold agreed, and Captain Edward Teach began a piratical career of his own. Meanwhile, because of the King's proclamation offering pardon to all pirates who would reform, Captain Thornigold returned to New Providence, where he surrendered to the mercy of the government there.

Teach soon had forty sizable guns, most of which were from recent captures, mounted on board his vessel. He named the craft the *Queen Anne's Revenge*. Near the island of St. Vincent's, he fell in with a ship named the *Great Allan*, commanded by Captain Christopher Taylor. A thorough job of pilfering was done on this fine vessel, with all valuable supplies removed to the pirate sloop. The crew members of the *Great Allan* were put ashore at St. Vincent's, while the ship was set afire.

An event now occurred which put Teach on a special pedestal in the annals of piracy. Falling in with the British man-of-war *Scarborough*, of thirty guns, Blackbeard so successfully fought the English warship that after an engagement of several hours in which blood flowed freely on the decks of both ships the Britisher withdrew and ran for the nearest harbor in Barbados. Pleased with his defeat of the English warship, Captain Teach sailed triumphantly for Spanish America, with his fame as a bold and dangerous pirate spreading rapidly around the blue waters of the Atlantic Ocean.

Shortly afterwards he fell in with a Major Stede Bonnet, an interesting pirate who had formerly been a gentleman of good reputation and estate on the island of Barbados. This man had taken up piracy for excitement and adventure. Unfortunately for Bonnet, however, he knew nothing of navigation, so Blackbeard tactfully suggested that the major come aboard the *Queen Anne's Revenge* to serve as lieutenant to Teach, while Teach would send an experienced master aboard Bonnet's own sloop, the *Revenge*.

"As you have not been used to the fatigues and cares of such a post," said Teach to Bonnet, "it would be better for you to decline it and live easy, at your pleasure, in such a ship as mine, where you will not be obliged to perform duty, but follow your own inclinations." Major Bonnet quickly saw the wisdom of Teach's statement, and exchanged places with pirate Richards, who took charge of the Bonnet sloop.

A short time later the pirates were loading fresh water at Turneffe, near

Blackbeard, alias Teach, the most ferocious pirate

the Bay of Honduras, when they saw a sloop enter the inlet. Captain Richards, hoisting the black flag of piracy, slipped his cable and ran out to encounter the stranger. The sloop was the *Adventure*, commanded by Captain David Harriot, who observed the black pirate flag on Richard's mast and ordered his own sails struck at once, finally coming to under the stern of the *Queen Anne's Revenge*. Harriot and his crew were quickly transferred to the larger vessel, and Israel Hands, whose name Robert Louis Stevenson borrowed for one of his pirates in *Treasure Island*, was given the command of the *Adventure*. We shall hear of Israel Hands again.

On April 9, 1717, the pirate fleet weighed anchor and left Turneffe, sailing to the Bay of Honduras, where they found a ship and four sloops. The ship was the *Protestant Caesar*, out of Boston, commanded by Captain Wyar. When Teach hoisted his pirate flag and fired his gun, Captain Wyar and every member of his crew fled ashore in their boat. The four sloops were quickly captured, whereupon the *Caesar* was ransacked and set afire, along with one of the sloops. Teach explained that the two vessels were destroyed because they came from Boston, where the inhabitants had had the unmitigated nerve to hang certain pirates who had been captured. Evidently the mention of the word *Boston* left a bad taste in the buccaneer's mouth.

Some time later the sea rovers cruising in waters around Grand Cayman, located about sixty miles westward of Jamaica, seized a small craft occupied in hunting turtles, which abounded in the waters nearby. Working northward toward the Carolinas on the Atlantic coast, they engaged and captured three more vessels. Soon the buccaneers sighted the shores of the North American mainland.

Arriving off the bar at Charles-Town, or Charleston as it is known today, they waited there several days until a ship came out. It was a vessel bound for London and commanded by Captain Robert Clark. The pirates took it in short order. The following day four more captures were made, a ship, a brigantine, and two pinks, and all the prisoners herded aboard the pirate vessels. This activity threw terror into the hearts of the inhabitants of Charleston.

At this time there were eight sails in Charleston Harbor, none of which dared to go out and risk capture by Blackbeard. Word also reached other ports that the notorious Edward Teach was near Charleston Harbor, so incoming commerce as well was suspended. It was a particularly trying period for the colonists of South Carolina, who had just finished a grueling war with the Tuscarora Indians.

Every ship and every man taken by Teach had been detained off the bar. Now Blackbeard showed not only his colossal nerve but his contempt for Americans in general by sending his representative, Captain Richards, right into the harbor and ashore in the center of the town, with a message demanding a chest of medicine for the pirate fleet. Teach could afford to be insolent, for aboard his ship as a prisoner was Samuel Bragg [actually Samuel Wragg—*Ed.*], one of the governor's councilmen. Richards told the people of Charleston that unless they sent the chest of medicine out to the fleet, all the prisoners would be murdered and every ship set afire. Meanwhile, Richards and the other two pirates strutted through the streets of Charleston, appearing wherever and whenever they wished.

The governor soon reached a decision with his councilmen. Since there was nothing else they could do but comply with the wishes of Blackbeard, the citizens of Charleston sent the pirate fleet an expensive chest of medicine worth at least three hundred pounds. When Teach received the chest he kept his word and allowed every prisoner to go free, after he had robbed them of their wealth, which totaled fifteen hundred pounds in gold and silver.

Northern Carolina was now the destination of the pirate fleet, which consisted at that time of Teach's "man-of-war," two "privateers" commanded by Richards and Hands, and a small sloop which served as a tender. According to historian Johnson, the pirate biographer, Teach now decided to break up his company, cheating and marooning those for whom he did not care and dividing the spoils with his friends. To this end he ran his own vessel aground, and had Captain Israel Hands do likewise. Thus the two ships were destroyed, and every pirate was forced to go aboard the tender, leaving the *Revenge* on the rocks. As the tender was purposely overloaded, Teach sailed to a sandy island some three miles off the mainland, and put ashore seventeen of the unfortunate pirates whom he did not care for. Fortunately Major Bonnet rescued the marooned men two days later.

Teach decided to take advantage of the proclamation of His Majesty about this time, so appeared before the Governor to obtain a certificate of his desire to retire from the pirating profession. Then followed a shameful act of Governor Charles Eden, who ordered a Court of Vice-Admiralty held at Bath-Town for the purpose of declaring Teach an honest privateer. This farce of justice was carried through according to law, thus enabling Blackbeard to lay claim to a vessel that he had captured from the Spanish some time before, although England and Spain were not at war when the capture was made.

The marital life of Captain Edward Teach was a trifle overcrowded, for he had acquired thirteen wives. Before he left Bath-Town he fell in love again, this time with a girl of fifteen. He asked Governor Eden to officiate at the marriage. The governor readily performed the ceremony, after which Blackbeard moved out for a few days to the plantation where his wife's people lived. The girl's happiness was short-lived, however, for Blackbeard invited his ruffian friends out to the plantation, where they all caroused, gambled, and drank night after night. The poor girl was finally made miserable with the pirates continuing their debaucheries.

Teach sailed away shortly afterwards, and tradition has it the pirates went far to the north on this particular voyage, running in at the Isles of Shoals off the New Hampshire coast. It is true that some of the characters who have made the Isles of Shoals their residence in far-distant times have been of the type which would not mind the presence of pirates, but at best the story of Teach there is based on tradition rather than recorded statements.

According to legend, Blackbeard often went ashore at the Isles of Shoals, having as his special abode Smuttynose Island. After a trip to England he returned to the islands with a woman whom he took ashore. A considerable portion of Blackbeard's silver treasure was buried at this time. Telling the girl to guard the treasure until his return, Teach sailed away with his pirate band, but never came back, continuing his career elsewhere. She lived here many years and finally died on this lonely island, where it was said her ghost haunted the Isles of Shoals for almost a century. Regardless of the truth of the story, there is no question but that Samuel Haley, in building a wall many years later, uncovered four bars of solid silver worth a fortune. Haley built a breakwater between his property and the adjoining island at Malaga after the discovery of the fortune, and many believe that part of the money used was from Blackbeard's treasure that Haley uncovered.

Let us return to the story of Blackbeard. Teach sailed for Bermuda in June 1718. Falling in with three English vessels, he took from them only such food and provisions as he needed, but shortly afterwards he came up with two French sloops bound for Martinique. Putting both French crews aboard one vessel, which he permitted to go free, Teach sailed the second ship to North Carolina, where he and the governor shared the spoils. Governor Charles Eden demanded that everything should be done legally, and so he had Teach swear that he found the French ship adrift at sea. The governor then convened a court, which declared the vessel condemned. This action allowed Governor Eden to have sixty hogsheads of sugar as his share while the governor's secretary, Mr. Knight, received twenty barrels for his efforts. The pirates were permitted to have the rest of the cargo, but the ship remained in the harbor, causing Teach a great deal of worry. He was afraid that other vessels might recognize her, so told the governor that the ship was leaking, and might sink to block up the inlet. Thereupon Governor Eden ordered Teach to sail her out, giving Blackbeard the opportunity to burn her to the water's edge, and the vessel sank in deep water.

Records of some of the queer incidents which took place aboard Blackbeard's ship have been preserved. One night Teach sat drinking in the cabin with Israel Hands and another man, when suddenly Blackbeard drew out two pistols and cocked them under the table. The other pirate observed what was going on, and quickly left the cabin, but Hands did not notice Teach's action. Blackbeard suddenly blew out the candle, crossed his hands under the table, and fired. Israel Hands received the full force of one of the pistols in his knee, which left him lame for the rest of his life. Some time later other members of the crew asked Blackbeard why he had injured one of his good friends. "If I do not now and then kill one of you, you'll forget who I am," was the astonishing reply.

Another time Blackbeard was drinking heavily, and suggested to the others that they try a little sport of a slightly different nature. "Come," said the leader, "let us make a Hell of our own, and try how long we can bear it." He then took three of the bravest of his followers down into the hold, where he closed the hatches. After filling up several large pots with brimstone, he set them on fire, and they all remained there breathing the suffocating smoke into their lungs until some of them shouted for air. Then he released the hatches and allowed the others to go up on deck, not a little pleased with himself that he had held out the longest.

An excerpt from this strange man's diary follows:

> *Such a day, rum all out:—Our company somewhat sober:—A damn'd confusion amongst us!—Rogues a-plotting;—Great talk of separation—so I looked sharp for a prize:—Such a day took one, with a great deal of liquor aboard, so kept the company hot, damned hot; then all things went well again.*

Teach's beard was the talk of two continents. Jet black, it completely covered his face, even growing around his eyes, giving him a fierce appearance that he made the most of. He would twist the ends into small pigtails, fastening them with hair ribbons and turning them about his ears. When going into battle he purposely tried to create an effect to overwhelm his adversaries with fear, wearing three braces of pistols hanging in holsters from his shoulders. Inserting hemp cord under his hat, Blackbeard would set the hemp ends afire, allowing them to burn like punk, making his eyes look fierce and wild, while his whole appearance suggested the Devil himself. There was one man, however, who had heard of the doings of the notorious buccaneer Edward Teach, and determined to kill this monster who preyed on all shipping up and down the coast. He was Lieutenant Robert Maynard of the British man-of-war *Pearl*. Maynard was thoroughly exasperated by the fear which Blackbeard created among some of the inhabitants of North Carolina and the tolerance with which he was treated by others.

When planters and traders along the coast were obliged to submit to the pirates going ashore and molesting their own wives and daughters, they met together secretly to plan a campaign of retaliation. Knowing that their governor was hand in hand with Teach, they expected no help in that direction, but decided to send a delegation of protest direct to Virginia.

Governor Alexander Spotswood of Virginia received the North Carolina planters with courtesy and kindness. He agreed that something must be done, and that it was useless to consult with Governor Eden of North Carolina. Therefore it was arranged that two small sloops should be hired, capable of running over the shoals where buccaneer Teach was lurking. It was also agreed upon that they should be manned by two crews chosen from the man-of-war vessels *Pearl* and *Lime*, then at anchor in the James River. The command of the expedition was given to pirate-hating Robert Maynard.

As the two sloops were made fit for sea, Governor Spotswood called an assembly, which agreed with him on a proclamation, excerpts from which follow:

A Proclamation
Publishing the Rewards Given for Apprehending or Killing Pirates.
Whereas, *by an Act of Assembly, made at a Session of Assembly, begun at the Capital in Williamsburg, the eleventh day of November*

Blackebeard and his men ashore at the plantation

in the fifth year of His Majesty's reign, entituled An Act to Encourage the Apprehending and Destroying of Pirates: It is, amongst other things enacted, that all and every person or persons, whom, from and after the fourteenth day of November, in the Year of Our Lord One Thousand Seven Hundred and Nineteen, shall take any Pirate or Pirates . . . shall receive . . . the several rewards following; that is to say, for Edward Teach, commonly called Captain Teach or Black-Beard, one hundred pounds; for every other commander of a pirate ship, sloop or vessel, forty pounds; for every lieutenant, master or quartermaster, boatswain or carpenter, twenty pounds; for every other inferior officer, fifteen pounds, and for every private man taken aboard such ship, sloop, or vessel, ten pounds; and, that for every Pirate which shall be taken by any ship, sloop or vessel, belonging to this colony, or North Carolina . . . like rewards shall be paid according to the quality and condition of such pirates. . . . And, I do order and appoint this Proclamation, to be published by the Sheriffs at their respective County houses, and by all Ministers and Readers in the several Churches and Chapels throughout this Colony.

Given at Our Council Chamber at Williamsburg, this 24th day of November, 1718. In the Fifth year of His Majesty's Reign.

GOD SAVE THE KING

A. SPOTSWOOD

Of course, the governor of Virginia must have realized that he had not the slightest jurisdiction over North Carolina, which he mentioned in his proclamation, but he probably decided that the legal sidestep was necessary because of the gravity of the situation. And he was right.

Lieutenant Maynard lost no time in getting the expedition ready for sea. Sailing from Kicquetan, on the James River, the two vessels reached the mouth of the Ocracoke Inlet, where the spars and masts of Teach's vessel were sighted. Although the proclamation had not been officially issued at the time Maynard arrived off the Inlet, Mr. Knight of North Carolina, who had his spies in Virginia, had already written to Black-beard, warning him of trouble brewing. When Blackbeard saw the sloops approaching, he stripped his vessel for action, and awaited his adversaries.

By the time Maynard had reached the vicinity of the pirate strong-hold, darkness was falling, so Maynard wisely anchored for the night.

The channel was intricate, and the shoals were many. When morning came, he sent a boat out ahead to sound, and followed slowly behind. In spite of this precaution the sloops grounded on several sandy spots, and Maynard ordered all ballast thrown overboard. Even the water barrels were emptied, for Maynard was determined to capture Blackbeard or die in the attempt.

Finally Blackbeard fired a shot in the direction of the two sloops, whereupon Maynard hoisted the King's colors and stood directly for Captain Teach's vessel. The pirate chieftain then cut his cable, planning to make a running fight of it. The sloops were without cannon, while Teach could use his, giving the pirates a definite advantage at first. Maynard was not deterred in the least by this, going ahead with his plans as if all were in his own favor. Finally the two opposing forces were close enough for hailing distance.

"Damn you for villains, who are you?" asked the exasperated pirate captain. "And from whence came you?"

"You may see by our colors we are no pirates," responded the resolute Maynard, who now felt fairly certain of his objective. Blackbeard then asked Maynard to send his boat aboard, so he could find out who he was. But Maynard was not to be tricked.

"I cannot spare my boat, but I will come aboard of you as soon as I can with my sloop," replied the British lieutenant. This so upset Blackbeard that he had to go below and swallow a glass of whiskey before he could reply. Returning to the deck, he glowered across at Maynard.

"Damnation seize my soul if I give you quarter or take any from you," the thoroughly angered buccaneer declared.

"I do not expect quarter from you, nor shall I give any," were Maynard's words. When we realize that he was about to tackle one of the hardest fighting pirates the world has ever known, and had nothing but small arms to do it with, while buccaneer Teach was armed with many cannon, we can understand why Robert Maynard was called a brave man.

Blackbeard's sloop, which had run aground, was soon floated off in the incoming tide, but the wind died down completely. Afraid that his prey would escape, Maynard ordered his men to the sweeps,* and in this manner he rapidly gained on the becalmed pirates. Suddenly, however, Captain Teach let go with a broadside, which did terrific slaughter to the poor men at the sweeps, exposed as they were while rowing.

---

*Sweeps are large oars used to propel and steer the vessel.—*Ed.*

When the smoke of the discharge had died down it was discovered that no less than twenty-nine were either killed or wounded in Maynard's two sloops.

It was a serious blow to the English officer's plans, and many another equally brave leader would have given up then and there. Maynard, however, was determined to capture or kill the great Blackbeard and forever rid the seas of his presence. The British lieutenant ordered all hands below, remaining on deck alone with the man at the helm, whom he told to crouch down as far as possible. The other sloop was out of the contest, temporarily disabled by the broadside. The wind now freshened a trifle, allowing Maynard's sloop to draw closer to the pirates. But it was a difficult course, the sloop grounding and sliding off time and again.

Maynard ordered two ladders placed in the hatchway so that the men could scramble from the hold when the signal was given. Closer and closer the sloop came to the pirates, who were awaiting them with hand grenades. When within throwing distance, the pirates lighted the short fuses on the grenades and tossed them over to the deck of the sloop, but as most of the sailors were below, the grenades exploded harmlessly. Blackbeard, when the smoke had partially cleared, looked over at the sloop.

"They are all knocked on the head except three or four," he exclaimed. "Let's jump aboard and cut them to pieces."

As the two ships came together, Blackbeard and fourteen of the pirates jumped across to Maynard's vessel. Then the men below decks raced up the ladders and the bloody conflict began. The tides of victory surged back and forth, with the sabers gleaming and flashing in the sun and the pistol shots sending out their fatal charges echoing across the water. The two forces fought on until almost every man was bathed in blood.

Edward Teach, alias Blackbeard, was in his last fight, although he probably did not realize it. Anxious to come to blows with the British upstart who had threatened his piratical kingdom, he gradually worked his way aft until he could see Lieutenant Maynard, who had also noticed the fearsome spectacle that he identified as Blackbeard, and was advancing to meet him. Having waited for such a long time to come to grips with this hated outlaw, who represented everything loathsome connected with the ocean, Maynard was not to be frightened by the truly dreadful apparition that came at him from out of the thinning smoke of gunshot and hand grenade.

Maynard and Blackbeard fired at each other simultaneously, but Blackbeard missed his aim, while Maynard wounded his adversary in the body. In spite of this the huge, lumbering form kept moving steadily forward, until suddenly he struck with a terrific sweep of his cutlass, which smashed into Maynard's sword with such force that it broke the weapon off at the hilt. Getting his balance again for a fresh lunge that would have done for the lieutenant, Blackbeard drew back his cutlass. As he started his second sweeping parabola, he was given a terrific blow in the throat by a British marine, and this telling wound deflected his own blow so that it struck Maynard's knuckles instead of killing him.

The result of the battle seemed to change time after time, but finally when Blackbeard had suffered twenty saber thrusts and five pistol wounds he was seen to waver. Just as he began to cock his last pistol, having fired three others previously, he was seized with a spasm. Tottering for a brief moment in helplessness, Blackbeard fell dead at the very feet of the man who had sworn to take him, Lieutenant Robert Maynard. By this time only a few of the buccaneers were left alive. When they saw that their leader was dead, the buccaneers quickly jumped over the side into the water, crying piteously for quarter. Maynard told them they could have mercy, but did not guarantee them against hanging later on. Back on the pirate ship, the sailors from Maynard's other sloop had finally gone into action, and the outlaws aboard Teach's vessel, who had seen Blackbeard go down to death and defeat, also asked for mercy.

It had been a glorious but fearful day for the British officers and sailors. Lieutenant Maynard deserved all the credit for the victory, for he had pushed ahead in the face of what seemed hopeless defeat to win one of the greatest encounters ever staged with pirates along the Atlantic coast. His subsequent conduct in continuing the fight after twenty-nine of his small force had been put out of action showed the highest form of bravery.

Blackbeard's plans miscarried aboard his own vessel, however. Had not Teach believed victory was certain when he boarded the Maynard sloop, the pirate vessel would have been blown up, for Blackbeard left explicit orders to set off the gunpowder should defeat seem imminent. Apparently victory changed to disaster in such a rapid and unexpected fashion that the giant Negro whose duty it was to blow up the ship if defeat threatened could not reach the powder magazine in time. Thus the outlaw vessel, with all its incriminating documents, was left secure for Maynard to go aboard and salvage. Among the documents which Maynard found were a great number of letters addressed to Teach from many leading citizens in various colonies along the Atlantic coast.

Finally, after all had been secured, Maynard ordered Blackbeard's head severed from his neck and suspended from the bowsprit of the victorious sloop. In this manner Maynard sailed into Bath-Town, where he and his ship excited the awe and amazement of the entire populace there. Sending his wounded men ashore for treatment, Maynard left at once for the governor's storehouse. Armed with the incriminating letters between Secretary Knight of Bath-Town and pirate Teach, involving twenty barrels of sugar for Knight and sixty for Governor Eden, Maynard boldly seized the eighty barrels piled up in the warehouse and ordered them taken away. Secretary Knight was so frightened at the

Blackbeard's head dangling over the water after his death

sudden turn of events that he actually fell sick with fear, and was literally scared to death at the consequences of his act and its discovery, dying a few days later.

With the ferocious head of the infamous Blackbeard still dangling from the end of the bowsprit, Maynard sailed out of Bath-Town and reached the James River, where the inspiring news of his daring exploit had preceded him. The sale of the pirate sloop and of certain effects and supplies of the pirates which were located ashore came to twenty-five hundred pounds, a tidy sum, in addition to the rewards paid for the apprehension of the pirates themselves. All of this small fortune, the equivalent of over ten thousand dollars today, was given to the survivors of the battle aboard the *Pearl*.

The result of the trial, which was held later in Virginia, was a foregone conclusion, with two exceptions. Israel Hands, ashore at the time of capture, was later apprehended and brought to the bar, where he was convicted. Sentenced to be hanged, he was told of the extension of King George's proclamation, and this condemned pirate in the shadow of the gallows had the cleverness to announce that he would agree to the king's offer and turn honest. The astonished justices in turn were forced to accept his statement as sincere, and pardoned him on the spot. Some years later pirate biographer Johnson heard that Hands had turned up in London, where he practiced for many years as a professional beggar.

Another pirate, Samuel Odell, was discovered to have been removed from a trading sloop the very night before the engagement. Having received no less than seventy wounds in the encounter, Odell was acquitted, and gratefully left the courtroom. He later recovered completely from the effects of his many injuries.

Nine of the pirates had been killed in the battle, with the two acquitted making eleven who were not hanged. All the other pirates, fourteen in number, were hanged with proper ceremony in the royal colony of Virginia. But the body of Captain Edward Teach, alias Blackbeard, did not grace any Virginia gibbet, for one of the most ferocious pirates of all time ended his career as he probably wished it would end, fighting a worthy opponent in the throes of a wild and thrilling conflict at sea.

We know next to nothing about Blackbeard's life before 1716, but he is believed to have been an educated man born into a respectable family around

1680. It's generally accepted that he was born in Bristol, but according to Philip Gosse in *The History of Piracy*, an anonymous author claimed in 1740 that Blackbeard was a native of Jamaica. We don't even know his surname for certain, as several variations of "Teach" or "Thatch" appear in various records. Teach is the accepted name, as it has appeared the most often.

Mark Wilde-Ramsing, project manager of the Queen Anne's Revenge Shipwreck Unit for the North Carolina Underwater Archaeology Branch, points out, "Much of the 'history' on Blackbeard is unsubstantiated. For example, there is no record of him having engaged the HMS *Scarborough* nor was Blackbeard still with Hornigold when *La Concorde* was captured. But they do make for a good story. The known facts are few and far between for the pirate."

Snow mentions that Blackbeard had thirteen wives. This is more or less true, but most of the marriages were probably not legally binding. They were usually performed aboard ship by the first mate, and the string of "wives" Blackbeard left behind in every port apparently was a sort of running joke to his crew.

It's said that on the eve of his final battle, one of his crew asked Blackbeard about the location of his treasure. "Nobody but the Devil and myself know where my treasure is, and the longer liver of the two shall have it all." If Samuel Haley really found silver bars in the Isles of Shoals, it can't be said for certain where they came from. But some still cling to the belief that Blackbeard buried treasure on the islands, and sightings of a ghostly woman in white (Blackbeard's abandoned wife?) have been attributed to several of the islands. Snow wrote in his1952 book *True Tales of Buried Treasure* that Prudence Randall of Lunging (also known as Londoner or Londoner's) Island, told him that "government men" who visited the island around World War II found indications that a substantial amount of silver was buried there. The History Channel series *History's Mysteries* featured a treasure hunt on Lunging Island, where some claim Blackbeard left his wife as well as his treasure. The hunt turned up nothing, but the legends and speculation continue.

After Maynard had Blackbeard's head severed from his body and the corpse thrown overboard, legend has it that the pirate's still-defiant headless body swam several circles around the sloop before it finally went under. Blackbeard's skull was displayed dangling from a pole at the mouth of the Hampton River for many years, and the location is still known as Blackbeard's Point.

The later whereabouts of the skull have been the subject of considerable debate. Robert E. Lee wrote that it was fashioned into the base of a large punch bowl that was "long used as a drinking vessel at the Raleigh Tavern." Pirate researcher John Walker wrote an article called "The Search for Blackbeard's Skull" in the May 1996 edition of the magazine *No Quarter Given*. In 1990

Walker had learned of a Judge Charles H. Whedbee, who claimed that the skull had been "fashioned by some local silversmith into a silver cup bearing the curse 'Deth to Spotswoode' engraved on the rim. . . . According to Judge Whedbee, it was used in a number of college fraternity initiations, both held and drunk from by him, on Ocracoke Island in the 1930s."

In 1958, Snow's friend Robert I. Nesmith published a book called *Dig for Pirate Treasure*. One of the book's chapters is "The Pirate's Skull." Snow had explained to Nesmith that the skull belonged to a college fraternity for some years, and that beginning around the time of the American Revolution it was exhibited at a tavern. In *True Tales of Buried Treasure*, Snow wrote that while in Alexandria, Virginia, in 1949 he had met with historian William Buckner McGroarty. A "chance remark" led to Snow's discovery in a nearby village of what he believed to be Blackbeard's skull, which "after considerable discussion, examination and appraisal," became his property. The skull acquired by Snow was complete, minus the jawbone, and had nothing engraved on it, although it was silver plated or painted. It can't be stated definitively whether or not the skull found by Snow was Blackbeard's, but it certainly made a vivid impression on the thousands of people who saw it at his lectures.

This 1709 cast bronze church or ship's bell of Spanish or Portuguese origin was recovered from Beaufort Inlet, North Carolina, in 1996. It is believed to have been on Blackbeard's ship, the Queen Anne's Revenge. *The bell may have been obtained when Blackbeard captured a Spanish sloop off the coast of Cuba. (Courtesy of Queen Anne's Revenge Shipwreck Project)*

The chapter in *Dig for Pirate Treasure* includes a whimsical and entertaining account of a conversation between Edward Rowe Snow and Blackbeard's skull during a raging thunderstorm. The pirate was about to reveal the whereabouts of his treasure to Snow, wrote Nesmith, when a flash of lightning knocked the skull to the floor and ended the conversation.

Blackbeard's treasure hasn't been found, but it appears that his ship, the *Queen Anne's Revenge* (originally the French slaver *La Concorde*), has. In 1988 a Florida-based research firm called Intersal, Inc., began searching for the remains of *Queen Anne's Revenge* and *Adventure* in Beaufort Inlet, North Carolina. In November 1996, a crew led by Intersal's project director, shipwreck researcher Mike Daniel, discovered a significant mound of cannons, anchors, and ballast stones. State underwater archaeologists agreed that the find was likely the remains of the forty-gun *Queen Anne's Revenge*.

To date the research team has taken more than three thousand photographs and recovered fifteen thousand of the estimated 1 million artifacts at the shipwreck site. Artifacts—including a wide variety of cannonballs and hand grenades, a bronze bell, medical and scientific instruments of the period, a blunderbuss barrel, wine bottles, pewter platters and food remains, and several cannons—will be on display in the summer of 2004 at the North Carolina Maritime Museum's *Queen Anne's Revenge* exhibit in Beaufort.

Edward Rowe Snow holding a skull said to be Blackbeard's (from Snow's True Tales of Pirates and Their Gold, *1957)*

CHAPTER 15

Major Stede Bonnet, the Gentleman Pirate

Major Stede Bonnet, a most unusual pirate, was originally a gentleman of leisure and wealth, living on the island of Barbados. Why he turned pirate is hard to understand, unless we believe Bonnet's claim that he craved excitement and adventure. He began his depredations with a small vessel of ten guns and a crew of seventy men whom he paid in regular fashion from his own pocket as though he were a master making a cruise.

Sailing away from Barbados in the dead of night, Major Bonnet headed the vessel for the Cape of Virginia. After plundering several ships, he continued his course to the northward, reaching Gardiner's Island, where he went ashore and purchased provisions as any other trader might have done. Soon afterwards he captured two other vessels.

About this time the major experienced great difficulty in deciding who should navigate the ship, since he himself knew nothing at all of this important science. Some weeks later he fell in with Edward Teach, alias Blackbeard. We have already told of his meeting with Blackbeard, of their decision to place a competent navigator on Major Bonnet's ship, allowing Bonnet to sail aboard Blackbeard's vessel, and of Blackbeard's subsequent trips in Bonnet's company. When Blackbeard decided to take advantage of the Royal Proclamation of Amnesty, Major Stede Bonnet held out a few days longer, going back on his own vessel. Finally he decided to give up. Bonnet sailed to Bath-Town and placed himself at the mercy of the king's magistrates.

A short time after he received his royal pardon, Major Bonnet went to the island of Saint Thomas, where he accepted a commission as a privateer against the Spaniards. Sailing back from Saint Thomas, Bonnet discovered seventeen members of Blackbeard's crew whom Teach had marooned on a lonely island, and rescued them.

While off the Virginia Capes, the major fell in with a vessel from which he took twelve barrels of pork and four hundredweight of bread, leaving in place of the provisions ten casks of rice and an old cable. Two days later he captured a vessel, which was carrying a cargo of rum, off Cape Henry. Bonnet chose several casks that were to his fancy and removed as well other badly needed articles from the cargo.

After this beginning, Major Stede Bonnet resumed his piratical course on the high seas. Changing his name to Edwards and then to Thomas, he became a hunter of ships as well as a hunted pirate. He soon encountered two tobacco vessels bound from Virginia to Glasgow, but the only thing of value that he could remove was several hundredweight of tobacco. The next day he captured a Bermuda-bound ship, which netted him twenty barrels of pork and two forced men. Another ship headed for Glasgow and several other vessels quickly fell to the determined major.

When the pirates reached the Cape Fear River, their ship sprang a bad leak. Finally refitted, she sailed out only to meet two vessels that had been sent after her by the council of South Carolina. A terrific battle followed, but the forces of the law were too strong for the pirates, who finally surrendered. The pirates were all manacled and imprisoned below deck but in some way Captain Bonnet and pirate Herriot made their escape.

The other members of the pirate crew were brought into Charles-Town [Charleston] and tried for piracy on the high seas. Of the twenty-six buccaneers, twenty-two were sentenced to be executed by the Court of Vice-Admiralty and four were freed. Meanwhile Colonel Rhet started out after Major Bonnet and his fellow pirate, spurred on by a reward of seven hundred pounds offered for the major's capture. Reaching Bonnet's hiding place late one afternoon, the soldiers under Colonel Rhet killed Herriot on the spot; Major Stede Bonnet was quickly captured and brought back to Charles-Town, to face trial.

The twenty-two condemned members of Major Bonnet's crew were taken out of prison on Saturday, November 8, 1718. Following the gentleman with the silver oar, the unhappy buccaneers reached White

Point, near Charles-Town, where they were given a chance to say their prayers. Then they were hanged. The twenty-two bodies outlined against the sky made a fearsome sight.

Four days later the trial of Major Stede Bonnet, which had commenced October 30, entered its final stages. It had been quite a problem, administering justice to this gentleman pirate, who was so different from the usual rough, uncouth, uneducated buccaneer. Much was made of the fact that he was brought up with all the advantages of a civilization that he was doing his part to destroy. The magistrate also stressed the fact that after taking benefit of the king's grace, Captain Bonnet captured eleven more vessels on which eighteen innocent victims were killed.

We quote part of Judge Nicholas Trott's final speech from the court records:

> *You being a Gentlemen that have had the Advantage of a Liberal Education, and being generally esteemed a Man of Letters, I believe it will be needless for me to explain to you the Nature of Repentance and Faith in Christ. . . .*
>
> *And therefore having now discharged my Duty to you as a Christian, by giving you the best Counsel I can with respect to the Salvation of your Soul, I must now do my office as a Judge.*
>
> *The Sentence that the Law hath appointed to pass upon you for your Offences, and which this Court doth therefore award, is*
>
> *That you the said Stede Bonnet shall go from hence to the Place from whence you came, and from thence to the Place of Execution where you shall be hanged by the Neck 'til you are Dead. And the God of infinite Mercy be merciful to your soul.*

So Major Stede Bonnet, gentleman pirate of Barbados, was taken from his cell in Charles-Town on December 10, 1718, to the gallows at White Point, where he was hanged. A contemporary illustration of the event is in the pages of this volume, showing Bonnet stepping off into eternity as the hangman's cart is driven away.

———————— ∾ ————————

Stede Bonnet was a most unusual pirate in many ways. He had no prior experience as a seaman, having been a major in the King's Guards. Charles

Major Stede Bonnet is swung out into eternity from the hangman's cart with flowers in his mana-cled hands, in Charleston, South Carolina.

Johnson in *A General History of the Pyrates*, blames Bonnet's sudden piratical career on a "Disorder in his Mind," perhaps brought about by an unhappy marriage. The *Boston News-Letter* reported that Bonnet roamed his vessel in his nightgown, and that he brought a large library to sea with him.

Despite his background as an educated gentleman landowner, Bonnet had a cruel streak. Some credit—or blame—Bonnet for inventing "walking the plank" as a punishment. This was actually a rare practice, Hollywood notwithstanding.

CHAPTER 16

Charles Gibbs,
Who Was Hanged at New York

Some pirates rise above the common level of their profession. In certain ways they have distinguished themselves so that they are classed in a different light from other marauders of the sea lanes. Such a desperado was Charles Gibbs, who was born on his father's Rhode Island farm in the year 1794. His father was a well-to-do citizen with an efficient, up-to-date farming property, and was respected and admired everywhere in the community.

Charles was his father's joy. Sending the lad to the best academy in the neighborhood, the elder Gibbs confidently awaited reports of his son's success with his lessons and deportment. Favorable reports, however, never arrived at the farm to gladden the heart of the fond parent, for after minor misdemeanors, Charles developed his capacity for causing trouble to such an extent that he finally was banished from the hall of learning and sent home for good. This was a severe blow to his father's pride, and he sought to reform the lad by giving him hard manual labor to perform on the farm.

Charles, however, soon began to commit acts of such outrageous nature in the neighborhood that the despairing father realized his boy was becoming a problem. If he heard of any new outbreak in the vicinity, it usually was the act of his son. Feeling between the two became more and more strained as the career of Charles continued, finally causing the boy to run away from home at the age of fifteen.

Evidently his thoughts for some time had been of the sea, and so his footsteps naturally turned to Boston, the sailing metropolis of New England. At that time the great man-of-war *Hornet*, commanded by Captain James Lawrence, was in the harbor. Charles obtained a berth aboard her. Life on an American warship seemed to be what he needed, for he remained on the *Hornet* until the outbreak of the War of 1812, and acquitted himself with glory when the *Hornet* defeated the *Peacock* several months later. So much a part of Lawrence's force did Gibbs become, that he was transferred to the ill-fated *Chesapeake* when his commander took over the vessel early in 1813.

The *Chesapeake* sailed out of Boston Harbor on June 1, 1813, and was defeated by the British warship *Shannon* off Boston Light in a fierce and bloody encounter. Gibbs fought by the side of his commander to the end. When brave Lawrence fell, shouting his immortal "Don't give up the ship," his men fought on but were finally overwhelmed. Although in the thick of the engagement, Charles Gibbs received but minor injuries, and was among those brought into Halifax a few days later.

The grim walls of Dartmoor Prison in England later received Gibbs and his shipmates. Here they lay in all the wretchedness and filth of Britain's most notorious jail until the end of the war. Finally returning to his home in Rhode Island, he announced his decision to forsake the cares and troubles of the sea for the steadier career of a farmer ashore. His parents, of course, were highly gratified at this turn of events, and treated him as a prodigal son. After a few weeks spent on the farm, however, Charles felt the call of the big town, and announced that he was going to Boston, where he would try to establish himself in some suitable trade. His father had a serious talk with him, and it was decided Charles should take $1,000 with him to Boston for the purpose of starting up in the grocery business.

It is true that he started a grocery store, but the neighborhood in which he established himself was that section of the town where the houses of ill repute were located. Gibbs soon obtained a license to sell liquor over the counter. Always fond of the opposite sex, his nearness to them now proved his downfall, for while they were very willing to purchase his stores and liquors, they did not often make a cash trade, and before long his modest fortune was gone. Utterly discouraged, Charles Gibbs sold out his entire stock for the sum of one hundred dollars and shipped away to sea.

Signing on the ship *John*, he worked his way to Buenos Aires, where he jumped ship. Gibbs followed his inclinations in the South American city until all his money had vanished, and then joined the crew of a privateer. Near the successful termination of a long cruise when sailing toward port, Gibbs evidently decided to turn pirate, for he stirred up the crew with complaints about their share of the prize money, starting much trouble between the officers and their men.

Finally the discontented men met with Gibbs and determined to mutiny. Choosing an opportune moment, Gibbs led the attack that succeeded in overpowering the officers and those of the crew who were loyal to them. All were forced below under hatches, but were humanely treated. Gibbs was not chosen the sole commander, but the pirates took turns in running the ship. When the mutineers reached the coast of Florida, they took all of the honest privateers and crew ashore, bidding them to shift for themselves.

The pirates then began their career in earnest. Sallying forth from a small inlet in the West Indies, they would fall upon an approaching ship, capture and murder the crew, and change the general appearance of the vessel. Their next move was to sail into Havana and sell the vessel for a substantial sum. Time and again this practice was repeated. Whenever the whimsy struck them and they felt lazily inclined, the pirates would run the captured vessel into the inlet that was their headquarters and burn the ship to the water's edge. As not one of the captured ships' crews ever returned to civilization to tell his story, more than five hundred souls must have been murdered in cold blood.

The pirates' secret was finally revealed when their capture of the American ship *Caroline* was observed by officers aboard the British man-of-war *Jarius*, then cruising in the vicinity. Following the pirates into their inlet, the commander of the *Jarius* ordered his crew ashore in longboats to attack the buccaneers, who were firing from a small battery erected on a nearby promontory. The marines organized a determined assault against the surprised marauders. For this sort of frolic the pirate gang had little stomach, fleeing ingloriously to the shelter of the woods. For some reason they were not pursued. Exploring the nearby area, the marines found no less than twelve vessels burned to the water's edge. When these ships are added to the number taken into Havana Harbor and sold, the pirates were probably responsible for from twenty-five to thirty ships that never returned to their owners.

Gibbs had long before distinguished himself as a leader and when the pirates fled into the woods, he was chosen to command. One night the pirates rowed out and boarded a Dutch vessel, anchored off shore, which was loaded with silver plate. The pirates divided the rich loot. The passengers and crew, numbering thirty, were all killed with one exception, a beautiful young girl of seventeen, who appealed to Gibbs. Falling on her knees before the pirate leader, the maiden begged for her life, and as he was attracted by her charms, Gibbs promised to save her. After the other people had been killed he sailed away to Cape Antonio, where she accompanied him ashore. Two months went by, during which the two were constantly together. This excited the jealousy and anger of the others.

Finally one of the sailors openly rebelled against Gibbs, grabbing the girl in his arms and taking his hatchet to dash her brains out. Drawing his pistol, Gibbs shot from the hip, and the pirate fell dead at his feet. It was not the end of the matter however, for the other pirates demanded a showdown. Gibbs reluctantly agreed to a meeting of the

Gibbs carrying away the Dutch girl (from The Pirates Own Book, *1837; Marine Research Society, Salem, 1924)*

buccaneers. As he was tiring of his liaison with the Dutch girl, Gibbs then promised that he would abide by the decision of the majority. A vote was taken immediately and it was agreed to poison the girl. This was done at once, and she died shortly afterwards in terrible agony.

Some time later Gibbs visited Havana. He was told that conditions were becoming increasingly difficult in his particular profession. Authorities were going to watch carefully any and all transactions along the waterfronts, and patrols were to sail up and down the coast around the pirate haunts, on the lookout for marauders of the deep. Upon mature reflection, Gibbs decided that it was an opportune time to return to his native land. Withdrawing $30,000 that he had on deposit in a Havana bank, he booked passage for New York City, where he arrived on Christmas Day, 1819.

Disgusted with city sharpers and their clever manipulations, Gibbs decided to visit the old world, and sailed from Boston to Liverpool a short time later. The charms of a lady in Liverpool so appealed to him that he never left the city while he was in England. Day and night her attractiveness enchanted him, until finally she tired of his slavish devotion, and fled from him with another man. This development embittered him against all England, and he sailed on the next ship for America.

Gibbs shooting a comrade (from The Pirates Own Book*)*

Arriving in the United States again, he wandered around various cities of this country, but was suddenly excited into action by the declaration of war between Argentina and Brazil. He took passage at once on a vessel bound for Buenos Aires, and on his arrival there sought an interview with the governor, who signed him on in the navy as a fifth lieutenant. Gibbs went aboard a warship of thirty-four guns, named the *Twenty-Fifth of May*.

After a number of skirmishes with the enemy in which he fought bravely, his abilities were recognized by Admiral Brown, who placed Gibbs in charge of a privateer schooner mounting two long twenty-four-pounders and carrying a crew of forty-six men. He made two successful voyages before he was captured by the enemy on the third, and taken to Rio de Janeiro, where he remained until the end of the war. His own words, taken from Gibbs's confession, which was published after his death, tell us what befell him.

> *After the lapse of about a year, which I passed in travelling from place to place, the war between France and Algiers attracted my attention. Knowing that the French commerce presented a fine opportunity for plunder, I determined to embark for Algiers and offer my services to the Dey. I accordingly took passage from New York in the* Sally Ann, *belonging to Bath, landed at Barcelona, crossed to Port Mahon, and endeavoured to make my way to Algiers. The vigilance of the French fleet prevented the accomplishment of my design, and I proceeded to Tunis. There, finding it unsafe to attempt a journey to Algiers across the desert, I amused myself with contemplating the ruins of Carthage, and reviving my recollections of her war with the Romans. I afterwards took passage to Marseilles, and thence to Boston.*

Gibbs next went to New Orleans. Soon after his arrival he found himself without funds, so shipped on board the brig *Vineyard*, commanded by Captain Thornby, bound for Philadelphia. Sailing from the Gulf port on November 9, 1830, the *Vineyard* was soon far at sea. The members of the crew learned of the existence aboard the vessel of $54,000 worth of Spanish dollars consigned to Stephen Girard, a merchant of Philadelphia. Gibbs was greatly excited on hearing of the treasure aboard, and he determined to seize the ship and appropriate the money for his own use.

After talking for a short time with a Negro seaman named Thomas J. Wansley, Gibbs convinced him that they should attempt to take the vessel. The other members of the crew were cautiously sounded out. Edward Church and James Talbot openly joined the conspirators; John Brown finally was persuaded, while the other three refused but agreed to remain silent. It was then five pirates against four honest men, and Gibbs's determination carried the day.

On the night of November 23 the blow fell. About midnight Captain William Thornby was standing a little forward of the companion hatchway, when Wansley came up the steps, carrying a lantern, which he placed on the deck. In his left hand he had a knife, but at the last minute he saw a pump-brake on the deck, which he seized. Swinging it high in the air, he dealt the unsuspecting captain a blow over the head, knocking the poor man unconscious. Gibbs and Wansley picked up the fallen man and dumped him unceremoniously into the sea.

The noise of the scuffle had attracted the attention of the mate, William Roberts, who rushed up the companion hatchway. Awaiting

Gibbs and Wansley burying their money (from The Pirates Own Book*)*

him were Gibbs on one side and Wansley on the other. They hit him simultaneously, and he staggered back down the steps. The two pirates were on Roberts at once, beating him unmercifully, after which he lapsed into unconsciousness. Roberts was also tossed into the ocean. Gibbs then announced himself as commander of the brig.

When daylight broke, the search for the silver dollars began. Finding the treasure intact between decks, the pirates divided their spoil and set to work sewing moneybags in which their respective shares would be placed. With seaman Dawes in charge of the wheel, the brig continued northward. The next evening Southampton Light was sighted, and Gibbs made plans to leave the ship. When more than ten miles out to sea he transferred to the longboat, with the three other pirates, while the honest men took to the jolly boat, carrying the small shares of money which the pirates had given them. The buccaneers carried the bulk of the treasure in the longboat, of course. Gibbs then applied the torch to the brig, which burned and sank.

The three honest men struck a bar while rowing toward the shore, overturned, and were drowned. The longboat hit the same sandspit, but carried over it successfully, landing later that day at Pelican Island, where the marauders at once buried the treasure in the sand. They then rowed across to Great Bar Island, where lived a man named Johnson. Pirate Brownrigg communicated with him. Brownrigg, a pirate by coercion, pretended that Johnson would cooperate with the cutthroats. But he had no intention of allowing them to escape.

Just as the pirates were being driven away by horse and wagon from the home of Mr. Johnson, Brownrigg chose the moment to announce that Gibbs and Wansley were murderers. Panicked by the sudden denunciation, the two ruffians were so overcome that they jumped out of the wagon and fled to the woods. A searching party was quickly organized, and started in pursuit. Late that night the buccaneers were discovered, huddling in a clump of bushes. They were taken to the local jail, together with Brownrigg and Dawes, and were conveyed to New York City the next day.

Realizing the game was up, the pirates talked freely in the conveyance that carried them from Flatbush to the city. Wansley told the whole story, occasionally prompted by Charles Gibbs. The two men implicated Dawes, but their testimony showed that Brownrigg took no part in the crime. Nevertheless, when the case came to court, both Dawes and Brownrigg were admitted as state's evidence, with Gibbs facing trial for the murder of Mate William Roberts, while the charge against Wansley was the murder of Captain Thornby. After due deliberation, both Gibbs and Wansley were found guilty as charged. Controlling his emotions, Charles Gibbs heard the verdict calmly, sitting with his hand between his knees, but Wansley went to pieces toward the end of the trial, and trembled violently when he heard that he was to hang.

Wansley was given a chance to speak. He mentioned the fact that he was colored, and said that it hurt his chances when white men were judges. White men, said Wansley, had stolen Africans from their own country, and there always had existed among the whites a strong dislike for the blacks. Then Wansley announced that he had said enough, but when urged to continue he did so. It was Atwill, one of those who later drowned, who first told him of the conspiracy to rob the vessel, said Wansley in his statement. "I felt no inclination to join them," said Wansley, "and so I told Church, who was the only one of the crew that I knew before I shipped in the Vineyard. Church told me by all means not to inform against the conspirators. If I had informed upon them I should have only been in the same situation in which I am at present. I have nothing more to say."

The judge then sentenced the two men to die by hanging on the next 22nd of April. Gibbs wrote two letters while awaiting his execution, both of them to the woman he had previously known in Liverpool, advising her to forsake her vicious life and seek repentance before it was too late. It was said at the time that the letters proved him to have a limited education, but nevertheless showed much innate talent.

The day of the execution arrived, Friday, April 22, 1831. Charles Gibbs and Thomas Wansley, in charge of the marshal, his aides, and thirty marines, made the walk to the gallows, which they reached at noon. Two clergymen prayed for their souls. Wansley also joined in the prayers, later chanting a hymn as the time drew near for his execution. Gibbs addressed the great crowd which had gathered.

> *The law believes me guilty of the charge, but I take my God, before whose tribunal I shall in a few moments be summoned, to witness that I did not murder the mate.*

The caps were quickly adjusted over the faces of the doomed men. Gibbs himself, by dropping a handkerchief, gave the signal for the trap to be sprung, and the two pirates were suspended between heaven and earth. It is said that Wansley died peacefully, without struggling, but Gibbs fought to the end. After hanging for two minutes he raised his right hand to his head, as if in some involuntary movement he was trying to remove the black cap, and partly succeeded in dislodging it before his hand dropped. Shortly afterwards he raised the same hand to his mouth, but then the hand dropped lifeless to his side and his struggles ceased. It has been said that when Gibbs was later cut down, part of his body was sent to Harvard College for preservation.

Thus ended the career of a brave man, who fought aboard the *Chesapeake* for his country in the War of 1812, became a prisoner of war at dreaded Dartmoor, started a grocery store in Boston, became a notorious pirate, again became a marine fighter in South America, and then after many years was attracted to piracy by chance and hanged for his evil deeds.

Like so many pirates before him, much of Charles Gibbs's life remains shrouded in mystery and contradictions. According to Don Carlos Seitz in *Under the Black Flag: Exploits of the Most Notorious Pirates* (1925), Gibbs's naval record is suspect. "In a 'confession' made by him before his execution," wrote Seitz, "he claimed to have served as 'James D. Jeffers' under the gallant James Lawrence on the *Hornet* and the *Chesapeake*. . . . The records of the Navy Department at Washington prove this to be entirely untrue." There was, however, a Charles Gibbs in the record in 1815 as a gunner for the British on the sloop-of-war *Pelican*, which was taken by the *Hornet* under Captain Nicholas Biddle. This Gibbs was taken prisoner and released at San Salvador the same year.

The Pirates Own Book, originally published in 1837, tells us that Gibbs was married and fathered a child while in Buenos Aires. The letters Gibbs wrote to his former lady friend from Liverpool were reproduced in *The Pirates Own Book*. An excerpt: "My breast is like the tempestuous ocean, raging in its own shame, harrowing up the bottom of my soul! But I look forward to that serene calm when I shall sleep with Kings and Counsellors of the earth. There the wicked cease from troubling, and there the weary are at rest!"

The Pirates Own Book provides descriptive detail on the pirates as well: "Gibbs was rather below the middle stature, thick set and powerful. The form of Wansley was a perfect model of manly beauty."

Although most sources name Cuba as the scene of the death of the young Dutch woman captured by the pirates, some versions of the story place it on a Florida Gulf Coast island now called Pavilion Key. The name is said to originate from a shelter that Gibbs had built to protect the captive before she was ultimately killed by poison.

Gibbs and Wansley were among the last pirates hanged in the United States. The place of the execution is sometimes said to have been Bedloe Island, now the site of the Statue of Liberty, but it was apparently Ellis Island, where large throngs gathered for the event. In his book *Dig for Pirate Treasure* (1957), Robert I. Nesmith reported that a sculptor made death masks of Gibbs and Wansley. "The casts have been lost," he wrote, "but a reporter for the *New Yorker* magazine recently turned up Gibbs's skull in the museum section of a New York Trade Society Library."

Seitz adds some intriguing information: "Gibbs was abnormally constructed. A peculiarly confidential portion of his person, preserved by petrification, was long used in class demonstrations by no less a personage than Oliver Wendell Holmes."

CHAPTER 17

The Pirates Who Were Executed at Philadelphia

Sometimes almost pitiful attempts at piracy have been made by wholly uneducated sea outlaws. Their weaknesses as regards sailing, navigation, and even the ability to read, were so great that once they had captured ships, they were unable to work out their subsequent problems successfully, and authorities found it easy to step in and capture them. One such case of piratical inadequacy occurred on the schooner *Eliza*, which left Philadelphia on August 27, 1799, bound for St. Thomas.

At this particular period in American history, it was hard to find sailors from the United States to sign on for a voyage, so when Captain William Wheland hired his crew, it consisted of two Americans— Thomas Croft, whom he appointed mate, and Jacob Suster. There were three foreigners, Jacob Baker, Joseph Brous, and Peter Peterson. A French gentleman named Charles Rey went along as supercargo. Rey had been a resident of St. Domingo up to the time of the revolution there. Moving to Philadelphia, he watched his fortune dwindle steadily, so he resolved to return to St. Domingo and try to regain part of his former immense holdings on the island.

Both Captain Wheland and Mr. Rey had poor opinions of the foreigners who had signed on, for the sailors seemed to have resentful manners and revengeful spirits. On the way down the Delaware River from Philadelphia, one of them, Peter Peterson, refused to obey the mate, so Captain Wheland struck him. When Baker rushed to Peterson's aid, Rey stepped in to protect the captain. Baker received a good beating, after which both he and Peterson promised to behave if they would be forgiven. In this Captain Wheland readily agreed, and for the next fourteen days there was no trouble at all.

At ten o'clock the night of September 12, Mate Thomas Crofts was standing his watch on deck. Both Rey and the captain had retired. Apparently the mate dozed off, for as far as can be gathered, the three foreigners came up on deck while he was asleep. Brous and Baker hit him over the head with an axe and threw him into the sea. Next, the men entered the cabin and crept up to the bunk where the sleeping captain lay. The axe swung again, catching Captain Wheland on top of the skull, while a sword was thrust into his arm. Terribly injured, but partially conscious, he reached for the pistols under his pillow.

The confusion awakened Charles Rey, who jumped from his bunk in the cabin and cried out, asking what the trouble was. Seeing the captain fighting the ruffians, he snatched up his pistol and ran for the three pirates, who retreated from the cabin. Awaiting him outside, they smashed Rey over the head with the pump handle, and he staggered back into the cabin. Again he attempted to leave. Another terrific blow hit him, and he collapsed. Rey, gathering his senses, looked over at the captain, whose entire body was bathed in blood from his painful wounds. Almost delirious himself from the murderous blows on his head, Rey crawled over to where the captain lay. The two men talked together quietly. They felt that another attempt would soon be made on their lives, and that they did not have long to live. After talking over his chances with the captain Charles Rey determined to make a last attempt to overcome the pirates. Seeing a light on deck, he believed he might have a chance to surprise the ruffians. Rey staggered to his feet and rushed out where the pirates were standing around a lantern, but he was no match for them. They beat him unmercifully with their weapons, hitting him long after he had fallen to the deck. The buccaneers were wasting their blows, however, for by that time he was dead.

Later that night Captain Wheland crawled up on deck to the Frenchman's dead body, where he wrenched the pistol from the lifeless grasp and retreated to the cabin prepared to defend himself. Early in the morning the pirates asked him to show himself, which he refused to do. Next they asked for liquor. The captain said he could not get any because of his wounds. Evidently the problem of navigation had been discussed, for the pirates then asked Captain Wheland if he would compromise with them, offering him his life if he would navigate the vessel. Captain Wheland agreed, for the plan was better than death.

Under this partial armistice, the pirates entered the cabin and dressed Captain Wheland's wounds. The pirates went out on deck and threw Rey's body overboard. They then called the only remaining crew member, Jacob Suster, who had been sleeping all through the mutiny. When he reached them, they brutally knocked him down with an axe and threw him overboard. As the wind was light, the vessel made little headway, and the helpless captain could hear the cries and screams of the victim for eight or ten minutes after he was cast into the sea, as they grew fainter and fainter, finally stopping altogether.

The pirates returned to the captain's cabin, where they washed the blood from the floor and seemed anxious to remove all signs of the fight. Later they cleaned up the deck as well, but with the coming of dawn the ruffians began to loot the property of the men they had thrown into the sea.

Daylight gave Captain Wheland hope, for he felt that the pirates were in desperate need of his knowledge of navigation, and because of this his life would be spared. He was worried about his two pistols, however, for he knew that he could not keep awake all the time and that they would be a powerful weapon in the pirates' possession. Debating at length with himself, he finally decided to toss the weapons overboard secretly. The pirates never discovered that he had done so and continued to believe that Captain Wheland still had the pistols in his possession.

The cutthroats now ordered Captain Wheland to set a course directly for the Spanish Main, but he deceived them easily, setting his own course. Day after day passed in this strange state of existence, with no one trusting any one else. The sails and rigging soon showed signs of the poor seamanship of the ignorant sailors. They knew, or thought they knew, that the captain was not physically able to handle a rope, and they were too lazy most of the time to do the work themselves, so considerable damage to the ship's fitting was done during this period.

The captain's arm was not as feeble as he pretended, however, for he tested it secretly day by day. His entire body was slowly gaining in strength. The pirates occupied themselves chiefly in rifling the vessel, breaking open packages or looting staterooms. As they grew more and more careless, Captain Wheland, always keeping in the background, awaited his chance to recapture the schooner.

On the 21st of September, nine days after the pirates had seized the ship, Wheland's opportunity came. Peterson and Baker had gone down into the fore scuttle to bring up some choice hams, of which they were very fond, while Brous was in the caboose, or galley as it is known today, getting the fire ready. Accompanied by the murdered Rey's dog, which followed him everywhere, Captain Wheland sauntered into the galley, holding in readiness a club he had picked up from the deck. Stepping behind Brous, he hit the pirate on the back of the head, knocking him to the deck. When Brous began to get up, Captain Wheland aimed another blow at him, but his bad arm prevented good delivery, and Brous rolled safely out of the way. Rey's bulldog now entered the fray, rushing at the pirate, who turned and ran in terror into the shrouds, where he climbed high up in the rigging.

Captain Wheland, pleased at his success, ran over to the fore scuttle, slipping his strengthened arm out of the sling completely for the coming effort. Grabbing an ax with both hands, he raised it over his head just as the pirates prepared to climb out of the scuttle. The sight of the apparently wounded man holding the ax with both hands completely bewildered the other two pirates. Instead of coming up on deck and trying to take the ax away, they ran down below into the scuttle again, so Captain Wheland immediately secured and locked the hatchway over the scuttle. Then he dragged a huge anchor and several other heavy pieces of timber over to the scuttle cover, piling them on the hatchway so that the men would be unable to get out of the fore scuttle even if they forced the lock.

Captain Wheland now turned his attention to Brous who was still clinging to the rigging, gibbering in French to the other pirates. Wheland told Brous that if he came down on the deck and allowed himself to be tied up, he would not be killed. But Brous had completely lost his nerve. It was a long time before he could get up enough courage to descend to the deck, but he finally climbed down. Falling on his knees, Brous took the captain's hand and kissed it several times, making the humblest of statements of gratitude and subservience. Captain Wheland, unwilling to trust the pirate's claims of complete surrender, chained the blackguard to the ring bolts on the deck.

Not wishing to antagonize the two men in the scuttle, he bored a hole in the hatch cover large enough to pour water down to them. There was plenty of food there anyway. From time to time the pirates attempted to break out but finally they gave it up. The two men believed that Brous had been killed, for he had promised to make no signal to them and kept his word. Of course, the captain realized that he might doze off and be murdered in his sleep should Brous escape, so he tried to keep awake constantly, day and night, never lying down.

On October 4 Captain Wheland sighted the island of St. Bartholomew's and by 7 P.M. was off the port, where he hailed a passing vessel and made known his unusual story. Commander John Peterson of the Swedish brig *Housare* then sent to his assistance two officers and ten men who brought the schooner *Eliza* safely into the harbor. Captain Campbell, of the American brig *Eagle*, met Captain Wheland there and offered to assist in any way. The two men went down to the American consul's office where Consul Job Wall arranged to have the three pirates put in irons aboard the *Eagle*.

His adventure at an end, Captain Wheland was then faced with a heavy salvage claim from the Swedish brig but Wheland pointed out that the American-Swedish treaty would allow only a fair amount to be paid for towing the *Eliza* into the harbor, and nothing else. After considerable discussion he made the payment of $200. Selling his cargo and loading a fresh one of sugar, Wheland hired on a new crew, and finally sailed away for home November 4, 1799. He arrived at Gloucester Point on the 25th of the same month.

The prisoners were taken to Philadelphia, where they were examined by Judge Peters. Confessing readily to the several murders, they claimed they were French prisoners in the service of the French Republic, and as United States and France were then at war, they had a right to seize any American ship and kill those who resisted. Judge Peters decided that as the pirates had voluntarily signed on an American vessel, they came under the jurisdiction of American courts. He ordered them to trial for murder and piracy on the high seas. It was then revealed that Peterson's real name was LaCroix, although he may have been Swedish, while the other two were actually Frenchmen. Baker's name was Boulanger, while Brous's was LaRoche.

They were tried in the circuit court at Philadelphia before Judges Peters and Chase on April 21, 1800. Captain Wheland, of course, as the only survivor of their murderous scheme, was the single witness against them, but after a short retirement the jury brought back the verdict, guilty. The pirates were sentenced to be hanged by the neck until dead.

On May 9, 1800, the three marauders of the deep were taken from their cells in Philadelphia out to Smith's Island opposite the great city of brotherly love, and executed for their crime of murder and piracy on the high seas.

———————————— ～ ————————————

Captain William Wheland's account of the events on board the *Eliza* in 1799 was published a year later as *A Narrative of the Horrid Murder & Piracy committed on board the Schooner Eliza, of Philadelphia, on the high seas by three foreigners . . . together with an account of the surprizing recapture of the said schooner, by Captain Wheland, the only person to escape from their Barbarity*. The confession of pirate Baker (Boulanger) was also published in Philadelphia in 1800. Baker/Boulanger was said to be Canadian by birth.

PART IV

THE WOMEN PIRATES

CHAPTER 18

Alwida and Mrs. Ching

Shrill cries of women pirates have echoed down through the corridors of time. The daughter of a Gothic king, Princess Alwida embraced the life of a sea rover to avoid marriage with Alf, the son of a Danish King. Embarking on a piratical voyage with a crew of young women, all attired in male garb, Alwida soon distinguished herself among the pirates.

She came to be such a menace to shipping along the coast that Prince Alf himself was sent out in pursuit of her, not knowing, of course, that the object of his search was Alwida. Killing most of the sea rovers, Alf forced Alwida to surrender. On removing her helmet, she revealed herself as the girl he desired to wed. Pleased with his ability in battle, the princess married Alf on board the pirate ship, and left the sea forever.

The Chinese woman pirate, Mrs. Ching [often spelled Cheng—*Ed.*], was a terror to all Europeans in the early years of the nineteenth century.

Ann Bonney [usually spelled Anne Bonny—*Ed.*] and Mary Read, however, are the two most interesting women pirates in history, and because of their activities along the Atlantic coast their adventures are included in detail.

CHAPTER 19

Mary Read and Ann Bonney,
Who Loved and Fought

This generation falls into the habit of thinking that the girls and young ladies of today are becoming more independent and active than ever before. Here is a story, however, of how two young women over two hundred years ago became experts at the world's most dangerous and exciting profession, that of piracy on the high seas.

Mary Read was an English girl whose mother married a sailor when she was very young. Perhaps the sailor decided it was a bad bargain, possibly there were other motives in his subsequent behavior, but he went to sea and never came back. A little later a "sprightly boy" was born. Shortly afterwards, Mrs. Read found herself again expecting an addition to her family, so in her embarrassment she moved away from home to a place in the country, where the little boy died. A few months later, Mary Read, who was to become a pirate, arrived in this world.

Mrs. Read stayed on in the country for a few years, until Mary was about four years old. All this time she had been very secretive as to her activities, never letting the folks back home discover that her boy had died or that another baby had been born. Her plan was to substitute this girl child of another man for her husband's baby son, so that she could return to her home. Her husband's mother was fairly well to do. Mrs. Read now decided that the time had come to attempt the deception.

Dressing Mary in the most appropriate boy's clothes which she could find, Mrs. Read taught the girl to consider herself a boy at all times. She started for her husband's family home after she had coached little Mary on what to say and how to act. As soon as she arrived in the city, which was on the coast of England, mother and daughter made their way to the house where she planned to carry out the ruse, and confidently knocked on the door.

They were soon invited in by the good lady, who was favorably impressed with the appearance of the stocky lad standing before her, so impressed, in fact, that she proposed that the two move in with her and live at the mansion. Of course, Mary's mother realized that the deception would be short-lived under such intimate circumstances, so told the kindly woman that she had made other plans. She intended to live down in the village where she had obtained employment and would consent to no other arrangement. The grandmother insisted that Mary receive a crown a week for support, which was exactly according to the plot. As the years passed, this ruse continued, but the grandmother finally died and the income stopped altogether. Mary's mother had informed the girl of her background, explaining why she was being raised as a boy and Mary agreed that the plan should be continued. Obtaining employment as a footboy, Mary grew stronger and stronger until, a few years later, she was manly enough in appearance to enlist in the Royal Navy, where she was put aboard a man-of-war.

Mary, however, evidently inherited a wandering disposition from her unknown father. We find her next in Flanders, where she joined a foot regiment as a cadet. With the ambition to become an officer dominant in her thoughts, she fought in every engagement with daring and bravery. She was not promoted in spite of her good record, as in those days commissions were almost always bought and sold.

After many battles Mary Read remained a cadet, so in her discouragement the girl left the service and enlisted in a regiment of horse marines. Mary soon became a favorite in her new regiment, gaining the esteem of all her officers. Occupying the same tent with her was a handsome young Dutch youth. Without declaring herself, she fell violently in love with him. This passion was so absorbing that it affected her soldierly bearing and the officers were quick to notice the change. Even her tent-mate considered that she had gone out of her head, while the others decided she should be discharged from the service because she seemed insane. Finally, in her desperation, she found a moment when the two were alone in the tent and revealed to the astonished lad that she was actually a girl. After his extreme surprise had been overcome, we are told that the lad easily reconciled himself to the situation, believing that his tent-mate would readily acquiesce in whatever suggestions he might make. But in this he was disappointed. He found that it was necessary to court Mary for his wife. He was entirely successful. Eventually the officers were informed of the amazing situation between the two troopers.

The romantic aspect of the affair so impressed the commanding officer of the regiment that he decided the wedding should be a memorable occasion. Almost every officer on the post honored the union by his presence. The gifts were handsome and costly. A few weeks later arrangements were completed whereby both were allowed to leave the regiment.

Returning to the coast of England, the two lovers set up an ordinary or tavern called the Three Shoes, and because of the notoriety they had received soon were doing a very lively business. But after a while, Mary's husband became ill and died. With the coming of peace, the soldiers and troopers left the army, and business became so bad that the young widow was forced to give up the ordinary. She crossed over into Holland, where she again assumed the guise of a man and enlisted in a regiment of foot soldiers quartered in one of the frontier villages. Within a few months, however, Mary tired of her duties, so she left the service, signing on as a sailor aboard a Dutch West Indiaman.

While at sea she soon demonstrated her abilities in a satisfactory manner, and the men never realized she was a girl. When nearing its destination, the ship was overtaken by English pirates who ransacked it for spoils. The only English sailor on board, Mary Read, was impressed into the pirate service, after which the buccaneers permitted the Dutch vessel to sail away.

Month after month Mary Read participated in the capture of many ships of all nations, so effectively demonstrating the manly qualities of hardihood and courage with the best of the other pirates that they were unsuspecting of her sex. Sloops, brigantines, and other vessels were captured up and down the Atlantic coast of North America, after which the pirates sailed for the West Indies.

When a royal pardon was announced for all pirates who would give up their unlawful pursuits, Mary Read was among those who decided to retire to an inactive life ashore. Moving to a pleasant island in the

Mary Read

West Indies, she lived for several months without incident, but gradually her food and money dwindled. Mary realized that she would have to seek some occupation before all her funds were exhausted. Hearing of a privateering expedition which was being outfitted by Captain Rogers in the Island of Providence, Mary Read signed on as a member of the crew.

Others aboard the ship included the infamous Captain Jack Rackam and his sweetheart, Ann Bonney. This strange couple had become enamoured of each other to such an extent that Ann had deserted her husband for pirate Rackam, and wherever he signed on as a pirate she always accompanied him in men's clothes. All three—Mary Read, Jack Rackam, and Ann Bonney—were aboard the same ship.

Ann Bonney had been a native of Cork, Ireland, the daughter of a respectable attorney and his serving maid. The three had gone to America, where the serving maid died, leaving Ann to manage the household. Although approached by offers of marriage from many respectable and wealthy young men it is said that her heart and not her head determined her choice, for she married a young sailor who admitted that he did not have a single shilling. Her father was so upset at the marriage that he turned Ann out of his house, and the couple then sailed to the

Mary Read kills her antogonist (from The Pirates Own Book, *1837; Marine Research Society, Salem, 1924)*

Island of Providence. While on the island, she became enamored of handsome Jack Rackam, and soon she had left her sailor husband forever. Pirate Rackam, who seems to have held a fascination for all women, then took Ann with him whenever he went on a buccaneering cruise, and during the heat of battle she fought as well as any man on the ship.

Such were the histories of the two people with whom Mary Read was soon to toss her lot. We shall now learn of the strange way in which the event occurred. Of course, Mary's fair skin, when seen among the privateering crew, most all of whom had beards, attracted the attention of Rackam's paramour. Ann Bonney was soon thinking of various ways to attract the good-looking young man. Naturally, Captain Jack noticed this wavering of devotion, and, not being used to competition, became extremely jealous. Ann finally made her desires known to the disconcerted Mary, who saw there was only one way out of the difficulty. She told Ann Bonney that she, also, was a girl. After overcoming her surprise and disappointment, Ann realized she must make the most of the situation. In an attempt to conceal what her true feelings had been, she explained to Jack Rackam that the only reason she and Mary had been familiar was that Mary was actually a woman and the two were befriending each other.

About this time the pirates aboard the privateer decided the opportunity was at hand to seize the ship from Captain Rogers. One night, as the watches were being changed, the buccaneers arose en masse. Outnumbering the honest sailors two to one, the pirates soon overcame all opposition. After the fighting ended, the buccaneers chose Jack Rackam to lead them.

Few changes were necessary to convert the privateer into a buccaneering galley, and the pirates fell to work with a will. A piratical cruise was then the order of the day. The buccaneers sailed along for several weeks under tropical skies, until a merchant vessel was overtaken. A terrific fight ensued during which almost every sailor aboard the merchantman was killed. Finally the survivors surrendered. Among them was the ship's young artist (or navigator, as he is called today).

The old story again presented itself. Mary saw the young man for the first time as he signed the ship's articles, and within a few days she was violently in love with him. Her passion soon became so pronounced that she decided to reveal to the navigator why she was so attracted. She told him she was a woman. Esteem and friendship on his part then

Ann Bonney

changed within a few days to the most ardent affection, and the two lovers were as happy as any two lovers could be on the decks of a pirate ship far at sea. Their happiness was short-lived, however.

One day the navigator and another member of the crew quarreled violently, deciding to fight a duel whenever land was reached. Some time later the buccaneers anchored off an island. The two men agreed that the coming day would be suitable for their encounter. Desperate in her fear that she might lose the man she loved, Mary Read openly picked a quarrel with the artist's opponent of the morrow, finally succeeding in agreeing on a duel for the following morning two hours earlier than that which her lover had chosen. Unbeknownst to the navigator, Mary Read left the ship before dawn, and engaged the pirate with both sword and pistol. Showing a method of fighting which far surpassed anything her opponent had ever encountered, Mary Read laid the other pirate at her feet. When the artist learned of this act of unqualified devotion on the part of his sweetheart, he went to her at once, and they pledged to each other a faith so binding, that according to pirate historian Johnson, they considered their attachment just as strong as "if the ceremony had been performed by a clergyman."

Captain Jack Rackam, sometime after he had discovered that Mary Read was a woman, questioned her about pirates in general. He could not understand why she could be interested in the profession.

"Why do you follow a line of life that exposes you to so much danger, and at last to the almost certainty of being hanged?" asked Rackam. Her reply was typical of her unusual life.

> As to hanging, I think it no great hardship, for were it not for that, every cowardly fellow would turn pirate, and so infest the seas that men of courage would starve. If it were my choice, I would not have the punishment less than death, the fear of which kept some dastardly rogues honest. Many of those who are now cheating widows and orphans, and oppressing their poor neighbors who have no money to obtain justice, would then rob at sea, and the ocean would be as crowded with rogues as the land, so that no merchant would venture out, and the trade in a little time would not be worth following.

One day in 1720, Captain Jack found himself caught by a Spanish man-of-war south of Cuba, where he had been careening his vessel. The Dons warped their great battleship into the channel that evening, completely blocking all possibility of the ship's escape. Captain Jack Rackam told the two women that the game was up, and they prepared to sell their lives dearly. Nearby the Spanish man-of-war, just a little farther out to sea, was a small English sloop, which had been captured as an interloper in Spanish water. A prize crew was then aboard.

Rackam called his fellow pirates together to explain his plan. They would launch their longboat, into which everything of value would be placed, and row in the dead of the night far to the south of the man-of-war, after which they would come up on the English sloop, and capture the prize crew. The program was carried out without a mishap. Captain Jack and his crew soon were aboard their prize, where they quickly silenced the Spanish crew, slipped cable, and sailed triumphantly out to sea. The following morning the Spanish man-of-war opened fire upon the pirate's ship, but in a short time they discovered the true state of affairs, and cursed themselves for the fools they had been.

Rackam had escaped this time, but his hourglass was slowly running out. In August 1720 he went to sea again, capturing several small craft and eventually reaching Harbor Island where the pirates stole fishing nets and tackle from schooners anchored off the shore. Sailing across to Hispaniola, they killed and ate many cattle from several French settlements along the coast. On the nineteenth of October off the island of Jamaica they captured a schooner, which was commanded by Master Thomas Spenlow. Reaching Dry Harbor Bay the next day, Captain Rackam stood in and fired a gun, causing the men on a sloop at the wharf to run ashore, but when they found out it was Captain Jack they all came back and even asked to be signed on.

Sailing around the western point of the island at Point Negril, Rackam came up on a small pettianger, or dugout, and invited the men to come aboard for a drink of punch. All nine members of the crew of the dugout accepted the invitation, coming on board fully armed, however. After a few drinks they put down their muskets and pulled off their cutlasses, deciding to enjoy their drinking without encumbrances.

At that very minute a sloop that had been outfitted by the governor of Jamaica sighted the pirate ship, and started at once in pursuit. The pirate lookout noticed the sloop, standing directly for them, and reported the state of affairs to Captain Rackam. Handsome Jack ordered the anchor weighed at once. Captain Barnet [or Barnett—*Ed.*], commander of the armed sloop, rapidly overhauled the pirate ship, whose captain soon realized this was one vessel from which he could not escape.

The sloop caught the pirate ship, and boarded it. A bloody engagement followed, but the soldiers and marines were too strong for the buccaneers. After a few quick skirmishes most of the pirate crew ran below decks. There were three exceptions, Ann Bonney, Mary Read, and another pirate whose name is not known. Captain Jack, to the scorn of Ann Bonney, fled below with the others. Without question Mary Read and Ann Bonney were braver than any other pirates aboard the ship that day, fighting on long after the other buccaneers had gone. The two women only surrendered after the hopelessness of their situation was realized. All the buccaneers were brought to Port Royal, Jamaica, given a quick trial, and sentenced to be hanged.

On November 15, 1720, Captain Jack Rackam was allowed to visit Ann Bonney. Expecting her to commiserate with him, Rackam was amazed when she began to scold her lover.

"I am sorry to see you there, Jack," said Ann, "but if you had fought like a man, you need not have been hanged like a dog." These were her last words to the man she loved, for the following day, November 16, Captain Jack Rackam was hanged at Gallows Point, Port Royal, along with eight in his crew. Handsome Jack and two others were given the after-death consideration of hanging in chains as a special honor to their wickedness. The nine men who had gone aboard Rackam's vessel for a drink were also finally sentenced to be executed.

Ann Bonney and Mary Read, then in prison, announced that they were expectant mothers. Therefore their execution was put off until such a time as they could be properly hanged. Poor Mary, however, grew sick in jail and died, her thoughts to the last of the handsome young navigator who ended his career at Gallows Point, Jamaica. Ann, more fortunate, outlived her companion, and actually disappeared from the prison about a year later. All we are sure of is that she was not executed, but whether her child was born in prison or out, the records of Jamaica do not tell.

This "Thelma and Louise" duo of the high seas has inspired books, plays, and songs for nearly three centuries. Much of what we known about Anne Bonny (as it's usually spelled) and Mary Read comes from *A General History of the Pyrates* by Captain Charles Johnson. Johnson (who, as mentioned earlier, may have been Daniel Defoe) drew from the published account of the trials of Jack

Rackam, Anne Bonny, and Mary Read, along with other contemporary sources. According to Tamara Eastman and Constance Bond's *Pirate Trial of Anne Bonny and Mary Read*, an examination of the source documents available today shows Johnson's account to be largely accurate.

Not much is known of Mary Read's early life other than the possibly fictional events outlined by Snow in this chapter. Anne Bonny was born Anne Cormac in Kinsale, County Cork, Ireland, in 1698 to lawyer William Cormac and his serving woman, Mary Brennan. A local scandal ensued, and within two years Cormac, Brennan, and young Anne had moved to South Carolina. William Cormac became a wealthy plantation owner in his new country, and Anne was raised in wealth and privilege. The many legends about her young life—for instance, that she stabbed a maid to death in a fit of anger—cannot be substantiated. At twenty she married James Bonny, a drifter and part-time pirate, very much against her father's wishes, as Snow notes.

Captain Jack Rackam was widely known as "Calico Jack" after his shirt and breeches of calico sailcloth. Captain Barnett of the sloop that overtook Rackam and his crew later described the fierce fighting of Bonny and Read while most of the men cowered below deck. The two woman screamed as they swung their cutlasses and fired their pistols. Legend has it that Bonny shouted for the men to come on deck and fight. When they refused, she fired into the hold and killed one of the pirates.

Tamara Eastman speculates that Mary Read died in childbirth. She died a few months after the trial and was given a proper burial, indicating that she may have been buried with the baby. What happened to Anne Bonny after the trial remains a tantalizing mystery. According to Eastman, her wealthy father probably bought her way out of prison. Records indicate that she married a gentleman from Virginia in 1721 and apparently lived the rest of her life in relative quiet.

The exploits of pirates on the Atlantic coast pale in comparison to the prodigious attacks led by Mrs. Cheng, or Ching, mentioned by Snow at the start of this chapter. Mrs. Cheng led as many as several hundred vessels and two thousand pirates into battle between 1807 and 1810. Among the many pirate-related artifacts acquired by Edward Rowe Snow was a dagger said to have belonged to Mrs. Cheng.

PART V

NEWFOUNDLAND AND NOVA SCOTIA

CHAPTER 20

Bartholomew Roberts, the Pirate Cavalier

Captain Bartholomew Roberts, in several ways the most remarkable pirate of all, was born in Wales. Unlike the typical buccaneer, he was a man who never touched intoxicating liquor, drinking nothing stronger than tea. He made his pirates retire at nine every night and was a strict disciplinarian in the matter of women, never allowing his men either to take liberties with them or have them aboard ship. The penalty for seducing a woman on board was death. Furthermore, the practice of betting, card-playing, or rolling dice was forbidden aboard his vessels. He was extraordinarily fastidious in dress and is said to have been a Beau Brummell even in the stress of battle. In religious matters he allowed the pirates to follow their own wishes, but was careful to let the musicians have a period of "Rest on the Sabbath."

In the year 1719 Roberts sailed from London as master of the *Princess*, bound for the Guinea coast to pick up a cargo of Negroes at Anamaboe. Reaching port, he was attacked in the harbor by another Welshman, the notorious pirate Howel Davis. Davis captured the *Princess* after a short fight. To the unlucky Roberts, Davis suggested that he might as well join up with the pirate crew. As there seemed to be no other alternative, Bartholomew Roberts reluctantly agreed. In the first stages of his career with Davis, he would have deserted had the opportunity presented itself, but gradually he became reconciled to his new calling.

One day the pirates arrived at the Island of Princes, off the African coast. Davis had in mind a sinister scheme to invite the governor aboard, capture him, and then, later, to subdue the island. This plan almost worked. But on the night before it was to be carried out one of the Negro captives swam ashore and revealed the plot to the residents. The next day when Davis and a small group of pirates unsuspectingly went ashore, they were ambushed by soldiers of the governor and killed. This was the end of the notorious Howel Davis. Crowding canvas upon the vessel, the pirate crew put to sea. After some discussion, Bartholomew Roberts was chosen as one of the candidates for leader. Incidentally, the pirates of long standing aboard Davis's vessel were known as Lords. When they addressed each other, it was often with the title "fellow noble." The underdogs of this pirate state were called Commoners.

There were several other candidates for the position of leader besides Roberts, including Simson, Antis, and Ashplant. Lord Dennis, one of the older pirates, made a long speech to the Lords, in which he stated that the election was not too serious a matter, for, according to him,

> *If one should be elected who did not act and govern for the general good he could be deposed, and another one substituted in his place. We are the original of this claim, and should a captain be so saucy as to exceed prescription at any time, why, down with him! It will be a caution, after he is dead, to his successors, of what fatal consequence any kind of assuming may be; however, it is my advice, while we are sober, to pitch upon a man of courage, and skilled in navigation,—one who, by his prudence and bravery, seems best able to defend this commonwealth, and ward us from the dangers and tempests of an unstable element, and the fatal consequences of anarchy, and such a one I take Roberts to be: A fellow in all respects worthy of your esteem and favor.*

It is said that every pirate of the "commonwealth" applauded this speech except one man, Lord Simson, who designed to make himself commander of the expedition. Finally Simson gave in, saying that he didn't care who was elected as long as he "was not a Papist, for I have conceived a mortal hatred of them, because my father had been a sufferer in Monmouth's rebellion." Then the vote was taken and Bartholomew Roberts was elected.

Roberts, on accepting the leadership of the pirate band, made a blunt speech, very much to the point. "Since I have dipped my hands in muddy water," said Roberts, "and must be a pirate, it is better being a commander than a private man."

A plan for revenging the death of Captain Howel Davis met with general approval, and a pirate named Kennedy was chosen to lead a landing party of thirty men. Returning to the island, they stormed ashore under a brisk cannonade from the ship's guns. The soldiers manning the fort fled into the depths of the woods behind the town. The pirates seized the fort, pushed the cannon into the sea, and returned to the ship unmolested. The suggestion was made to Roberts that the town be stormed and burned. But when he reminded the enthusiasts that a large force of men was probably hiding in the woods and could pick them off at leisure, the idea was abandoned.

The pirates hoisted anchor and sailed away to the southward. Shortly afterwards a Dutch Guineaman was captured, looted, and set free. Next an Englishman was taken. Every man on this ship voted to join Roberts' commonwealth of pirates. As soon as they fired the vessel, the pirates made sail for Anamaboe to procure water and repair the ship. Once the vessel was refitted and ready for sea again, the Brazilian coast was chosen by vote of the crew as the next scene of action. After a voyage of twenty-eight days, Captain Bartholomew Roberts sighted the shores of South America at the Bay of Bahia. Ill luck accompanied the venture for about nine weeks, not a sail being sighted on the blue waters of the

Captain Bartholomew Roberts and two of his ships

rolling seas. At last, off the Bay of Los Todos Santos, a huge fleet of Portuguese vessels came into view. Heavily loaded, the ships were en route to Lisbon, but were anchored offshore, awaiting the arrival of two Portuguese men-of-war.

With a reckless courage and abandon characteristic of the man, Captain Roberts sailed in among the great fleet. Singling out for special attention the most likely sail, he ordered his crew below deck and edged gradually closer as if he were the forty-third member of the fleet. Later that day he communicated with the captain of the vessel he planned to loot, ordering him aboard the pirate vessel.

When the frightened captain of the Portuguese ship obeyed this blunt summons, Roberts saluted him by explaining that they were both gentlemen of fortune and all he wished of him was information as to which was the richest vessel in the fleet. If the Portuguese captain complied, he would be restored to his own vessel; if not, he would be summarily executed. The harassed captain pointed out to a vessel of forty guns, telling Roberts that she carried 150 men. Roberts replied he would sail over at once, using the Portuguese captain as a decoy.

Approaching the treasure ship, Captain Roberts ordered the Portuguese prisoner to hail the captain of the vessel, ask after his health, and invite him aboard. The ruse was apparently successful. The other captain replied that he would come aboard presently. But something seemed amiss. Roberts noticed an unusual rushing to and fro on the decks of the Portuguese craft. Suspecting a trick, he ordered his men to open fire at once, and lowered boats full of pirates to board the treasure ship. In an astonishingly short time Roberts had captured a very rich prize. There were 40,000 moidores of gold aboard, besides sugar, skins, tobacco, and other valuable commodities. The gold alone was worth about $130,000, a moidore being valued at $3.27.

After making this rich haul, the pirates sailed for a safe retreat to relax in comfort and revel in luxury. They chose the Devil's Island on the river Surinam, where a warm reception was accorded them by the governor. He entertained them lavishly, and all was well.

However, provisions were needed and the pirates were informed of a brigantine from which they could supply themselves. Roberts started in pursuit of the brigantine, but when the quarry was located she showed a clean pair of heels. After eight days Roberts, short of food and water, abandoned the idea of catching the brigantine. Sending his dinghy back to the Devil's Island colony, Roberts lay off the shore day after day awaiting her return. Finally, in his desperate need for water, he tore up the cabin to make a raft, on which his men paddled and poled their way to shore.

But the worst was yet to come. The dinghy finally returned from the island. The delay, they told him, was caused by Lieutenant Kennedy's

Pirates carousing ashore. The Pirates Own Book suggests specifically that the illustration shows "Captain Roberts' crew carousing at Old Calabar River."

running off with both the other ships of the pirate fleet. Captain Bartholomew Roberts blamed himself for the situation. Left with a small sloop, his two larger vessels gone, he was forced to new ventures.

Sailing out again in search of victims, he captured two sloops, from whose stores he was enabled to provision himself for a long voyage. The voyage scarcely began, however, before he fell in with a vessel from Bristol, England, which he plundered and allowed to sail away. A few days later Captain Rogers of Barbados, aboard a vessel of twenty guns, caught up with pirate Roberts, who little thought she was anything but a merchantman. Roberts closed in. When within range his cannon roared over the choppy seas. In quick response, Captain Rogers' ship belched flame and smoke, and three hearty British cheers sounded out over the intervening water. It was a rude awakening for Roberts, who suddenly became aware of his mistake. Following a bitter engagement lasting for the better part of two hours in which losses on both sides were heavy, Roberts decided that he had had enough of it. He ordered his yards braced and sheered off. His vessel, being the better sailer, enabled him to shake off pursuit and escape from the English gunboat.

Roberts concluded that West Indian waters were becoming decidedly unhealthy. Far to the northward lay the great island of Newfoundland, with its rugged cliffs rising two and three hundred feet out of the water. At the extreme southern tip of Newfoundland, between Cape Pine and Mistaken Point, lies beautiful Trepassey Bay, leading into Trepassey Harbor. To this new and presumably safer field of operations, Roberts turned the prow of his vessel.

After a peaceful voyage over summer seas, the rugged shores of Newfoundland finally appeared on the horizon. Approaching more closely, Roberts observed the masts of twenty-two ships anchored in the harbor. In his customary audacious fashion, he sailed directly into the harbor, his trumpets blaring and his drums beating. Trumpets and drums, he believed, would so awe the inhabitants that when the black flag of piracy was unfurled the fishermen would be easy prey.

He had not miscalculated. Cannon boomed, musketry rattled. The black pirate vessel became a living volcano belching smoke and flame! Panic spread throughout Trepassey Harbor and when the guns ceased fire every vessel except one was either sunk or afire. Without fear of molestation, Roberts went ashore to pillage the houses and destroy the plantations. The ship that Roberts had saved was from Bristol, England, and this vessel Roberts later exchanged with a Frenchman he had captured. The residents of Trepassey never forgot the day when pirate Roberts came to Trepassey.

Following this raid Roberts returned to tropical waters. Vessel after vessel, ship after ship, he captured and destroyed, until he finally decided to take his chances at the settlement of Martinique. He was familiar with the Dutch system of hoisting a jack should they desire to trade with the natives, and Roberts followed their practice when reaching a point offshore.

Twenty-one small vessels came sailing out to him for barter. Treacherously he destroyed them, one by one, as they reached the pirate ship. Only the last one did he save, and on this he placed the crews of all the others and sent them ashore. A strange incident took place here. Three of the pirates who decided to go on a little expedition of their own choosing were speedily recaptured by a vessel that Roberts sent in pursuit. The three men were tried for their lives as deserters; two were hanged and one was freed.

Shortly afterwards the pirates went for another cruise, capturing a vessel on which a clergyman was sailing. Having no chaplain on board, the pirates thought the clergyman should join forces with them. The clergyman refused. They explained to him that all he would have to do was to make punch and say prayers for them. He would be allowed to carry along whatever he called his own. It is not known whether or not the clergyman went aboard, for Roberts never forced a man to join up against his will. However, it is hard to imagine a clergyman who would go aboard Roberts' vessel willingly. One account has it that the prelate begged to be excused and was finally allowed his freedom in exchange for three prayer books and a corkscrew.

Captain Roberts was coming to the end of his rope, but he was to leave a record never equalled again in all the annals of buccaneering: the capture of at least four hundred ships in his career of piracy.

Sailing through the same waters was a determined English naval officer named Captain Chaloner Ogle, who was commander of the warship *Swallow*. In his cruising from port to port he was keeping much better track of Roberts than the pirate had any reason to believe. It so happened that when Roberts ran into Parrot Island to careen the two ships which he possessed at that time, Ogle was not far behind. Off Cape Lopez Captain Ogle learned of Roberts' whereabouts and sailed at once for Parrot Island.

Arriving off the beach, Captain Ogle, by a ruse, tempted Roberts to send his ship in chase. The *Swallow* pretended to flee from the pirate vessel. Once out of sight of shore, however, Ogle turned on his pursuer just as the black flag was being raised confidently aloft. The severe cannonading of the gunboats effectually silenced the pirate guns. The buccaneers struck their colors, pulling down the black flag and throwing it overboard that it might not rise in judgment over them.

Roberts himself was next on the British captain's list. Returning to Parrot Island a few days later, Ogle sailed boldly into the bay. It was early in the morning. Captain Bartholomew was enjoying a breakfast of hot West Indian pickles, known as salmagundi, when the news reached him that the *Swallow* was coming up the bay. Somehow he seemed to have a presentiment that he might not survive the encounter. At any rate he gave explicit orders to his subordinates to throw him overboard at once should he be killed or seriously wounded in the battle.

Roberts questioned one of his men, who had formerly been a member of the crew aboard the *Swallow*, as to the sailing qualities of the craft. Perchance he might run for it and escape, but it was not to be.

In pursuance of his habit and in accordance with his motto, "a short life but a merry one," Roberts went below to change into his battle regalia. Putting on the most expensive garments in his wardrobe, made of magnificent red damask, he hung several fine pistols, handsomely carved, from his shoulders, and placed around his neck a costly solid gold chain, from which a cross of diamonds was suspended. As a finishing touch he donned his gala hat with a red peacock feather. It was the tenth day of February in the year 1722, an eventful date in piratical journals.

Ominously the British man-of-war nosed slowly up the bay. When he realized that she was after him, the pirate ordered the ship's cable cut and sailed out to engage her in a running battle. Fighting began. The cannonading was terrific, with neither side gaining the advantage. Scuppers ran red with blood. Hoarse cries mingled with the thunder of artillery and small arms. Powder and smoke drifted over the heaving vessels. It was a desperate and bloody engagement. Suddenly a burst of grapeshot hit the pirate ship. Captain Bartholomew Roberts fell mortally wounded, shot through the throat. A stream of blood spurted from his mouth, and without a word he died. When the pirates saw that their leader was dead, in accordance with his command they threw him overboard. Thus ended the career of the most successful pirate of them all. The officers and men of the pirate vessel, deprived of their brave leader, lost their courage and soon surrendered to Captain Ogle.

Bartholomew Roberts, during his unusual lifetime, held that in honest labor there are low wages and hard work, while a pirate always had liberty and power. At least he escaped the fate of his men who, after their surrender to Captain Ogle, were hanged or gibbeted at Cape Corso. He died a violent death, it is true, but it was in the heat of battle as he had wished.

Pirate Bartholomew Roberts was born John Roberts around 1682 near Haverfordwest in southern Wales, but later changed his name to Bartholomew, leading to the classic pirate nickname "Black Bart." In *Under the Black Flag*, pirate historian David Cordingly says that Roberts was a "stern, disciplined man with a natural flair for leadership and the ability to make bold decisions." It is apparently not mere legend that Roberts took more than four hundred vessels during his career; the figure is corroborated by contemporary reports and newspapers. He was a far more successful pirate than the more famous Blackbeard, and despite his gentlemanly appearance was as ruthless and cruel as any.

Comprehensive articles drawn up by Roberts and his crew were reproduced in *A General History of the Pyrates*. One of the articles called for the "lights and candles to be put out at eight o'clock at night." Any pirate wishing to drink after that hour was required to do it on the open deck. This effort by Roberts to curtail the pirates' rampant consumption of alcohol was "ineffectual," according to Johnson.

The articles also called for the pirates to keep their pistols and cutlasses "clean and fit for service." Johnson wrote that the crewmen tried to outdo each other with their beautiful guns, for which they paid as much as thirty or forty pounds per pair at auction. The pistols were slung with "coloured ribbands over their shoulders in a way peculiar to these fellows, in which they took great delight."

According to Cordingly, the battle that resulted in Roberts' death was fought in "driving rain, with 'lightning and thunder and a small tornado.'" Fifty-two of the pirates captured after Roberts' death were hanged.

Captain Chaloner Ogle was knighted after his defeat of Roberts, and he eventually became an Admiral of the Fleet. Cordingly informs us that the crew of the *Swallow* didn't realize they were entitled to a bounty for taking Roberts until they read it in 1724 in Johnson's newly published *A General History of the Pyrates*. Three years after doing battle with Roberts' crew, they received their reward.

CHAPTER 21

The Husband and Wife Pirates of Nova Scotia

Halifax, Nova Scotia, was the scene of a strange court case in November 1809. On the sixteenth of that month Edward Jordan and his wife were brought to trial in the courthouse for murder and piracy on the high seas.

Jordan was a fisherman at Percé in the Gaspe Peninsula, living in that beautiful country with his wife and four children. It is all the more surprising that in what appeared to be a happy family the mother and father actually were pirates.

On July 15, 1809, Captain John Stairs of the fishing schooner the *Three Sisters** sailed from Halifax to Percé with John Kelly his mate, and two seamen, Thomas Heath and Benjamin Matthews. Aboard the vessel were two passengers, Edward Jordan (who later turned pirate) and Patrick Cinnet. Jordan was returning home to arrange for the shipment of fish aboard the same craft. After a journey of two weeks, the schooner reached her destination, and the loading of the cargo began. By September 10 about six hundred quintals of fish had been stored. Captain Stairs planned to sail for Halifax late that afternoon. Edward Jordan and his entire family were to make the voyage with him.

---

*Snow's original text refers to this schooner as the *Eliza*, but we have changed the name throughout to the *Three Sisters*, to reflect information that's become available since the original publication of this book.—*Ed.*

The schooner sailed along the coast until September 13. On that date the vessel was somewhere between Cape Canso and White Head. When Captain Stairs went below to get his quadrant to take the sun between eleven and twelve in the morning, Thomas Heath followed him. Captain Stairs stood for a moment near the cabin table directly under the skylight. A noise from above attracted his attention. Looking up through the skylight, he saw Edward Jordan leaning down with a pistol in his hand.

Jordan, aware that he was discovered, fired. An orange flame flashed from the muzzle. The charge passed close to Captain Stairs, grazing his nose and the side of his face, but entered the body of Heath standing behind him. Thomas Heath fell to his knees.

"Oh, my God, I am killed," he screamed, and collapsed on the cabin floor.

Captain Stairs, recovering slowly from the shock of the incident, made his way to his trunk for his pistols. The lock had been forced! The pistols were gone! Thoroughly alarmed, he searched frantically for his cutlass. It also was missing!

Grimly determined to face the situation, Captain Stairs hastily mounted the ladder, encountering Jordan, pistol in one hand, axe in the other, just about to descend. Stairs seized him, pinioning Jordan's arms so that the pirate could not move. Begging Jordan not to kill him, Stairs pushed him backwards. Jordan managed to free his arm and cocked his pistol. Stairs promptly grabbed the weapon by the muzzle and threw it overboard, at the same time roaring to Mate Kelly for help. Kelly, unknown to Captain Stairs, had been won over to Jordan's plans for taking over the schooner, and kept out of sight completely. Loyal Ben Matthews, however, in spite of the fact that he had already been badly wounded, attempted to answer the captain's cry for help. Staggering along the deck, the poor man collapsed as he attempted to come to the aid of the struggling captain.

Rolling over and over in their fight, Captain Stairs and pirate Jordan were evenly matched. Finally Stairs pulled the axe away from Jordan, slinging that weapon also into the ocean. Captain Stairs renewed his calls for Kelly, but the effect was opposite to what he had hoped. As his shouts continued Jordan's wife appeared, armed with a boat hook handle. Striking the handle against Captain Stairs repeatedly, she screamed as if she were possessed.

"Is it Kelly you want? I'll give you Kelly!" she shrieked, and hit him again. Making a superhuman effort, Captain Stairs pulled himself away from the panting Jordan, and crawled forward. By this time Heath, shot by Jordan when the latter stood at the skylight, had died, and with Kelly nowhere in sight and Matthews unconscious, things looked bad for Captain Stairs.

Jordan obtained another axe, and made his way to Matthews, where he struck the unconscious form several times with the murderous weapon. While this was taking place Captain Stairs, with a tremendous effort, dragged a hatch cover to the side of the ship and heaved it overboard, whereupon he jumped in after it. He later declared that he thought he might as well drown as be shot. Perched on his raft, he watched Jordan and Kelly walk over to the side of the ship. When Jordan aimed at Stairs, Kelly told him that the captain would drown within a few hours anyway, so Jordan put away his pistol, and Stairs drifted out of range.

Captain Stairs watched the *Three Sisters* disappear in the distance, but within a short time his heart was gladdened as another sail rapidly came into view. Tacking close to him, the schooner's helmsman maneuvered the vessel within a few yards of the floating hatch cover so that Captain Stairs could climb safely aboard. He was soon telling his strange story.

The vessel that saved him was an American schooner bound for Hingham, Massachusetts. Since the Yankee commander had lost his pilot by impressment at Halifax on the outward journey, he flatly refused to run into that port. He did agree to put the captain ashore near Cape Sable, however. The wind changed and this proved impossible. Stairs perforce remained aboard the schooner for several days, until finally the vessel passed Boston Light and anchored off Hingham.

Captain Stairs thanked his rescuer and then journeyed to Boston, where he lost no time in interviewing the British consul. The story of his capture by the husband and wife pirates was published in the local papers and the British consul sent letters to various ports along the Atlantic Coast to be on the lookout for Jordan and the *Three Sisters*.

Back on the fisherman, pirate Jordan took command, after throwing overboard the victims of the fight. From all available testimony it seems that Mate John Kelly readily accepted the situation and agreed to cooperate with the pirates. The children, still aboard the ship, apparently were innocently unaware of all that was taking place.

A short time later the *Three Sisters* sailed into Little Bay, an inlet on Fortune Bay. Two seamen of the settlement, William Crew and John Pigot, were invited to join the ship. Certain signs indicated that she was on the "runaway account," according to Pigot's testimony later, "for the fish was not stowed properly, but carelessly tossed about, and the hatch cover was missing."

Declaring that they would not sign on, Pigot and Crew returned ashore with a man who called himself John Stairs, but who in reality was John Kelly, the mate. When, after repeated urgings Pigot still refused to go on the schooner, Kelly drew him into the countinghouse of a man named Thorn where Jordan was hiding. Jordan demanded the reason for Pigot's refusal to help. Bluntly, Pigot answered that it was not his wish to go. Jordan went out, to return shortly with Thorn and a justice of the peace. The justice of the peace was induced to declare that unless Pigot went aboard, he would be tied to a flagstaff, punished, and according to Pigot's statement, "have man of war for my money." At this poor Pigot went aboard and reluctantly signed on.

The *Three Sisters* set sail at once for St. Mary's, where the ship lay at anchor for several days, after which Jordan decided to run up the coast in search of a navigator who could sail them to Ireland. Jordan finally fell in with a navigator named Patrick Power. Power seemed dubious about joining the crew of the *Three Sisters*, but on October 19, 1809, was induced to pilot the *Three Sisters* to Ireland for the sum of eleven pounds a month, Jordan signing the agreement in the name of John Tremain, one of the actual owners of the schooner.

While the vessel was getting ready for sea, John Kelly and Jordan came to blows about Jordan's wife, whose attractiveness started trouble many times on the journey. When Kelly drew two pistols, Power took them away from the sailor, and went up on deck. He was followed by Margaret Jordan, who asked Power to throw the pistols overboard. Without question Mrs. Jordan was familiar with several of the men aboard the ship.

"You know not the mischief they have done!" was her surprising remark when Power asked her why she wanted the pistols thrown overboard. He refused to obey her. Leaving the woman, he went below to Jordan, trying to pacify him. Jordan shouted, "Don't let my wife come to bed with me; if you do I shall kill her."

Kelly later rowed away in the boat, and never came back. His subsequent history is unknown, but evidently he was as guilty as the Jordans. About this time Jordan cut the schooner's cable, and the jib was hoisted. An hour later a sail was sighted, which proved to be His Majesty's schooner *Cuttle*.

Commanded by Lieutenant Bury, the *Cuttle* actually had been sent along the coast to look for the *Three Sisters* in response to the appeal sent out by the British Consul's office in Boston.

Jordan by this time had become very uneasy, and repeatedly asked the others what they thought the oncoming stranger might be. When told that she was a King's schooner, he cried out in alarm: "The Lord have mercy on me, what will my poor children do?" He then ran down into the cabin, but came up shortly afterwards, instructing everyone to say that they were bound for Halifax. Finally the *Cuttle* drew near, and signaled that she was sending a boarding party over to the *Three Sisters*. A boat arrived under the command of Mr. Simpson of the *Cuttle*, who announced that Captain Stairs was still alive and that the game was up for Jordan and his wife. At the time of capture there were six new crew members, all of whom had been recruited since the murders. The *Three Sisters* sailed into Halifax Harbor a few days later under escort, and the pirates were lodged in the local jail. The trial began the following month. After much testimony, in which Jordan's guilt was definitely proved, he was charged as follows:

> EDWARD JORDAN—*The Gentlemen Commissioners, before whom you have been accused of Piracy, Felony, and Robbery, have deliberately examined the articles of charge exhibited against you; and having maturely weighed and considered the several evidences produced against you . . . have agreed that sentence should be pronounced against you for the same accordingly.*
>
> *You,* EDWARD JORDAN, *shall be taken from hence to the place from whence you came, and from hence to the place of execution, there to be hanged by the neck until you are dead— and may God Almighty have mercy upon your soul.*

Edward Jordan's co-partner in the piracy, his wife Margaret, was pronounced not guilty. The court decided that Margaret Jordan's part in this strange drama of the sea was so hard to ascertain that, as she was the mother of several children who would be orphans unless she lived, she was freed. Her husband, however, was taken from the jail on the twentieth day of November, 1809, and executed.

The trial of the Jordans was Canada's first piracy trial. Margaret Jordan submitted a written defense stating that she had married Edward Jordan in Ireland ten years earlier, and that she had been severely mistreated by him ever since they had moved across the Atlantic.

According to her testimony, when the *Three Sisters* arrived in Percé, Margaret Jordan had expected her husband to bring cloth to be made into clothing for their children. He brought none, so Mrs. Jordan approached Captain Stairs for a piece of calico. This apparently aroused a jealous rage in her husband. Jordan later found Stairs visiting his wife in her berth, which quickly led to the shooting that killed Thomas Heath. Margaret went to the deck and found her husband fighting with the captain. According to a report on the trial in the *Quebec Gazette*, "She did not deny but that she might have struck Stairs when engaged with her husband, as she was in such a state of mind as not to know what she was doing; but she could appeal to the Almighty, and say that she was innocent of the crimes with which she then stood charged."

The *Quebec Gazette* reported after Jordan's execution by hanging, "We are informed by the Reverend gentlemen who attended him in his last moments, that he appeared deeply sensible of the enormity of his crimes, and died sincerely penitent." The body of Edward Jordan was tarred and gibbeted at the entrance to Halifax Harbor.

PART VI

SEARCHING FOR BURIED PIRATE TREASURE

CHAPTER 22

The Lure of Pirate Gold

Buried treasure always holds a fascination for the adventuresome person. There are only a few individuals who have not contemplated the possibility of finding a fabulous hoard of gold or silver buried in the sands of some interesting beach or inlet along the Atlantic coast. Nevertheless, treasure, as a rule, eludes most of those who hunt for it.

As far as Americans in search of buried treasure are concerned, the only man who really found so substantial a sum that it more than repaid his expenses was Sir William Phips. His discovery of a Spanish galleon in the West Indies in 1686 brought him wealth and the Royal Governorship of Massachusetts. Phips conveyed to the surface the equivalent of at least $1,250,000 in gold and silver. Phips received more than $80,000 as his share.

True, there have been other successful treasure hunts, but most of them have cost the seeker more than the find was worth. Three efforts to locate and bring up the purser's safe on the ill-fated *Portland* failed to find much of value, while more than a score of attempts to discover buried chests were equally unsuccessful. Without question, at least a third of a million dollars has been spent vainly in efforts to reach the famous Oak Island treasure supposedly buried more than one hundred feet below the surface of the Nova Scotia island.

The ancient timbers of the pirate ship *Whidah* are now in the barn of artist Edward A. Wilson of Truro, Massachusetts, where I saw them during the summer of 1944. Of course, they were from the superstructure washed ashore, and not from the hull of the vessel itself, which still lies buried underwater in the sand off the Cape, close to where Cyprian Southack located the vessel on his map.

John Howard Nickerson of Chatham deserves much praise for his rediscovery of the *Whidah* during the summer of 1923. Walking along the bank with his son at dead low water one Sunday, he observed a discoloration in the water. Descending to the sand, he undressed and swam out to the location. His feet touched the hull of the old pirate ship, and he stood erect, the water reaching his armpits. Diving down, he examined the hull of the *Whidah*, and discovered the projecting trunnion of one of the old guns of the famous pirate ship.

Two Sundays later he returned to the beach with a hacksaw and swam out to the wreck again. Finding the trunnion, he went underwater with the hacksaw and began to saw methodically. After descending time and again underwater to the cannon, coming up at intervals for a breath of air, Nickerson sawed the bolt through, and the trunnion was brought up to the surface. Made of lignum vitae, the trunnion was little the worse for its immersion of two hundred years.

Diver Bill George putting the helmet on diver Al George, who is about to descend to the floor of the sea off Chatham to examine the pirate treasure ship while Lawrence P. Wolfson stands by. Two large cannon and a quantity of silver have been brought up.

While strolling along the beach in the vicinity of Plymouth, Massachusetts, Ben Lay of Colebrook, New Hampshire, came across a chest of money evidently uncovered by a recent northeast gale. The treasure consisted of gold and silver money, and included coins dated from 1769 to 1845. No explanation has ever been given, but Ben Lay still has the treasure.

During a hike along Cape Cod south of Chatham in the summer of 1944, I came upon the wreck of what is believed to be an old pirate galleon. Two great cannon have already been removed from her, besides a considerable amount of money. Laurence Peter Wolfson of Everett is now conducting extensive diving operations at the treasure ship, and reports that his discoveries of late are particularly gratifying.

Orin A. Arlin, who is more familiar with the coastline from Gloucester to Salisbury, Massachusetts, than any other living man, came across a peculiarly marked rock one day with the letter "A" enclosed in a circle. He has reason to believe that £40,000, the equivalent of around $175,000, lies buried in the vicinity.

Artist Edward Arthur Wilson is best remembered for his book illustrations, including those for *Iron Men and Wooden Ships* (1924) and *The Pirate's Treasure, or, the Strange Adventures of Jack Adams on the Spanish Main*, which he also wrote, in 1926. Wilson illustrated more than seventy books, including many maritime adventures. There's no way of knowing if the timbers in Mr. Wilson's barn in Truro were from the *Whydah*, but this seems doubtful to Ken Kinkor, director of the Whydah Museum in Provincetown. When he became involved with the *Whydah* project in the mid-1980s, Kinkor learned that the story had been looked into, but the barn was gone by that time.

According to Kinkor, what John Howard Nickerson actually recovered in 1923 was a deadeye, which was used for adjusting the tension of the ship's rigging. "Given that deadeyes did not change much over time, and the number of wrecks which occurred in that vicinity, there is no way of knowing whether or not Nickerson actually recovered the deadeye from the *Whydah*," says Kinkor. "That the deadeye was made of lignum vitae is not necessarily an indication that it was, or was not, from the *Whydah*. Deadeyes were subjected to a lot of abuse, and ordinary woods would simply not stand up."

Kinkor adds that the sale of "pirate artifacts" in Chatham grew into quite a little cottage industry for a while. "I've seen photos and physical examples of a

Edward Rowe Snow on Cape Cod looking for treasure with a metal detector (from True Tales of Buried Treasure, 1952)

number of 'pirate chests' which, when their provenience was examined, all led back to Chatham one way or another," says Kinkor. "It is my theory that some unsung craftsman was consciously constructing these chests in an antique style for the tourist market of the '20s and '30s. Either that craftsman, or another individual, would then add a famous pirate's name/signature to the chest. The chests in question are pretty convincing. The forger(s) blew it, however, by using the same pirate's signature for two different chests."

CHAPTER 23

Pirate Treasure Found Near Boothbay, Maine

George Frederick Benner of East Boston had a fascinating experience many years ago concerning a pirate's treasure. The story begins at Middlesex, Vermont, around the year 1880. His aunt, Emeline Benner Lewis, was at home one stormy October evening when an ancient seafaring man, resembling a pirate in general appearance, called at the cottage, asking permission to store a small sea chest until his return. Mrs. Lewis consented, and the trunk was placed in the attic. The years went by, and the sailor never returned.

Young George Benner often called at his aunt's cottage, and every year he asked the lady if he could open the chest to find out what was in it. The good woman always refused, claiming that the mariner might come back. Finally, around the year 1900 she admitted that the sailor was probably dead, and gave George permission to open the trunk.

Besides the usual sailor's trinkets, there were a whale's tooth, an old quadrant, a few shells, a copy of Scott's *The Pirate*, and several letters. One letter dated at Bristol, England, in 1830, was the only clue to the sailor's home. The most important find, however, was a piece of folded vellum. George opened it, revealing a map of the Kennebec River in Maine, with a star on a small bay. Underneath the star were these instructions:

Stand abrest qurtsbolder bring top in line with hill N 1/2 m it lise 12 fathom N E near big trees under stone.

The map, according to Benner, was about 150 years old. The following fall young Benner and a friend chartered a small boat and sailed to Boothbay, Maine. The day after their arrival they started up the river early in the morning, exploring the bank hour after hour, until they came to a large quartz boulder which glistened in the sun. The men ran their boat ashore and searched the vicinity half a mile to the northward, but were only able to locate a single tree. By this time the afternoon sun had set, and they decided to return to Boothbay to await the next day.

Leaving Boothbay with the arrival of dawn, they soon found the great rock and again went ashore. When they walked over to the tall tree and discovered the remains of another large elm nearby, they decided they might be on the right trail. By sinking their crowbar into the earth every few feet, the two men located a large flat stone that was a few inches under the surface, and after straining and tugging, lifted the stone high enough to roll it over. Another smaller stone was more easily removed. There, exposed to the sunlight, lay a cask, the top stove in, covered with a fine green mold. Excitedly plunging their hands into the rotting cask, they brought up handfuls of decayed wood and discolored coins, which proved to be gold! The keg was entirely filled with coins except for a roll wrapped in badly rotted canvas. They knelt there with hands full of gold, stunned for a moment at their find. With a quick glance around to see if anyone were watching them, the successful treasure hunters threw the treasure into the new canvas bags they had brought with them, and beat a hasty retreat to the boat. Nervous because of the large treasure in their possession, they agreed that it would be safer to travel right to Boston aboard their craft and thus avoid embarrassing questions.

Starting down the coast at once, Benner and his friend reached Boston two days later, and tied up at the Northern Avenue Public Landing. The two men soon made arrangements for the treasure to be taken to a well-known bank, where experts examined and counted the hoard. When they opened the canvas roll, a pearl necklace and a diamond-studded gold cross nine inches high were revealed.

The bank finally reported that the sum of $20,000 awaited the two men, an amount which they divided equally. Benner's friend finished college with part of his share, but lost the remainder of his money through stock manipulations. George Frederick Benner still is alive and active on the streets of Boston today, his brisk manner and quick step belying the fact that he has long since passed the biblical allotment of years.

An article by Anthony J. Pallante in the April 2001 issue of *Lost Treasure* magazine claimed that the treasure described in this chapter had been buried by a lieutenant of the pirate Bartholomew Roberts. Like so many similar compelling and romantic stories of buried treasure, this one is impossible to substantiate—but it certainly appeals to the treasure seeker in all of us.

Barbara Rumsey of the Boothbay Region Historical Society has written, "In Boothbay just about every island is reputed to have treasure buried on it, and I suppose the same is true of all the other seaside communities. Many people are unwilling to give up the fantasy of pirate treasure dotting our islands, or don't even allow it may be fanciful. I don't agree but I try not to be a spoilsport every waking minute." Regarding this particular story, she adds, "The Kennebec is not a Boothbay river—the Kennebec is ten miles west of Boothbay. If the supposed treasure seekers got to Boothbay and went up a river, it would be either the Damariscotta or the Sheepscot Rivers which define the east and west sides of the Boothbay peninsula."

CHAPTER 24

A Successful Cape Cod Pirate Treasure Hunt

An old resident who lives in Chatham, Massachusetts, has just revealed a most unusual story of Cape Cod treasure. Time, place, and size of fortune, details which are usually rather indefinite in accounts of treasure, are all convincingly presented as evidence of the truth of this story. The name of the man who found the treasure chest, about how much he obtained from it, and where he found it are known. It is possible to tell approximately, within a few rods, the present location of the chest, which still holds a sizable fortune.

The story starts more than a hundred years ago in the tailor shop of one of Chatham's leading citizens, whom we shall call John Eldridge. Having a prosperous tailoring business, Eldridge was well known to all the residents of Chatham and the nearby towns as an honest and hardworking person. One day a friend, Arthur Doane, came into the shop and asked Eldridge if he were busy. The tailor said that he was working, but that if Doane wanted to talk with him he could come on out back where Eldridge was cutting out a suit of clothes on the large table in the back part of his shop. Doane followed the tailor into the workroom and sat down. His eyes seemed to glisten attentively as the huge scissors in the hands of his friend described their pattern on the cloth. Arthur Doane seemed strangely restless, but, Cape Cod fashion, Eldridge did not query him needlessly, knowing that Doane would come to the point sooner or later. Finally Arthur, a fisherman by trade, asked a question.

"Is it possible to change foreign coins into American money?" faltered Doane in a tense voice.

"Why, yes, there are places in both Boston and Philadelphia, where I go for my cloth," answered the surprised tailor. "Why do you ask?"

"I have a reason," responded the now excited fisherman, who then lapsed into a stony silence.

John Eldridge bided his time, waiting for the thought reflexes which had frozen up inside Arthur to thaw and assert themselves. Finally Doane seemed to decide his course and reaching into his pocket, brought out a coin. About the size of a half-dollar, it was made of gold. Grabbing it carefully between the thumb and forefinger of his right hand, he rapped the coin's edge significantly on the cutting table.

"Can you do anything with this?" Arthur queried. He was trembling now, the excitement causing small beads of perspiration to come out on his brow. "Can you turn it into American money?"

Laying aside his scissors, Eldridge took the gold piece and examined it carefully. It was a Spanish coin, slightly smaller than those of our own which are worth twenty dollars. He turned it over slowly, and then handed it back to the fisherman, who now appeared to be sorry that he had revealed his secret.

"Why, yes, I can cash it the next time I go up to Boston or over to Philadelphia," said John slowly. "But where did you get it?"

"Never you mind where I got it. Just tell me if you will change it for me."

John stood motionless for a minute or two, his eyes on his friend, and then thoughtfully agreed to obtain American money for the Spanish piece, whereupon Arthur pulled five more similar coins from his pocket.

"Get me money for all six coins," he cried, and ran out of the shop in a panic, seemingly afraid to trust himself further.

Perplexed, Eldridge watched his friend out of sight, and after putting away the coins for safekeeping, resumed his work. Some time later in the month he visited a coin dealer in Philadelphia, where he was told that the gold content in the Spanish pieces was very satisfactory and that he would receive approximately twelve dollars a coin.

As soon as he returned to Chatham with the American money, John Eldridge sent word to Arthur Doane to come to the shop. A few hours later, the excited fisherman reached the tailor and heard of his good fortune. Taking his money, after leaving a small amount for Eldridge's expenses, Doane left the tailor shop without revealing in any way how, where, or when he had obtained the gold. A few weeks went by, and Doane again appeared in the shop, this time with another six gold coins.

"What is this all about?" asked John curiously. "How do I know that this money is honestly obtained?"

"Never mind that," returned Arthur. "I have come by it honestly, never you fear. If you will change these six coins when you go up to the city, you won't have to worry. You may trust me in that."

And thus the strange arrangement was made, with John going in to either Boston of Philadelphia every few weeks. The weeks quickly turned into months and the months to years. Eldridge made his unusual pilgrimages to the coin dealers of both cities, and the prudent man never suggested that they were curious, although they must have been puzzled about the source of the driblets of six, eight, and ten coins that reached them at regular intervals. Probably between $1,200 and $1,700 a year was redeemed by the coin dealers in this way over a period of forty-six years, making a total treasure of about $60,000.

Meanwhile, Arthur Doane prospered and married. His only son, born in due time, was unfortunately paralyzed. As the boy grew up he was a common sight in Chatham, as he manfully pulled his withered left leg after him while making his way along the main street of the town. Neither he nor anyone else knew, however, of his father's good fortune, which enabled him to add to his income from the fishing business.

In 1876 Eldridge's young grandson, who still lives at Chatham, was leaving the tailor shop, when suddenly the boy shouted, "Here comes Arthur Doane." The youth darted back into the shop and hid in the rear room. Doane entered the tailor shop, deposited a small pile of coins on the table, and went out without a word. The youth came out from his hiding place in time to watch his grandfather place the gold coins in his strong box.

Four years later Doane became bedridden and sent word to the tailor that he wished to see him. Eldridge hastened to the bedside of the crippled fisherman, who asked everyone else to leave the room.

"Sit down, John," said the sick man, "for it is a story of unusual nature I am going to tell you."

Eldridge seated himself comfortably in the creaking rocker beside the huge feather bed, and waited for Doane to continue.

You have waited more than forty-nine years for this story, John, and I know I haven't been very fair in not telling you about it before. But gold does strange things to ordinary people when they find it, and I guess I'm just as ordinary as the rest of them.

When I told you that afternoon so many years ago that the money was honest money, it was only partly true. I probably had just as much right to it as the men who buried it where I took it from. Anyway, it is too late now to do anything about that. What I called you over for was to tell you the whole story so that you can get the money for me.

"You may remember that day when I brought the first six coins in to you?" asked Doane. Eldridge nodded, and the bedridden man went on.

Well, at that time I was on a banker, fishing out from Chatham. There was a girl I was going with (I won't tell you her name), and I was especially anxious to spend as much time with her as I could. The captain would let me go up and see her, and then I would have to meet the schooner at the North Chatham Beach. Well, one night I arranged to meet the banker at four o'clock the next morning. I spent the evening with my lady friend, leaving her around midnight, to set out on the lonely trip to the rendezvous on the beach.

It must have been three o'clock when I was within a mile and a half of the meeting place, that I saw a light in the distance. Naturally I was curious, and walked stealthily over to the location where the light was. As I approached, I soon heard the sound of voices speaking in hushed tones, and then the rattle of picks and shovels.

Lying on my stomach and straining to look through the darkness, I could see that there were several fierce-looking men shovelling sand into a partly filled hole as fast as they could. They seemed to be talking in a foreign language, but one man appeared to be an American. I was greatly excited by this time, for I had hopes that they had been burying something of value in the sand. Otherwise why should they choose such a lonely location where no one would bother them, and go there in the middle of the night?

Arthur Doane went on with his story, pausing now and then to take a drink. He told how the men finished smoothing over the sand and then started away, taking their lantern with them. He remained near the filled-in hole, too interested in what they had buried to leave. Even after four o'clock arrived he decided to forget the fishing boat and let his shipmates sail away to the banks without him.

Daylight found him huddling behind a low clump of bushes, peering out on the ocean, where two schooners were visible. His own vessel, hull down, was rapidly disappearing, while another schooner, of a type rarely seen in northern waters, was slowly making her way from the vicinity of the beach, evidently with the men aboard who had buried the treasure.

The fisherman decided to settle the affair then and there. Waiting another hour to make sure he was not observed, he came out from the thicket and began scooping the sand up with a large plank he found nearby. After he had been digging energetically for two and a half hours, his improvised shovel struck the hard surface of a box, which proved to be a chest, about six feet long and two and a quarter feet wide. At this discovery, he was excited beyond sanity. He jumped down into the hole and started scraping madly with his fingers against the hard edges of the chest. At length when he found the lock, he seized his plank and forced the catch open.

Doane threw back the cover. He was confronted with bag after bag of heavy coins. Opening one of the canvas sacks, he brought out a handful of the glittering gold. Quickly he retied the hemp rope that secured it, placed the bag down on the sand beside him, and planned his campaign of action.

> *I knew that the safest way was to do it all alone. So many people have lost out by telling what they thought would remain a secret. Thinking it all over carefully, I slowly worked out what I would do. Then I arose, replaced the lid of the huge chest, covered it with sand, and walked out over the dunes.*
>
> *Almost a quarter mile away (375 yards as I paced it) there was a great sand dune fairly near the ocean whose crest was so placed it was easy to identify. At the base of this sand dune, which was due east of a grove of trees over on Strong Island, I began to dig. Hour after hour passed. I was so tired that there were times I wanted to quit. Finally, the hole was seven feet deep, and I went back and opened up the chest again. Taking a bag in each hand (they were very heavy), I trudged across the sand to the dune, where I piled the bags up at the edge of the hole. Time after time I made the journey. It must have been noon when the last cumbersome canvas money bag was safe near the dune. The chest itself was my next problem, for I didn't wish to leave a trace if the pirates should come back and dig.*
>
> *After considerable tugging and tipping it end over end, I pushed and*

dragged the great box to my new hiding place. Then I found the hole was just a bit too short, so another fifteen minutes' digging was necessary.

I was completely done in after this. Hungry, tired, and ready to quit, I threw myself down on the sand. But in a short time I was thinking of the mass of wealth around me. You can be greatly refreshed by thoughts of castles in the air, and I was enjoying quite a few. A half hour later I was ready for work again.

The pit was now eight feet deep. I then pulled the heavy chest over to the hole and carefully eased it into place. Opening the great cover, I propped it up with a gyzarium, and in less than an hour I filled the chest with the bulky canvas coin bags I had piled up on the banking I left out about sixty coins which I later took home.

Closing the cover, I secured the latch. Then I shoveled desperately for a long time, filling in the sand over the chest. I was pretty scared about then, for I noticed two men landing from a dory, far down the beach. They paid no attention to me, however. In fact I don't think they even saw me.

After smoothing the sand so that no one could tell I had been digging there, I broke up my plank into small pieces and scattered it around the sand dunes. By the time I had returned to the place where the treasure chest lay buried, I collapsed exhausted on the sand and knew no more.

When I awoke the stars were shining. There was no moon, but I could see fairly well. By the position of the Dipper, I knew it must be around midnight. I felt for the sixty coins and found them intact. Evidently no one had discovered my secret during the long sleep I had enjoyed. I returned to town around two in the morning, and hid the money in my bureau drawer, which I locked.

"You know the rest of the story, how I came to you with the six coins, and how you had them changed into United States money," concluded Doane as he lay back on his pillow to rest. When he had gained enough strength to raise himself again, he took a string that had been around his neck. Attached to the string was a key.

"Go over to the bureau and open the top port-side drawer," Arthur directed. Eldridge unlocked the drawer and pulled it open. There he found eighteen gold coins. "Those are all I have left, now," said Arthur. "When you have cashed them, no more are in the house, so you'll have to walk out on the dunes and get some."

Because of the exertion of telling the long story, Doane was quite worn out by then. John finally had to agree to visit the hoard within a few days to pacify his sick friend. Arthur then relaxed into a peaceful sleep, and Eldridge left shortly afterwards.

The following Sunday Eldridge made the long journey out to the beach, where he soon located the dune which bore due east of the grove of trees on Strong Island. He began to dig. John was successful the first attempt, for within an hour he struck the top of the chest. Opening the cover with little difficulty, for it was not locked, he saw that there were seven bags of the golden coins. After removing one of them, he closed the chest and covered over the hole. He then started for home. As soon as he entered his residence, he poured the golden hoard out on top of his dining room table and counted the coins, replacing the treasure in the bags when he had finished. The next day John Eldridge left for Philadelphia, where he exchanged the Spanish coins for $4,300. On his return he placed the money in the local bank.

After a few weeks he again visited Arthur Doane, telling him what he had done. Arthur was strangely upset.

"It may seem queer to you," said Doane, "but I don't think we are going to have any further luck in the matter. I think that taking the entire bag of coins seemed greedy." Eldridge tried to calm the sick man's fears, but it was no use. While appreciating the efforts John had made in his behalf, Doane was restless and disturbed. Later that year he grew worse and passed away. As his son and wife had died some years before, he was the last of the family.

Eldridge then planned to visit the treasure hoard and remove the remainder of the fortune. On the very day before he had arranged to make a trip to the outer beach, a terrific storm blew in from the northeast, causing great damage to property in and around Chatham. The bank near the former site of Chatham Light had all washed away, and the next day came reports of silver coins found near the spot where the lighthouse had stood.

The discovery of the silver coins made Eldridge wonder if his treasure chest, which then probably contained around $25,000 in gold, was safe from the ravages of the sea. As he hurried out to the sand dunes, he saw with sinking heart that the entire beach had washed away in the storm. Walking down to the location where he obtained his cross-bearing with Strong Island's grove of trees, he looked around him in dismay. Nothing remained. The chest, which was far too heavy to wash very far, had evidently sunk deep in the sand during the storm. After many futile weeks of searching, Eldridge finally gave up in despair. There have been others who have dug on the low tide sands for the golden coins, but not a single trace of the money has been uncovered to this day.

Thus the story of a successful treasure hunt at Cape Cod also may inspire some reader in the future to try to locate the missing chest, which, it is believed, still contains enough gold coins to permit the finder to enjoy moderate prosperity for his efforts, if luck is with him.

Somehow, I have a feeling that the chest will never be uncovered. Perhaps it will join the much richer cache of pirate gold located a few miles to the northward at the scene of the wreck of the pirate ship *Whidah*, which has lain undiscovered for more than two hundred years. The spirits of the notorious Bellamy, the infamous Blackbeard, and the despicable Low must indeed rest uneasy wherever they are at the knowledge of such great sums of pirate gold lying hidden and unknown on the silvery beaches of the Atlantic coast.

Some have written that the source of the gold in this story was smuggling, and that the romantic buried treasure tale was simply a cover story. Like so many similar stories, the veracity of the tale is lost in the haze of passing time. But these stories appeal to our innate belief that any one of us could stumble onto untold riches while strolling on a lonely beach, an essential ingredient in our coastal New England culture.

Bibliography from the 1944 Edition

NEWSPAPERS
American Weekly Mercury
Boston Gazette
Boston News-Letter
Boston Post
Essex Register
New England Courant

PUBLISHED VOLUMES
Colonial Society. *Publications.*
Dow, G. F., and J. H. Edmonds. *Pirates of the New England Coast, 1630–1730* [1923].
Ellms, Charles. *The Pirates Own Book* [1837].
Esquemeling, Alexander O. *History of the Buccaneers of America* [1634].
Gosse, P. *The Pirates' Who's Who* [1924].
Jameson, John F. *Privateering and Piracy in the Colonial Period* [1923].
Johnson, Charles. *General History of the Pyrates* [1724].
Johnson, Charles. *General History of the Lives and Adventures of the Most Famous Highwaymen, to Which Is Added Voyages and Plunders of the Most Notorious Pyrates* [1734].
Lewis, Alonzo. *History of Lynn.*
Macauley, Thomas B. *History of England.*
Mather, Cotton. *History of Some Criminals Executed in the Land.*
Paine, Ralph D. *The Book of Buried Treasure* [1911].
Roberts, George. *The Four Voyages of Captain George Roberts* [1726].
Stockton, F. R. *Buccaneers and Pirates of Our Coasts* [1917].

UNPUBLISHED SOURCES
Massachusetts Archives, Boston
Public Record Office, London, England
Suffolk Court Files, Boston

Index

About the Author

Edward Rowe Snow (1902–1982) was descended from a long line of sea captains. He sailed the high seas, toiled aboard oil tankers, and worked as a Hollywood extra—all before attending college. Later he worked as a teacher and coach, and as a reconnaissance photographer during World War II. His education and work prepared him well for his legendary writing career—which was part maritime history, part show business.

The *Islands of Boston Harbor*, his first book, was published in 1935. In all, Snow wrote nearly one hundred books and pamphlets, illustrated with many of his own photographs. He also contributed newspaper columns to the *Quincy Patriot Ledger*, the *Boston Herald*, and the *Brockton*

Edward Rowe Snow in the late 1960s with a treasure chest found on Matagorda Island, Texas. (From Snow's True Tales and Curious Legends, *1969)*

Enterprise. In the 1950s his radio show *Six Bells* was heard on dozens of stations, and he made many other appearances on radio as well as on television.

Snow is fondly remembered as the "Flying Santa." For forty years he flew in small planes and helicopters over the lighthouses of New England, dropping Christmas parcels for the keepers and their families. His efforts to preserve the islands of Boston Harbor as public lands are less well known. After his death in 1982, the *Boston Globe* lauded his support for conservation: "There are many political leaders and environmentalists who can justly share the credit for the preservation of the harbor islands, but among them Mr. Snow will hold a special place as a link to their past and a guide to their present."

Snow married Anna-Myrle Haegg in 1932. They had one daughter, Dorothy Caroline Snow (Bicknell), two granddaughters, and one great-grandson. The young people who grew up "at his feet," reading and listening to his tales of New England maritime history, are countless.